AF477787

International Political Economy Series

General Editor: **Timothy M. Shaw**, Professor of Human Security and Peacebuilding, School of Peace and Conflict Management, Royal Roads University, Victoria, BC, Canada

Titles include:

Hans Abrahamsson
UNDERSTANDING WORLD ORDER AND STRUCTURAL CHANGE
Poverty, Conflict and the Global Arena

Andreas Bieler, Werner Bonefeld, Peter Burnham and Adam David Morton
GLOBAL RESTRUCTURING, STATE, CAPITAL AND LABOUR
Contesting Neo-Gramscian Perspectives

Morten Bøås, Marianne H. Marchand and Timothy M. Shaw (*editors*)
THE POLITICAL ECONOMY OF REGIONS AND REGIONALISMS

Paul Bowles, Henry Veltmeyer, Scarlett Cornelissen, Noela Invernizzi and
Kwong-leung Tang (*editors*)
NATIONAL PERSPECTIVES ON GLOBALIZATION

Paul Bowles, Henry Veltmeyer, Scarlett Cornelissen, Noela Invernizzi and
Kwong-leung Tang (*editors*)
REGIONAL PERSPECTIVES ON GLOBALIZATION

Sandra Braman (*editor*)
THE EMERGENT GLOBAL INFORMATION POLICY REGIME

Giorel Curran
21st CENTURY DISSENT
Anarchism, Anti-Globalization and Environmentalism

Martin Doornbos
INSTITUTIONALIZING DEVELOPMENT POLICIES AND RESOURCE STRATEGIES IN
EASTERN AFRICA AND INDIA
Developing Winners and Losers

Martin Doornbos
GLOBAL FORCES AND STATE RESTRUCTURING
Dynamics of State Formation and Collapse

Bill Dunn
GLOBAL RESTRUCTURING AND THE POWER OF LABOUR

Myron J. Frankman
WORLD DEMOCRATIC FEDERALISM
Peace and Justice Indivisible

Marieke de Goede (*editor*)
INTERNATIONAL POLITICAL ECONOMY AND POSTSTRUCTURAL POLITICS

Graham Harrison (*editor*)
GLOBAL ENCOUNTERS
International Political Economy, Development and Globalization

Patrick Hayden and Chamsy el-Ojeili (*editors*)
CONFRONTING GLOBALIZATION
Humanity, Justice and the Renewal of Politics

Axel Hülsemeyer (*editor*)
GLOBALIZATION IN THE TWENTY-FIRST CENTURY
Convergence or Divergence?

Takashi Inoguchi
GLOBAL CHANGE
A Japanese Perspective

Kanishka Jayasuriya
STATECRAFT, WELFARE AND THE POLITICS OF INCLUSION

Dominic Kelly and Wyn Grant (*editors*)
THE POLITICS OF INTERNATIONAL TRADE IN THE 21st CENTURY
Actors, Issues and Regional Dynamics

Mathias Koenig-Archibugi and Michael Zürn (*editors*)
NEW MODES OF GOVERNANCE IN THE GLOBAL SYSTEM
Exploring Publicness, Delegation and Inclusiveness

Craig N. Murphy (*editor*)
EGALITARIAN POLITICS IN THE AGE OF GLOBALIZATION

George Myconos
THE GLOBALIZATION OF ORGANIZED LABOUR
1945–2004

John Nauright and Kimberly S. Schimmel (*editors*)
THE POLITICAL ECONOMY OF SPORT

Morten Ougaard
THE GLOBALIZATION OF POLITICS
Power, Social Forces and Governance

Richard Robison (*editor*)
THE NEO-LIBERAL REVOLUTION
Forging the Market State

Fredrik Söderbaum and Timothy M. Shaw (*editors*)
THEORIES OF NEW REGIONALISM

Susanne Soederberg, Georg Menz and Philip G. Cerny (*editors*)
INTERNALIZING GLOBALIZATION

Ritu Vij (*editor*)
GLOBALIZATION AND WELFARE

International Political Economy Series
Series Standing Order ISBN 0–333–71708-2 hardback
Series Standing Order ISBN 0–333–71110-6 paperback
(*outside North America only*)

You can receive future titles in this series as they are published by placing a standing order.
Please contact your bookseller or, in case of difficulty, write to us at the address below with
your name and address, the title of the series and one of the ISBNs quoted above.

Customer Services Department, Macmillan Distribution Ltd, Houndmills, Basingstoke,
Hampshire RG21 6XS, England

Regional Perspectives on Globalization

Edited by

Paul Bowles
Professor of Economics and International Studies, University of Northern British Columbia, Canada

Henry Veltmeyer
Professor of Sociology and International Development Studies, St Mary's University, Halifax, Canada

Scarlett Cornelissen
Senior Lecturer, Department of Political Science, University of Stellenbosch, South Africa

Noela Invernizzi
Professor, Development Studies Program, Autonomous University of Zacatecas, Mexico

Kwong-leung Tang
Professor, Department of Social Work, The Chinese University of Hong Kong, China

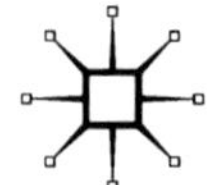

First published 2007 by
PALGRAVE MACMILLAN
Houndmills, Basingstoke, Hampshire RG21 6XS and
175 Fifth Avenue, New York, N.Y. 10010
Companies and representatives throughout the world

PALGRAVE MACMILLAN is the global academic imprint of the Palgrave Macmillan division of St. Martin's Press, LLC and of Palgrave Macmillan Ltd. Macmillan® is a registered trademark in the United States, United Kingdom and other countries. Palgrave is a registered trademark in the European Union and other countries.

ISBN–13: 978–0–230–00466–5
ISBN–10: 0–230–00466–0

This book is printed on paper suitable for recycling and made from fully managed and sustained forest sources. Logging, pulping and manufacturing processes are expected to conform to the environmental regulations of the country of origin.

A catalogue record for this book is available from the British Library.

Library of Congress Cataloging-in-Publication Data
Regional perspectives on globalization / [edited by]
Paul Bowles . . . [et al.].
        p. cm. – (International political economy)
    Includes bibliographical references and index.
    ISBN–13: 978–0–230–00466–5 (cloth)
    ISBN–10: 0–230–00466–0 (cloth)
    1. Globalization–Economic aspects. 2. Economic development.
3. Neoliberalism.   I. Bowles, Paul.
HF1359.R432 2007
337–dc22   2006050182

10   9   8   7   6   5   4   3   2   1
16   15   14   13   12   11   10   09   08   07
Transferred to Digital Printing in 2011

Contents

List of Figures and Tables

Figures

Tables

Notes on the Contributors

Carlos G. Aguilar is Facilitator of the Grupo de Agricultura y Comercio de la Alianza Social Continental (Agriculture and Trade Group of the Hemispheric Social Alliance) (ASC) and member of the Encuentro Popular in Costa Rica.

Galal Amin has taught economics at the American University in Cairo since 1979. He has worked as Economic Advisor to the Kuwait Fund for Arab Economic Development (1974–8) and as Visiting Professor at UCLA (1978–9 and 1985–6). He has written many books in English and in Arabic on the economics, politics, cultural and social life of Egypt and the Arab World. They include *The Modernization of Poverty, Whatever Happened to the Egyptians?* and most recently *The Illusion of Progress in the Arab World: A Critique of Western Misconstructions.*

Andreas Antoniades is Tutorial Fellow in International Relations and Visiting Fellow at the Centre for International Studies at the London School of Economics and Political Science. He is the author of articles and chapters on the biopolitics of globalization, epistemic communities and hegemonic discourse theory.

Walden Bello is a Professor of Sociology at the University of the Philippines and Executive Director of Focus on the Global South, a research and advocacy institute based in Bangkok, Thailand. He is the author of *Dilemmas of Domination: The Unmaking of the American Empire, Deglobalization* and 12 other books as well as numerous articles that have appeared in international journals, magazines and newspapers. He received the Right Livelihood Award (also known as the Alternative Nobel Prize) for his work on globalization.

Paul Bowles is Professor of Economics and International Studies at the University of Northern British Columbia, Canada. He is also affiliated with universities in Australia, China and Mexico. He has published in the areas of globalization, regionalism, development and the political economy of China's reforms. His latest book is *Capitalism.*

Scarlett Cornelissen is Senior Lecturer in the Department of Political Science at the University of Stellenbosch, South Africa. She has published on aspects related to cities as emergent major actors in the international economy, global tourism and the political economy of sport management.

Wim Dierckxsens is a researcher at the Ecumenical Research Department in San José Costa Rica and is a Director for Latin America of the World Forum for Alternatives (WFA).

Eric Helleiner is CIGI Chair in International Governance and Associate Professor of Political Science at the University of Waterloo, Ontario. He is the author of *Towards North American Monetary Union?* and *States and the Reemergence of Global Finance*, and is co-editor of the journal *Review of International Political Economy*.

Noela Invernizzi is Professor in the Development Studies Program, University of Zacatecas, Mexico. She is author of *Flexible and Disciplined: Brazilian Workers after Industrial Restructuring* and she is co-editor (with G. Foladori) of *Disruptive Nanotechnologies*.

Nasreen Khundker is Professor of Economics at the University of Dhaka, Bangladesh. Her research and publications include the informal sector, technical change, globalization, gender, employment and workers' rights. She has worked as a consultant for international organizations, as well as the government of Bangladesh.

Mary Njeri Kinyanjui is Senior Research Fellow at the Institute of Development Studies, University of Nairobi, Kenya. She is an economic geographer with a focus on industrial development, micro and small enterprises, and gender. Her research is conducted mainly in urban areas and she has been involved in the study of trade and justice in Malawi, Kenya, Tanzania and Uganda. Her latest book is *Social Capital*.

Felix Kiruthu is Lecturer in the Department of History, Archaeology and Political Studies at Kenyatta University, Nairobi, Kenya. He is an economic historian with a focus on urban history, the history of micro and small-scale enterprises in Africa, as well as labour history.

Jacek Kochanowicz is Professor of Economic History at Warsaw University and a Professor of History at the Central European University in Budapest. He has been a Visiting Professor at Chicago University and the University of Washington and a Fellow at the Institute for Advanced Study in Princeton. He has written on the Polish peasantry, on comparative modernization and on the post-communist transformation.

Kehinde Olayode is Lecturer in the Department of International Relations, Obafemi Awolowo University, Ile-Ife, Nigeria. He specializes in governance and developmental issues in Africa, civil society and democratization, and has a number of publications to his credit.

Amadu Sesay is Professor of Social and Political Studies at Obafemi Awolowo University, Ile-Ife, Nigeria, and a visiting professor at the Centre for Black African Studies at the University of Bordeaux. Her recent publications include *An Uncertain Today*, *A Tomorrow Under Siege* and *Ethnic Militias and the Future of Democracy in Nigeria*.

Kwong-leung Tang is Chair and Professor of Social Work at the Chinese University of Hong Kong. He is the author of *Social Welfare Development in East Asia* and editor of *Social Development in Asia*.

Lisa Thompson holds the position of Director of Research in Southern African Studies at the School of Government, University of the Western Cape. She is a research leader for a number of international research networks, including the Development Research Centre on Citizenship, Participation and Accountability, located at the Institute of Development Studies, University of Sussex, UK.

Henry Veltmeyer is Professor of International Development Studies at the University of Zacatecas, Mexico, and St Mary's University in Halifax, Canada. Recent publications, co-authored with James Petras, include *Unmasking Globalization*, *System in Crisis* and *Social Movements and State Power*.

Paulo Fagundes Vizentini is Professor of International Relations and a Researcher at the Centre of Strategy and International Relations at the Federal University of Rio Grande do Sul, Porto Alegre/RS, Brazil. He is also a Visiting Professor at São Paulo University and Leiden University. He recently co-authored with Marianne Wiesebron *Free Trade for the Americas?*

Acknowledgements

We would like to thank the following for contributing to making this book possible. Tim Shaw, the series editor, provided encouragement and advice throughout the project. Robert Stewart translated the chapters on Central America and the Caribbean and on South America. Translation costs were met by the Office of the Vice President Research at the University of Northern British Columbia. Phillipa Grand, Hazel Woodbridge and Keith Povey saw the book through the production process. We thank them all.

Galal Amin's chapter develops research that was commissioned by the Human Development Report Office. It draws upon material previously published as 'Globalization and Human Development in the Arab World' in *Globalization with a Human Face*, Background Papers Vol. II, Human Development Report, 1999, Human Development Report Office, UNDP, New York. We acknowledge permission to use the material here.

Every effort has been made to trace copyright holders of material produced in this book, but if any have been inadvertently overlooked the publishers will be glad to make the necessary arrangements at the first opportunity.

P.B.
H.V.
S.C.
N.I.
K.-l.T.

List of Abbreviations

ADB	Asian Development Bank
AFTA	ASEAN Free Trade Area
APEC	Asia Pacific Economic Cooperation
ASEAN	Association of Southeast Asian Nations
BRICs	Brazil, Russia, India, China (emerging economies)
CBI	Caribbean Basin Initiative
CUFTA	Caribbean–US Free Trade Agreement
DRC	Democratic Republic of Congo
EAC	East African Community
ECOWAS	Economic Community of West African States
EMU	Economic and Monetary Union (EU) (of 12/15/25/27 states)
EU	European Union
FDI	foreign direct investment
FTAA	Free Trade Area of the Americas
GDP	gross domestic product
HDI	Human Development Index
HIV/AIDS	human immunodeficiency virus/acquired immune deficiency syndrome
IADB	Inter-American Development Bank
IBSA	India, Brazil, South Africa
IFIs	international financial institutions
ILO	International Labor Organization
IMF	International Monetary Fund
IPE	international political economy
LDCs	least-developed countries
MAI	Multilateral Agreement on Investment
MNCs	multinational corporations
MST	Landless Workers Movement in Brazil
NAFTA	North American Free Trade Agreement
NEPAD	New Partnership for Africa's Development
NGOs	non-governmental organizations
ODA	official development assistance
OECD	Organisation for Economic Co-operation and Development
PRSPs	poverty reduction strategy papers
SAARC	South Asian Association for Regional Cooperation
SACU	Southern African Customs Union

SADC	Southern African Development Community
SADCC	Southern African Development Coordination Conference
SAFTA	South Asian Free Trade Area
SAP	structural adjustment programme
UN	United Nations
UNCTAD	UN Conference on Trade and Development
UNDP	UN Development Programme
US	United States
USAID	US Agency for International Development
WTO	World Trade Organization

1
Introduction

Paul Bowles and Henry Veltmeyer

Thematic overview

Globalization, according to Tony McGrew, 'has colonized the intellectual imagination of the social sciences' (2001: 293). There is plenty of evidence to support such a statement. Entering the word 'globalization' into the Google Scholar search engine results in a list of nearly 400,000 references. Academic Search Premier lists close to 50,000 articles with 'globalization' in their titles and Books In Print, nearly 13,000 titles.

Impressively large though this literature is, the 'colonization of the imagination', at least in print form, has been largely monopolized by scholars of Western academia. It is their interpretations of globalization that have been the dominant ones; it is they who have set the agenda and established the parameters of the discussion. In other words, the vast literature on globalization is not itself global but heavily skewed in favour of the core countries. Scholte (2000: 40) has made the same observation, albeit more pointedly, when he writes that 'the protagonists in globalization debates are disproportionately urban, white, middle-class, Judaeo-Christian, English-speaking men resident in the North (especially the US and the UK)'.

It is not surprising, therefore, to find calls for more inclusive debates. For example, Taylor (2005: 1025–6) introduces a recent paper by stating:

The purpose of this article is to try and suggest how to do global I[nter-national] P[olitical] E[conomy] 'better' within globalization studies. This springs from a belief that a great deal of extant studies are marked by a restricted theoretical and empirical base, which precludes such studies from being truly global. They are, in the main, predicated on selected examples from the core, i.e. the OECD countries, with an occasional nod in the direction of experiences outside the familiar. Certainly, within most IPE work on globalization, there are intermittent references to Asia and Latin America (usually from the perspective of capital flight and currency collapses) but almost no mention at all of Africa, South Asia, the Pacific region or Central Asia. That this neglect impoverishes the discipline is self-evident.

Taylor has a point. Using the (unscientific) method of Google Scholar searches, 'globalization' with 'Netherlands' scores more hits than with 'Russia', with 'Canada' more than with 'China', with 'Denmark' 50 per cent more than with 'Nigeria', with 'Europe' twice as many as with 'Latin America' and with 'US' four times as many as with 'Indonesia'. The 'globalization protagonists', to use Scholte's term, tend to come from the core countries and, as such, what they write about tends to be an academic mirror of the world distribution of wealth and power.

One of the primary motivations for this volume, and the companion volume *National Perspectives on Globalization*, is to address this imbalance. That is, to provide a space for a global dialogue on the meaning of globalization. For this reason, this collection includes essays from scholars all around the world, drawn from 12 regions, each providing perspectives on what constitutes globalization for them. These 12 regions are home to approximately 85 per cent of the world's population. They include the highly populated regions of East Asia, South Asia and South East Asia as well as the smaller geographic and population regions of Central Europe, and Central America and the Caribbean.

The comprehensive geographical scope of the regions analysed means that a defining feature of the approach taken here is to include analyses of globalization from regions which span the 'development divide'. While Taylor is correct in suggesting that much of the existing IPE literature has a bias towards coverage of the core, it is still the case that there is a substantial literature from the development and area studies fields which analyse globalization in the South and in other regions around the world. This volume includes analyses from both the North and the South, a relatively rare occurrence, and which in itself provides fertile ground for comparative analysis. Thus, we include here a chapter on Western Europe as well as on East Africa, for example. Furthermore, in the existing literature on the South, the impacts of globalization are typically the focus of attention. Here, we have asked authors to consider not simply impacts but what globalization means and how it should be theorized from the perspective of their region.

To complement the analysis of 'regional perspectives' provided here, the companion volume provides 'national perspectives' and focuses on

11 countries that include some of the most important countries in terms of population and power. These countries account for over 55 per cent of the world's population, and include the most populous countries in South East Asia (Indonesia), East Asia (China), South Asia (India), Africa (Nigeria), North America (the US) and South America (Brazil), as well as the UK and Russia. Taken together, these two volumes fill an important void by providing contributions towards a theorizing of globalization from a wide range of countries and regions and by bringing together theorists from around the world.

Implicit in the approach taken here is that 'globalization studies' needs to be informed by perspectives drawn from specific country or regional contexts. Such an approach might seem at odds with much of the analysis of globalization which places emphasis on concepts such as 'globality', 'deterritorialization', 'transnational' and 'supraterritoriality', terms which suggest that what distinguishes the contemporary period of globalization is precisely its ability to transcend the concerns, constraints and context of specific territories. While it would be foolish to deny the rise of cross-national flows of information, resources and organizations, it would also be foolish, in our opinion, to fail to pay due recognition to the fact that political entities – states – and regional contexts continue to shape both the processes of globalization and how those processes are interpreted. The study and understanding of globalization must, we argue, be rooted in the specificities of particular contexts.

The theorizing and analysis of globalization is enhanced by taking into account regional contexts for several reasons. Firstly, as Mittelman (2000: 4), for example, has argued, 'globalization proceeds through macro-regionalism sponsored by states and economic forces seeking to open larger markets as a means toward greater competitiveness'; and he identifies a number of 'global regions'. In similar vein, others have referred to the process of 'continental globalization' in the context of North America indicating that regionalism is the vehicle through which globalization is delivered. In Mittelman's view, regional analysis is important because

there is no single wave of globalization washing over or flattening diverse divisions of labour both in regions and in industrial branches. Varied regional divisions of labour are emerging, tethered in different ways to global structures, each one engaged in unequal transactions with world centres of production and finance and presented with distinctive development possibilities. Within each region, sub-global hierarchies have formed, with poles of economic growth, managerial and technological centres, and security systems. (2000: 41)

According to this analysis, not only are regions therefore central to the dynamics of globalization, being the units through which globalization's effects and impacts are felt, but these regions themselves are distinctive in character. Thus, 'it would be fruitless to seek to define a single pattern of regional integration' (ibid.). European formalism, East Asian familialism and diasporas, and hegemony in the Americas all appear in the literature as plausible lines of demarcation. The point here is that 'globalization' needs to be theorized within different regional contexts; the articulation of the processes of globalization and regionalization may differ substantially and this will be missed by approaches which focus only on the 'supraterritorial'.

Gamble and Payne (1996) distinguish between processes of regionalization, defined as being primarily technologically or market led, and of regionalism, defined as being state led. For them, 'state projects like regionalism typically seek to accelerate, to modify, or occasionally to reverse the direction of social change which emergent structures like globalization and regionalization represent' (1996: 250). This reinforces the point that regionalisms differ and need to be examined separately.

A second reason for taking into account regional contexts is that the differences between regions are evident not only in the processes of regionalization and regionalism, but also in their histories and their positions within global capitalism. Western Europe and South America, for example, have played quite different roles in the evolution of global capitalism over the past 500 years, and how the current phase of globalization is understood and analysed is likely to be influenced by this. Regions have different economic, social, military/security and political histories that will condition how 'globalization' is viewed and theorized. They have different histories of migration and diaspora formation, different histories as conquerors and conquered. Their contemporary experiences will also vary significantly with the meaning of 'globalization' reflecting these differences. Thus, the understanding of globalization in the Arab World is likely to be influenced by its history and current experiences in ways that are quite distinct from, for example, the understanding in Central Europe. East Asia's rise in global prominence may lead to a different theorizing of globalization than in West Africa, for example, where marginalization has been a recurrent theme. Are the agents of globalization seen similarly from South Asia as in North America? Furthermore, within each of these regions there will be significant differences. It would be a mistake therefore to homogenize these regions: intra- as well as inter-regional dynamics need to be examined and analysed.

Arising from the importance of the difference of histories, we have explicitly asked authors to consider the periodization of globalization.

That is, to consider from the perspective of their region if and when a distinctive contemporary phase of globalization began and which agents were active in this process. A common theme among Western treatises on globalization is that the 'contemporary phase' is dated from the early to mid 1980s. Typically this dating is supported by appeal to the revolutionizing impact of new information and communications technology (ICT) and the shift to neoliberalism associated with the politics and economics of Thatcherism and Reaganism. This latter shift was itself a response to the profit crisis and impasse in capital–labour relations in the 1970s. This account has mostly been applied to the core countries and regions. In this volume, we not only have authors analysing the accuracy of this account for the core regions but we are also able to assess the extent to which it is plausible as an account of the origins of the contemporary phase of globalization outside of the core.

It is these central issues and questions which the 12 region chapters, and the volume as a whole, addresses. Each author was asked to answer the question 'What is globalization?' from the perspective of his or her region. The answer to this question provides the title to each of the chapters. The question proved more difficult to answer in some regions than in others. For some regions, the authors believe that the answer is self-evident and that the main analysis of globalization needs to concentrate on the impacts of, and resistance to, globalization. The more theoretical question about the nature of globalization is, we discovered, a western/core preoccupation and one which demands little discussion in those regions of the South where the answer of 'neoliberalism' is quickly established. The chapters therefore reveal a range of emphasis reflecting what the authors themselves view as the most important aspects of the globalization debate. For some, it is providing a new analysis of globalization, for others it is establishing its impacts, and for others it is emerging forms of resistance. In presenting their views, we have allowed authors considerable latitude to define for themselves what they consider to be the main issues for the analysis of globalization starting from the context of their own region.

The analyses are, of course, personal perspectives as well as regional perspectives. There is no such thing as 'the' perspective from a particular region but rather 'a' perspective. Different individuals within any region might come to radically different assessments about the processes of globalization as they affect their region. The authors in this volume all present 'critical' analyses. They are 'critical' in a dual sense. Firstly, in an academic sense, in that they not simply present information but also provide interpretations and analyses of that information. Secondly, those interpretations and analyses are critical in a political sense. This is not a book which celebrates globalization as a (bourgeois) utopia. Rather one commonality of the contributors is that they are all drawn to the subject by a need to understand 'globalization' in order to counter its effects. They are all therefore 'critical' of globalization, although they do not represent any single political position.

The authors share a 'political economy' approach, that is, one which takes both economic and political factors into account when explaining globalization. That said, it is clear that disciplinary backgrounds also play a role in influencing the way in which globalization is analysed. For example, those coming from an economics background are more inclined to see globalization as represented by the rise in cross-border flows of goods and capital. This leads to a more empirical approach being taken to globalization with its meaning being derived from the effects of economic integration on national and regional economic and social well-being. Those contributors coming from a political science and international relations background, in contrast, are more likely to approach the issue from a structural analysis of power within the international system. Thus, while there are some common elements, disciplinary backgrounds are also evident in the chapters. We have not sought to harmonize the chapters in this respect and to impose a common framework, even though we did ask all writers to address a common set of questions. As a result, readers coming to the volume from different disciplinary backgrounds may find some chapters more to their taste than others. However, we deliberately sought contributing authors from a range of social-science disciplines even though we realized that how a political scientist would analyse globalization might differ, for example, from how an economist or a sociologist would. We retained this disciplinary range in the belief that if our intention in this volume is to provide a 'global dialogue' on globalization, a part of that dialogue should also be between disciplines.

The contributing authors are all academics, most of whom are working in the region on which they are writing. This is not because we subscribe to the facile position that 'only a European can write about Europe', for example, but because the intention of the volume is to bring together analyses grounded in different regional contexts; that grounding is often best realized by those living and working in that context.

The book therefore brings together specialists on globalization from 12 major regions in the world. The book is organized geographically with the first three chapters providing perspectives from three regions in the Americas. The first chapter, on North America, is written by Eric Helleiner, an author with political science training. This is followed by a perspective from Central America and the Caribbean by social activists Carlos G. Aguilar and Wim Dierckxsens. Paulo Vizentini, a political scientist from Brazil, provides a South American perspective. Moving to Europe, international relations academic Andreas Antoniades provides a perspective from Western Europe, while historian Jacek Kochanowicz writes on Central Europe. A perspective from that group of countries representing the geographic and cultural region which we call here the Arab World is provided by Galal Amin, an Egyptian economist. Part of the Arab World includes North Africa and the rest of the African continent provides three other regional chapters: historians Mary Kinyanjui and Felix Kiruthu provide an East African perspective, and political scientists Amada Sesay and Kehinde Olayode (on West Africa) and Lisa Thompson (on Southern Africa) round out the analysis of the continent. Economist Nasreen Khundker from Bangladesh provides a perspective from South Asia, while sociologists Walden Bello and Kwong-leung Tang provide perspectives from South East Asia and East Asia respectively.

The chapters offer a rich dialogue – with regions from the North and South represented, with a 'transition' region included and with authors from multidisciplinary backgrounds, although many would prefer 'political economist' to describe their intellectual location. In the concluding chapter we draw out the implications of these regional studies for our understanding of globalization.

Synopsis

Eric Helleiner, in Chapter 2, addresses the question as to whether there might be a distinctive 'North American' perspective on globalization, a question that also relates to North America itself: Does it (i.e. Canada, the US and Mexico) constitute a region? His answer in a nutshell is that there is in fact a distinctive North American perspective on the meaning of globalization, one forged in the very context of the region's creation. In effect, the emergence of the globalization discourse in the 1980s was timely in that it coincided with an impetus to forge links among the three national economies on the North American continent, and to seek thereby a 'regional' entry into the global capitalist economy.

In Chapter 3 Wim Dierckxsens and Carlos G. Aguilar turn towards another area of the Americas, raising serious questions about regional identity as well as conditions of integration into the global economy. They attempt to bring into analytic focus the diverse countries of Central America and those that comprise the Caribbean basin: that large number of mostly small island states and economies and those countries on the northern rim of South America that share a 'Caribbean' culture. Of course, all these countries hardly constitute a coherent 'region'. In fact, they comprise a most diverse mix of cultures, societies, economies and polities that happen to be located longitudinally between what we have for heuristic and analytic purposes identified as 'North' and 'South' America. The question that the authors address is whether these diverse cultures, societies and economies share a particular location in the globalization process, and whether in this regional context there is a shared perspective on the globalization process.

Paulo Fagundes Vizentini, in Chapter 4, turns towards 'South America', a set of countries and economies more easily grouped together as a region, comprising as they do of Brazil, the largest economy in the region and a Portuguese-speaking society, and a number of countries that share a legacy of Spanish colonialism and a struggle for national independence. A number of societies in the region also share in a historic and ongoing struggle of diverse indigenous peoples and nationalities, mostly located in the Andean highlands and the Amazonian subregion, against class exploitation, oppression and social exclusion. In this regional context the author focuses on the contemporary process of neoliberal capitalist development and globalization, and on the forces that have been unleashed in the process. The author's South American perspective is defined by the workings in the region of a global process of economic integration and the impact of this process on diverse countries. In short, the author argues that the 'new economic model' of neoliberal capitalist development throughout the region is in crisis.

In Chapter 5 Andreas Antoniades turns to Western Europe, a 'region' that, like much of North America (the US and Canada), is located at the centre of the world capitalist system, and thus presumably the countries in this region have experienced a very different, if not distinct, globalization process from that experienced in Central and South America, which are located on the periphery of the system. For the purposes of his analysis, Antoniades considers 'Western Europe' to be 'the politico-economic area covered by the European Union before its eastward expansion (i.e. the EU15)'. In this regional context the author argues that a Western European perspective on globalization is formed by the interplay between two competing discourses/projects. The first proclaims that Europe, instead of participating in or contributing to an international 'race to the bottom' in economic, social and environmental terms, must intervene in (and humanize) globalization by defending its social model, values and standards of living and working. The second proclaims that globalization is unavoidable and irresistible, not something that can be shaped; the only option is for countries to position themselves and strike the best deal they can.

In Chapter 6 Jacek Kochanowicz turns to Central Europe, a 'region' forged and shaped by a legacy of actually existing socialism and a process of 'transition' since the late 1980s and early 1990s towards capitalism. In this regional context, 'globalization' might be seen as a transmission belt hitched at high gear to a process of economic integration into the 'new world order'. The process, from the author's 'Central European' perspective is one of rapid 'transformation' – radical change of hitherto prevailing forms of economic and political organization. As Kochanowicz sees it, this process of transformation, like the collapse of state socialism itself, is the direct outcome of globalization in its neoliberal form, arguably the most advanced form of capitalism and imperialism. The focus of the chapter is on what this means for societies in this post-communist world.

In Chapter 7 Galal Amin turns towards several 'cultural encounters' of an 'uneven kind' to provide a perspective on globalization from the Arab World: an opening up of societies and economies located in the Middle East, a region that finds itself at the very centre of what some view as 'a clash of civilizations' but that others see as cultural and economic imperialism, the project of an imperial state to dominate the world system and hegemonize its forces – and this by force if necessary (and it is seen to be so). The author traces out several important and recent shifts from one area and 'centre' to another in a historic 200-year process of 'globalization'. As reflected in the title of the chapter, this process has been most 'uneven', with less than salutary results for the people and countries that make up the Arab world.

The next three chapters focus on Africa: West, Southern and East. In Chapter 8 Amadu Sesay and Kehinde Olayode examine the extent to which West Africa has participated in the globalization process and question the assumptions underlying the unbridled optimism about the capacity of unregulated markets to sustain economic growth and respond to problems of poverty and inequality. In other words, the chapter attempts to answer these important questions: Do the developing countries of the region have the opportunity, interest or ability to actualize the benefits promised by globalization? How are the issues of globalization and equity played out in the region? Will further integration of West Africa into international capitalism help countries in the sub-region to create the internal socio-political, economic and ideological conditions that will enable them to satisfy the exigencies of nation building and development?

In Chapter 9 Lisa Thompson takes a look at the contradictions that beset the process of globalization in Southern Africa, with reference here to the 14 countries that make up the Southern Africa Development Community (SADC), a regional organization founded in 1980 but reformed in 1992.

In a nuanced analysis of globalization's diverse, and indeed contradictory, regional outcomes, she makes the point that while the dynamics of what is new about globalization might refer to supranationality, the fundamental *developmental* impact of globalization is definitely territorial. This (globalization, both supraterritorial and territorial) means that 'globalization processes do not necessarily have a homogeneous . . . impact'. The chapter elaborates on this point from a Southern Africa perspective.

In Chapter 10 Mary Njeri Kinyanjui and Felix Kiruthu consider the workings of globalization on the countries that constitute 'East Africa': Kenya, Uganda and Tanzania, three countries that share common borders as well as Lake Victoria, the largest fresh-water lake on the continent, and – most importantly – a common history as former colonies or protectorates of the British Empire. From the perspective of this regional connectedness and common history, the authors argue that globalization essentially has meant 'imperialism': the imposition on countries of practices and policies that reflect the interests of 'outside powers'. As the authors construct it, the process of globalization or imperialism has unfolded in three distinct phases, the most recent of which ('super-imperialism') entails the agency of the World Bank and the International Monetary Fund (IMF) – 'currently the prime movers of global capitalism in East Africa' – as well as the World Trade Organization (WTO) and the multinational corporations. Together, these institutions represent the current configuration of globalization and have a major impact on shaping developments in the region.

With Chapter 11 the book turns to Asia, the most populous region of the world including what the World Bank (1993) termed the 'East Asian Miracle' – the emergence of countries that have exhibited historically unprecedented rates of rapid economic growth accompanied by productive and social transformation. The emergence of 'newly industrializing countries', first Japan and South East Asia, and more recently China and India, has sustained a more sanguine or positive view about globalization than that which prevails in Latin America and Africa, where its negative outcomes and effects are evident. As a result of these developments the debate about globalization in its most recent regional configuration and neoliberal form has been joined by scholars all over the world, some of them in this volume.

In Chapter 11 Nasreen Khundker takes us to South Asia, a region that encompasses some of the poorest countries in the world outside sub-Saharan Africa, and India, a poor country that in recent years appears to have joined the race to the top under the aegis of neoliberal globalization. South Asia comprises the countries of Afghanistan, Bangladesh, Bhutan, India, the Maldives, Nepal, Pakistan and Sri Lanka. These countries are also members of the South Asian Association for Regional Cooperation (SAARC), established in 1985. The main argument of this chapter is that in the South Asian context, 'globalization' is the realization of the neoliberal agenda of free trade and pro-market economic policies, with uncertain outcomes for development. In her analysis of the mixed outcomes of 'enforced globalization' in its neoliberal form the author emphasizes its historic roots in the colonial period and the neocolonial character of its current sponsors: 'global institutions such as the World Bank and the IMF, and more recently, the WTO'. The chapter examines the meaning and content of globalization in this context (the construction of, and integration into a new world economic order), as well as its outcomes for the South Asia region and its development implications.

In Chapter 12 Walden Bello takes us on the roller-coaster ride that globalization has been for the countries that make up South East Asia. Some of the countries in this region were among the first to experience a process of accelerated integration into the world economy under the aegis of Japanese capital. However, the period of rapid growth and relative prosperity brought about or associated with this early form of globalization (its form, neoliberal or otherwise, still at issue) did not last. In 1997 the region was hit by a wave of highly mobile and volatile capital released, as Joseph Stiglitz, former chief economist at the World Bank, has argued, by the self-interested and system-supporting (imperialist) misguided policies promoted by the IMF. The result was a financial crisis, the momentous conditions and effects of which (relative stagnation, large-scale poverty, inequality) countries in the region are still seeking to escape. The chapter examines the contradictory dynamics of this situation for countries in the region, providing thereby a perspective from South East Asia.

In Chapter 13 Kwong-leung Tang provides not a dissimilar perspective from East Asia. As Tang constructs the heated debate that has surrounded globalization in this regional context, it is mainly seen in economic and political terms, and in these terms a 'hotly contested terrain' rather than a 'neutral process'. On this intellectual battleground, the central focus of the chapter, liberal economists seek to establish the claim that economic liberalization promotes growth and reduces poverty while their many critics contend that the neoliberal regime of liberalization only fosters conditions that ensure the continued production of poverty in the developing countries by shrinking their prospects of economic growth. In this debate, reconstructed here in the context of East Asia, we have the contours of an ideological and political divide found across the world. Globalization is indeed a highly contested concept, pointing towards radically divergent ideas about epoch-defining changes and world developments.

To sort out and make sense of these divergent ideas, to provide a series of regional perspectives on associated 'developments', is one of the reasons for constructing this book and presenting it to our readers.

References

Gamble, A. and A. Payne (eds) (1996) *Regionalism and World Order*. New York: St Martin's Press.

McGrew, T. (2001) 'Review of "Globalization: A Critical Introduction" by Jan Aart Scholte', *New Political Economy*, 6(2): 293–301.

Mittelman, J. (2000) *The Globalization Syndrome: Transformation and Resistance*. Princeton: Princeton University Press.

Scholte, J. (2000) *Globalization: A Critical Introduction*. New York: St Martin's Press.

Stiglitz, J. (2002) *Globalization and its Discontents*. London: Penguin.

Taylor, I. (2005) 'Globalization Studies and the Developing World: Making International Political Economy Truly Global', *Third World Quarterly*, 26(7): 1025–42.

World Bank (1993) *The East Asian Miracle: Economic Growth and Public Policy*. New York: Oxford University Press.

2

A Rhetorical Weapon? A Perspective from North America

Eric Helleiner

Is there a North American answer to the question 'What is globalization?'. At first sight, any answer seems difficult because the very idea of Canada, the United States and Mexico representing a coherent regional political-economic unit is such a new one. It was born primarily in the age of globalization itself with the creation of the North American Free Trade Agreement in 1994.

In this chapter, I shall argue that this coincidence of timing is in fact significant. At the time of the NAFTA debates, both supporters and opponents invoked 'globalization' as a key force that was contributing to the birth of the North American region. Indeed, it was during these debates that 'globalization' first entered in a serious way into the political discourse of the three countries. In this context, the word acquired a distinctive meaning across North America. Thus, there *has* in fact been a distinctive North American perspective on the meaning of globalization, a perspective forged in the context of the region's creation itself.

At the same time, the unity of this perspective should not be overstated. As I highlight in the last two sections of the chapter, opponents of NAFTA have always seen globalization as a wider phenomenon than do its supporters, one that encompasses not just economic but also political and social phenomena. Moreover, as those opponents have increasingly built global activist alliances, the distinctiveness of North American debate on globalization has been eroded.

The birth of the North American region

Before the current age of globalization, the idea that 'North America' might be a region with a common perspective on any political-economic issue was rarely considered. This is not to say that economic integration involving the three countries was not extensive. But this integration had two distinctive features that discouraged analysts from seeing North America as a coherent political-economic community. The first was that economic integration proceeded not in a regional framework but rather in the context of two bilateral relationships: that between the US and Canada, and that between the US and Mexico. Second, even within these two bilateral relationships, economic integration was characterized by very few formal intergovernmental agreements.

In the US–Canada context, it is necessary in fact to go back as far as the Reciprocity Treaty of 1854–66 between the US and the Canadian colonies to find a precedent for the kind of comprehensive free-trade deal that was introduced in 1989. The Reciprocity Treaty had a relatively short life and was cancelled by the US in 1866 in response to protectionist interests in that country. After several efforts to renew the treaty, politicians in the newly created country of Canada soon turned towards a more nationalist economic policy in 1879. Their 'National Policy' supported a more integrated national economy along East–West lines with the creation of a tariff to support local manufacturing and the building of the pan-Canadian railway. Although the renewal of free trade with the US continued to attract large support within the country, the cause was decisively rejected in the elections of 1891 and 1911. But even under the National Policy, economic ties with the US continued to grow. This was true not just in the area of trade but also investment, as many US firms were tempted in the late 19th and early 20th century to jump over the tariff wall and establish production within Canada.

Economic linkages between the two countries grew rapidly in the interwar years, but, again, driven largely by private-sector initiatives rather than formal treaties. Indeed, Canadian politicians strengthened their formal links to Britain's imperial economic bloc during this period. This political initiative in fact only increased the attractiveness of Canada as a location for US firms to invest in, since they were able to export to the entire Empire market from manufacturing branch plants they established in Canada.

In the post-1945 years, trade and investment ties accelerated even further, and they did so once again largely without the help of a formal free trade or investment treaty between the two countries. The main exception was the Auto Pact of 1965 which provided free trade the auto sector, subject to the provision that a portion of North American automobile production remained in Canada. Initiatives to create a more comprehensive bilateral agreement to foster integration – including one as early as 1947–8 – were resisted by the Canadian government. By the 1970s and early 1980s, the Canadian government was in fact actively resisting further economic integration through various high-profile initiatives including regulations on foreign investment, support for Canadian-owned firms in sectors such as energy and cultural industries, and official efforts to diversify Canada's trade away from the US (Clarkson, 1985; Williams, 1994).

The history of US–Mexican economic integration since the late 19th century was also characterized by few formal agreements. Economic ties between the two countries accelerated rapidly for the first time during the presidency of Porfirio Díaz (1876–80, 1884–1910) who actively encouraged foreign investment and export-oriented development. After the Mexican Revolution of 1911–17, economic policy moved in a more nationalist direction. The constitution of 1917 directly challenged the dominant role of foreign investors in sectors such as agriculture and mining by declaring the land and subsoil wealth of the country as belonging to the nation. During the presidency of Lázaro Cárdenas (1934–40), the Mexican government sought to implement this goal through various initiatives such as land reform involving expropriation of foreign holdings and the nationalization of the foreign-owned oil industry in 1938. Cárdenas also made more serious efforts to promote Mexican industrialization through state support and tariff protection.

These efforts to promote industrialization with state support accelerated during World War II and the early post-1945 years. But so too did economic ties with the US in the form of growing Mexican exports to the US as well as foreign direct investments by US firms to establish manufacturing plants in Mexico behind the national tariff wall. The US and Mexican governments made few efforts to formalize the growing private economic ties between their two countries in this period. But there were some exceptions. The first most important exception was the 1942–64 Bracero Agreement which encouraged migrant labour flows from Mexico to the US. The agreement was initially meant to help the US address labour shortages in its agricultural sector during the war, but it remained in place after the war, encouraging hundreds of thousands of Mexican seasonal workers to find employment in the US every year. It served not only US corporate interests but also the Mexican government's goals of finding employment for rural labour and earning extra foreign-exchange earnings.

In the 1960s, the US and Mexican governments also began to foster the growth of 'maquiladora' sector in the northern Mexican border zone that came to be dominated by US manufacturers producing for the US market (Sklair, 1989). Even this important initiative, however, was not characterized by a formal bilateral agreement. Instead, it involved two separate unilateral national initiatives: 1) the creation of the 806/807 provisions in US trade law in 1962 that enabled imports produced with US parts and components abroad to have tariffs applied only on the value added abroad; and 2) the Mexican government's establishment of the Border Industrialization Program in 1965 that enabled the duty-free import of parts and machinery to the sector. The latter was established soon after the Bracero Agreement had been terminated in 1964 by the US (in response to the mechanization of US agriculture and growing domestic opposition to Mexican seasonal labour) partly in order to provide employment opportunities for the large numbers of Mexicans in the border region who were suddenly left without work.

There were not many more such official initiatives from the US and Mexican governments to promote economic integration in this period. Indeed, by the 1970s, Mexican economic policymakers were actively resisting the growing economic ties between the two countries. As in Canada, the Mexican government turned in an increasingly economic nationalist direction during this period, making efforts to diversity its export markets, tighten regulations over foreign companies and promote national ownership in key sectors of the economy.

In short, then, North American economic integration before the 1980s was characterized by two separate bilateral economic relationships – between the US and Canada, and the US and Mexico – neither of which was supported by many intergovernmental trade or investment treaties. It was not until after the late 1980s that this feature of North American economic integration was transformed and a more formal and trilateral 'North American economic region' was born. The first initiative in this direction came with the creation of the Canada–US Free Trade Agreement (CUFTA) in 1989, an agreement that provided a comprehensive framework for trade and investment flows between the two countries for the first time in the post-war period (Tomlin and Doern, 1991). Then, in 1994, all three countries created the North American Free Trade Agreement which built directly on the framework of CUFTA. The NAFTA was significant not only in formalizing Mexico's commitment to deepening economic ties with the US but also in creating a trilateral framework for economic integration across North America for the first time in the three countries' histories (Mayer, 1998; Cameron and Tomlin, 2000).

Globalization's contribution to the birth of North America

Why did these changes suddenly take place in the late 1980s and early 1990s? A detailed analysis is beyond the scope of this short chapter, but it is important for our purposes to recognize that supporters of North American free trade in all three countries invoked 'globalization' as one of the central rationales for their project. In what ways was globalization significant in this respect and what meaning was ascribed to the word?

Let us begin with the perspective of Canadian supporters of CUFTA/ NAFTA. The initiative to create CUFTA came first from the Canadian government in 1985. Backed by the recommendations of a Royal Commission, Brian Mulroney's Conservative government launched free-trade negotiations with the US between 1985 and 1987 and then success-fully fought an election in 1988 in which the CUFTA became the central issue. A central motivation for CUFTA was that of improving the com-petitiveness of the Canadian economy in an increasingly 'globalized' world. Globalization in this context referred to the rapid growth of international trade and investment flows.

Expanding international trade, it was argued, ensured that Canadian firms could no longer rest secure in a sheltered domestic market. Not only did they face more intense foreign competition, but their success increas-ingly relied on selling to larger markets abroad that would enable greater economies of scale to be realized in their production processes. Canadian-based firms also recognized that their ability to compete required them to become more closely linked with globally integrated webs of produc-tion that large firms abroad were cultivating in the 1980s and 1990s. Canadian policymakers also began to worry that the ability of Canada to maintain a high standard of living was reliant on the country's ability to attract internationally mobile investment from the foreign firms involved in these new global webs (Tomlin and Doern, 1991; Cameron and Grinspun, 1993).

From a Canadian perspective, CUFTA would help Canada adjust to this new global economy in a number of ways. By reducing tariff barriers, the agreement would provide a competitive jolt to protected Canadian-based firms. It would also help to restrain US trade protectionism, thereby guar-anteeing a larger market for Canadian firms and helping to attract for-eign direct investment to locate in Canada. And finally, the investment provisions of the deal would guarantee more predictable and friendly investment rules for foreign firms in Canada as well as Canadian firms investing in the US. The decision of the Canadian government to join the US–Mexican free trade negotiations in the early 1990s was also driven by the desire to attract foreign investment. If the US secured free-trade agreements with both Canada and Mexico, it was feared that inter-nationally mobile firms would locate in the US because this location provided access to the two markets. To avoid a situation where the US made itself the centre of a kind of 'hub-and-spoke' arrangement of bilateral trade deals, Canadian officials pressed for a trilateral agreement (Cameron and Tomlin, 2000).

These arguments invoking globalization as the rationale for a North American free trade agreement were put forward not just by Canadian conservatives and business leaders. They even found support among more centre-left policymakers. Liberal leader Jean Chretien, whose party had opposed CUFTA during the 1988 federal election, was a prominent convert after attending a 1991 policy conference whose keynote speaker was Robert Reich – his 1991 book *The Work of Nations* became very influential in this period. In the book, Reich argued that traditional statist policies favouring national champions had become futile in the new global age where investment was so mobile and where firms were becoming incorporated into transnational webs. Reich had previously been one of the leading US advocates of Japanese-style industrial policy. Now he argued that globalization had left this strategy outdated: 'We are living through a transformation that will rearrange the politics and economics of the coming century. There will be no national products or technologies, no national corporations, no national industries. There will no longer be national economies' (Reich, 1991: 1). In this new context, he called for more liberal trade and investment policies combined with a state support for education, job training and infrastructure.

Chretien embraced this new policy framework – which soon came to be associated with 'Third Way' politics – as Clinton would soon too. And Chretien's defence of his decision to change the Liberal Party policy to support CUFTA – and subsequently NAFTA after his election as Prime Minister in 1993 – invoked Reich's arguments directly: 'In the world of tomorrow, the old concepts of right and left do not mean anything. Protectionism is not left-wing or right-wing, it is simply passé. Globalization is not right-wing or left-wing. It is simply a fact of life' (*The Globe and Mail*, 1991).

The Mexican government relied on quite similar arguments when explaining its decision to first propose the idea of NAFTA in 1990 to US authorities. Since the outbreak of its debt crisis in 1982, the Mexican government had increasingly turned its back on statist economic policies in favour of more neoliberal ones promoted by the IMF. This had been not just because of the short-term need to satisfy international creditors. Equally important was a broader re-evaluation in Mexican technocratic circles of the merits of its past policies in the context of rapidly growing global investment and trade flows. The import-substitution industrialization strategy of the past was now seen to have fostered inefficient industries that were not fit to face the competitive realities of the new global economy. The highly regulated nature of the Mexican economy was also seen to discourage internationally mobile capital.

The NAFTA initiative was undertaken by President Salinas who was a US-trained economist renowned for his embrace of the IMF's neoliberal policy agenda. Indeed, in his view, the central case for NAFTA was that it would help to lock in the neoliberal Mexican economic policy regime. This, in turn, would help to attract mobile investment. He was particularly worried that the fall of the Berlin Wall was diverting the attention of international investors, particularly those in Europe, towards Eastern European countries. But the investment he hoped to lure to Mexico was not just foreign investment but also the flight capital of Mexicans that had left the country during the economic uncertainties of the previous decade (Cameron and Tomlin, 2000).

Globalization was also invoked prominently by supporters of North American free trade within the United States. The signing of CUFTA generated very little debate within the US, but NAFTA provoked much more domestic controversy. Indeed, the NAFTA debate has been described as one of the most controversial foreign economic policy debates within the US during the entire post-war period (Mayer, 1998). Although the Bush administration initially negotiated the deal, it fell to the Clinton administration to implement it after its election in 1992. After it succeeded in negotiating side agreements on labour and environmental issues with Canada and Mexico, the Clinton administration chose to back the deal.

A central plank in their case for NAFTA was that the agreement was necessary to help the US meet the challenges of the new global economy. The arguments of Robert Reich – who became Clinton's Labor Secretary and close confidant – were particularly prominent. Many US NAFTA supporters also argued, in a more neo-mercantilist manner, that the creation of a regional economic bloc was necessary to counter the growing economic competitive threat posed by the European Union and the East Asian region. NAFTA would guarantee US firms a larger market as well as access to resources in Canada and Mexico and a cheap labour pool in Mexico. This line of argument prompted US officials to press during the NAFTA negotiations for such provisions as tougher local content rules in the auto sector in order to defend the US Big Three firms (General Motors, Ford and Chrysler) against Japanese companies. Because they were keen to welcome Japanese investment, the Canadian and Mexican governments were much more wary of efforts to create such an 'insider/outsider' distinction (Molot, 1993).

In all three countries, then, the case for the creation of a more formally integrated North American economic bloc drew heavily on the phenomenon of globalization. This was a phenomenon that had not previously held a prominent place in the political discourse of these countries. It was now put front and centre by supporters of NAFTA. In each of Canada, Mexico and the United States NAFTA advocates all shared a similar understanding of the meaning of globalization. It was, to them, primarily an economic phenomenon involving the rapid growth of global trade and investment flows and provoking more intense competitive pressures around the world. In this way, the birth of North America itself as a political-economic region coincided with the emergence of a pan-North American answer to the question of 'what is globalization?'.

The perspective of the opposition

This answer was in fact partially shared by the opponents of North American free trade in the three countries. Given how globalization was invoked so often by CUFTA/NAFTA supporters, it is hardly surprising that the word also figured prominently in the analyses of those who sought to block these agreements. Indeed, opposition to CUFTA/NAFTA quickly became synonymous with opposition to 'globalization' (or even 'continental globalization'). The creation of these regional trade agreements came to be seen as both an embodiment of globalization and as an effort to further entrench and expand its influence in North American society (e.g. Cameron and Grinspun, 1993).

To CUFTA/NAFTA supporters, the notion that globalization could be 'opposed' was a fanciful one since it was an inexorable economic process driven largely by unstoppable technological pressures. Opponents agreed that it was an economic process involving an intensification of trade and investment flows. But they did not agree that the phenomenon was such an inevitable one. In their view, it was a political project being driven by an increasingly cosmopolitan class of big business and policy elites inspired by neoliberal ideology.

In the words of many opponents, what globalization supporters sought was the establishment of 'corporate rule' on a global scale (Nader *et al.*, 1993; Barlow and Campbell, 1991). This would be achieved not just by unleashing the competitive pressures of globalized markets but also by constraining the power of nation states through binding international treaties that locked in neoliberal policies. CUFTA and NAFTA were seen as prime examples of an initiative to implement this kind of 'neo-constitutional' constraint on state policymaking. (For a discussion of neo-constitutionalism, see Bakker and Gill, 2003.)

In this way, critics of North American free trade actually shifted the meaning of globalization in an important way. To them, the term was wider than just an economic phenomenon. It was also a socio-political process involving the emergence of a new transnational class that was bent on constructing new anti-democratic international governance mechanisms. From this perspective, globalization was contributing both to the growing inequality within and between countries and to the erosion of national autonomy, democracy and social and environmental standards.

Given this analysis, it is no wonder that the opposition to CUFTA/ NAFTA inspired such a diverse collection of domestic groups. In Canada, the negotiation of CUFTA generated one of the most broadly based coalitions in the country's recent political history that involved labour, the women's movement, environmentalists, native groups, social democrats and nationalists. Organized through bodies such as the Council of Canadians and the Pro-Canada Network, these groups were united in the view that CUFTA signalled an effort by Canadian elites to dismantle the country's more European-style socio-economic model in favour of a more neoliberal US-style of capitalism (Ayres, 1998).

The anti-NAFTA coalition in Mexico assembled a similar range of groups (although the scale of the opposition was muted somewhat by the long-standing close relationship with the ruling party of many of the country's unions and lobby groups). Many of them saw NAFTA as an abandonment of the social, nationalist and democratic goals of the Mexican Revolution of 1911–17. In their view, Mexico's subordination to the US would only be enhanced as the country became primarily a source of cheap labour and energy resources for US firms. Free trade would lead to the 'maquiladorization' of the entire manufacturing sector and would wipe out the livelihood of peasant farmers (Cameron and Grinspun, 1993). It was, in the words of the Zapatistas in the southern Chiapas province, a 'death sentence' for the small farmer.

In the US, oppositional forces to NAFTA were even wider. They included not just a coalition of left-wing groups who worried about job losses and downward pressure on US labour and environmental standards. Equally important were many groups on the right led by Ross Perot (1993) and Pat Buchanan (1998). Tapping into the long-standing populist tradition in US politics, Perot, Buchanan and their supporters associated NAFTA and globalization with the loss of American sovereignty and its standard of living. The title of Pat Buchanan's 1998 book summed up this latter perspective well: *The Great Betrayal: How American Sovereignty and Social Justice Are Being Sacrificed to the Gods of the Global Economy*. His critique of global corporate rule often bore a striking similarity to that put forward by the left: 'A transnational [corporation] has no heart or soul. It is an amoral institution that exists to maximize profits, executive compensation, and stock dividends. If the bottom line commands the cashiering of loyal workers after years of service, it will be done with the same ruthless efficiency with which obsolete equipment is junked' (Buchanan, 1998: 55).

What alternative to CUFTA/NAFTA did these groups put forward? Some recommended a reinvigoration of a more nationalist kind of economic policy as the best mechanism for challenging the globalization project. During the CUFTA debate of the late 1980s, many Canadians opposed to the agreement favoured an intensification of the efforts launched in the 1970s and early 1980s to develop a Canadian economy more autonomous of foreign, especially American, influence (Barlow and Campbell, 1991). Many Mexican opponents of NAFTA also called for a return to the import-substitution industrialization policies of the post-war period. In the US, the nationalist option had particularly wide and populist appeal. Indeed, figures such as Buchanan on the right or Ralph Nader on the left combined their rejection of NAFTA with a broader attack on US participation in the Bretton Woods institutions (Rupert, 2000).

Other opponents argued that a more effective alternative to CUFTA/NAFTA was to accept the reality of North American integration, but to press for a different kind of regional trade and investment agreement. This line of thinking was initially pressed most vigorously by the Mexican opponents of NAFTA. After a decade of neoliberal reforms, they recognized the difficulties involved in efforts to return to post-war nationalist policies. Led by Cuauhtémoc Cárdenas, they called for a Continental Trade and Development Pact that would embody a more European style of regional integration. The Pact would include: a social charter to harmonize labour and environmental standards at a high level, human rights guarantees, labour mobility, tri-national industrial policy and special support for subsistence agriculture and poor regions of North America (Cavanagh, 1992).

Although Cárdenas himself moved away from many of these ideas when he ran (unsuccessfully) for the Mexican presidency in 1994, they soon became a rallying call for many NAFTA opponents in Canada and the US. If regional integration could proceed along these lines, it could represent a kind of *resistance* to globalization, rather than a reinforcement of it. This line of argument had some limited impact on the Clinton administration and the Chretien government, both of whom refused to endorse NAFTA unless it was accompanied by labour and environmental side agreements. But the limited content of these agreements – and their subsequent record – was very disappointing to those pushing for a more social democratic EU-style of regional integration (Mayer, 1998).

One final alternative to NAFTA was to press for global change. If NAFTA was a product of globalization, did it not make more sense to attack the latter directly through the cultivation of global alliances that could challenge this political project of policy and business elites around the world? Once again it was a group of Mexicans – in this case the Zapatista movement – which provided an initial inspiration for many who took up this cause. Not long after the launch of their initial rebellion in Chiapas on the day that NAFTA came into force, the Zapatistas invited activists from around the world to a 1996 conference called the First Intercontinental Encounter against Neoliberalism and for Humanity. The conference was attended by 3,000 people from 43 countries, and was followed up by two others with the same title in Berlin in 1996 and in Spain in 1997. The transnational networks built in these and other subsequent contexts provided the basis for the coalitions that later helped to target successfully the OECD's Multilateral Agreement on Investment in 1998 and the WTO's Seattle Ministerial meetings in 1999 (e.g. Seoane and Taddei, 2002).

Canadian opponents of NAFTA have subsequently played a particularly prominent role in the development of a global movement challenging the neoliberal globalization project. Figures such as Maude Barlow, Tony Clarke and Naomi Klein have become well-known names to activists around the world for this reason. The high profile role of Canadians may reflect in part the political reality of the difficulties of cultivating support for nationalist or regionalist responses to NAFTA in the Canadian context. Barlow and Clarke had in fact embraced much more of a nationalist stance during the CUFTA debate of the late 1980s and had been politically defeated. Subsequent developments also revealed to the Canadian left that the prospects for Cardénas's social model of North American integration were slim.

Towards a more nuanced (and less distinctive) understanding of globalization

The support for this movement in Canada and elsewhere in North America has been important in widening the meaning of 'globalization' even further in the region. Initially, the movement was described both by its detractors and many of its supporters as an 'anti-globalization movement'. But the inaccuracy of this label was soon pointed out given that one of its central goals was to cultivate global alliances. The objective, in other words, was to encourage a 'globalization' of the forces of resistance to the 'neoliberal' globalization project of policy elites. While the latter was often referred to as 'globalization from above', the former quickly came to be known as a kind of 'globalization from below' (e.g. Brecher and Costello, 1994).

In this way, 'globalization' ceased to be merely something to be opposed by anti-neoliberal activists in North America. In this aspect of its social dimension, it was increasingly something to be embraced. As their influence grew, many of the more reformist transnational activists also became increasingly keen to promote greater 'political globalization'. They hoped to strengthen new kinds of global governance as a mechanism for containing the power of globalized markets and corporate power. The commitment of North American activists to building this kind of global social-democratic alternative was shared by many of the groups they encountered from Europe and Latin America in contexts such as the World Social Forum.

At the same time, those involved in the globalization-from-above networks were also forced to embrace a more nuanced understanding of globalization. As globally linked activists became more and more successful in challenging the neoliberal project across the world, it became increasingly difficult to argue that 'globalization' was simply an unstoppable economic phenomenon to be celebrated. It clearly had an important social component that could no longer be ignored: the transnationally linked 'internet warriors' who saw 'globalization' as a much less positive phenomenon. This element threatened to slow down, or even stop, what had previously been portrayed as a juggernaut of economic globalization.

By the turn of the century, the North American debate on globalization had thus become much more nuanced and complex. It had also become less distinctive. Characteristic of the North American perspective on globalization in the mid-to-late 1990s had been its highly politicized and binary nature. Depending on one's perspective in the CUFTA/NAFTA debates, globalization had been either good or bad. Full stop. Elsewhere in the world, it had often assumed a more ambiguous and overtly less politicized meaning.

Conclusion

What is 'globalization', then, from a North American perspective? In all three countries, the word entered political discourse in a prominent way at the very moment that a more formal North American community was being formed for the first time. The timing was not accidental. 'Globalization' was a phenomenon invoked as a rhetorical weapon by both sides in the intense debate that accompanied the creation of North American free trade. To both supporters and opponents of CUFTA/NAFTA, globalization was one of the key forces prompting the three governments of North America to embrace a regional free-trade agreement. Globalization, in other words, helped to bring North America into being.

But the equating of the creation of North America with globalization has meant that the term has acquired certain particular North American meanings for both supporters and opponents of CUFTA/NAFTA. For the supporters, globalization was associated primarily with growing global trade and investment flows and intensifying competitive pressures across the world. For the opponents, globalization was also an active socio-political project of globalizing elites who sought to promote global economic integration and lock into neoliberal policies via international treaties. From this latter standpoint, CUFTA/NAFTA was both a product of globalization – in all of its economic, political and social dimensions – and one of its more prominent manifestations.

At the same time, globalization soon assumed for North American opponents a more positive social meaning that was associated with their growing links with activists around the world who were opposed to neoliberal policies. This development marked the breakdown of the binary nature of the North American debate on globalization that been born in the CUFTA/NAFTA debates. Globalization was no longer something to be clearly opposed or supported by those who had been involved in the CUFTA/NAFTA debates. In this way, North American discourse on globalization became less distinctive and more open to engagement with the debate that was taking place in other regions of the world.

References

Ayres, J. (1998) *Defying Conventional Wisdom: Political Movements and Popular Contestation against North American Free Trade.* Toronto: University of Toronto Press.

Bakker, I. and S. Gill (eds) (2003) *Power, Production and Social Reproduction.* New York: Macmillan.

Barlow, M. and B. Campbell (1991) *Take Back the Nation.* Toronto: Key Porter Books.

Brecher, J. and T. Costello (1994) *Global Village or Global Pillage: Economic Reconstruction from the Bottom Up.* Boston: South End Press.

Buchanan, P. (1998) *The Great Betrayal: How American Sovereignty and Social Justice Are Being Sacrificed to the Gods of the Global Economy.* Boston: Little, Brown.

Cameron, M. and R. Grinspun (eds) (1993) *The Political Economy of North American Free Trade.* Montreal: McGill-Queen's University Press.

Cameron M. and B. Tomlin (2000) *The Making of NAFTA: How the Deal was Done.* Ithaca: Cornell University Press.

Cavanagh, J. (1992) *Trading Freedom*. Toronto: Between the Lines.

Clarkson, S. (1985) *Canada and the Reagan Challenge* (2nd edn) Toronto: James Lorimer.

Globe and Mail, The (1991) 'Today is Tomorrow to Yesterday's Men', 26 November, p. A18.

Mayer, F. (1998) *Interpreting NAFTA*. New York: Columbia University Press.

Molot, M. (ed.) (1993) *Driving Continentally: National Policies and the North American Auto Industry*. Ottawa: Carleton University Press.

Nader, R., *et al.* (1993) *The Case Against Free Trade: GATT, NAFTA, and the Globalization of Corporate Power*. San Francisco: Earth Island Press.

Reich, R. (1991) *The Work of Nations*. New York: A. A. Knopf.

Rupert, M. (2000) *Ideologies of Globalization*. London: Routledge.

Seoane, J. and E. Taddei (2002) 'From Seattle to Porto Alegre: The Anti-Neoliberal Globalization Movement', *Current Sociology*, 50, 1, 99–122.

Sklair, L. (1989) *Assembling for Development: The Maquila Industry in Mexico and the United States*. London: Unwin and Hyman.

Tomlin, B. and G. Doern (1991) *Faith and Fear: The Free Trade Story*. Toronto: Stoddart.

Williams, G. (1994) *Not for Export* (3rd edn). Toronto: McClelland & Stewart.

3
A Neoliberal Project: A Perspective from Central America and the Caribbean

Wim Dierckxsens and Carlos G. Aguilar

From the perspective of Central America and the Caribbean, the latest phase of globalization is best understood as a project to impose neoliberalism. This latest phase started in the early 1980s as the debt crisis engulfed the region. In this chapter we outline the contours of this project and also illustrate how it is being resisted by a different kind of globalization – a globalization from below as new social movements have sprung up across the region.

The reason for focusing on this short period of time is that it is the period during which neoliberal policies have been applied, policies that are of cardinal importance for the understanding of the current ongoing crisis in the area. We will refer in detail to Central America (although only briefly to the regionally ambiguous Mexico) and only in general terms to the Caribbean. Of course, neoliberal policies have been applied with different degrees of intensity, and their timing and consequences have differed from one country to another; nevertheless, the characteristics that we will highlight here are aspects that have set the course of the economy and politics with relative independence from the particularities that a more detailed study would highlight.

Although it is true that many aspects and problems that we are currently facing are not new in our region, it is also a fact that the policies imposed by the Washington Consensus and the long period of military intervention of the United States have intensified tendencies, structures and processes that strengthen the bonds of dependence (now not only on external markets but also on the growing role that transnational corporations play in our countries) and add to inequality, impunity, corruption, violence and the exclusion of the larger part of the population.

The chapter is divided into three parts. The first part discusses the policies that paved the way for the current crisis. We refer particularly to the national debt, the structural adjustment programmes and the period of the 'transition to democracy' in the Central American region. In the second part, we review how this milieu contributed to the strategy of commercial liberalization that began in the mid 1990s and which was strongly supported by international finance organizations, such as the World Bank Group (WBG), the Inter-American Development Bank (IADB) and the World Trade Organization (WTO), and implemented through initiatives such as the Caribbean Basin Initiative (CBI). This second part addresses the proliferation of free-trade agreements in the region, developed after the crisis of previous initiatives such as the Central American Common Market and the integration of the Isthmus Countries and the countries that belonged to the Caribbean Community and Common Market (CARICOM).

The third and final part discusses the resistance that has grown up in the region as a product, in part, of the reconstitution of social movements in the wake of the low intensity war of the Reagan Administration, but also as a product of the rupture of the neoliberal consensus and the efforts of certain parts of the transnationalized bourgeoisie which seeks to maintain and strengthen the agenda of a corporate globalization that excludes the majority.

The origins of the neoliberal project in the area: foreign debt, structural adjustment and restricted democracies

Economic expansion in the Central American Region since the 1950s has been characterized by periodic cyclical recessions owing to falls in the prices of the main export products and to the imbalances created by the import substitution model. The result of these trends and policies led to the increased foreign debt of the 1980s, which became an essential factor in understanding part of the problems of the region.

As some researchers have pointed out, this process of increased indebtedness is strongly tied to a development matrix centred on agro exports and the dynamizing role of social groups connected to this sector, a matrix that resulted not only in unequal development but also in supporting a social and political structure that is strongly polarized and exclusive.

In the short years of the 1960s, the Central American public foreign debt became 30 times higher (a period characterized politically by dictatorships and the absence of democratization processes in the whole region). In this sense, we should not be surprised at the fact that 'since the mid seventies, serious macroeconomic misalignments became noticeable owing to the lack of capacity of the dependent agro export model to adjust to the simultaneous processes of the slowing growth of the world economy and the increase in the international prices of hydrocarbons and their derivatives' (Timossi, 1989: 20).

The intense recession that followed in the 1980s was not only the beginning of the strengthening of the opening-up process of Central American economies but also served as a justification for the intervening roles of the main international financial institutions. According to data from the Economic Commission for Latin America and the Caribbean the import/GDP ratio reached 34 per cent in 1980 and export/GDP ratio 30 per cent, almost double in 30 years.

However, it is important to point out that which authors such as Torres-Rivas call the 'new elements' of this crisis. First, although the region was being dragged through problems of structural underemployment and unemployment in all the rural and agricultural areas, this time unemployment also affected urban sectors. Second, there is the question of unmeasured inflation in the region, partly because of the spending activities of local levels of government which occurred without central-government sanction (undoubtedly, the most dramatic case was that of Nicaragua). The third characteristic concerns the level of foreign debt (Torres-Rivas, 1982: 34–6). From the late 1970s until 1981, foreign debt increased at an average annual rate of 31.5 per cent accompanied by currency depreciations of around 35 per cent, capital flight and central-government deficits (Timossi, 1989: 21–3).

The situation is seen to be dramatic when we consider that the level of debt grew with policies that economically drained the region, with the gradual decline of the integration instruments of the Common Market, and with the collapse of interregional commerce. The economic aid received was allocated more by the geopolitical interests of the United States and the social and political conflicts of the region rather than as an element of economic stability.[1]

What we know today as the debt crisis signified a deeper crisis: that of the development models of the capitalist system for dependent countries and their agro-export economies. The debt was the catalyst for the introduction of policies orchestrated by aid from the US Agency for International Development Association (AID) through its Economic Support Fund (ESF), by the dispositions of the Washington Consensus and their structural adjustment programs and stabilization plans, by the low intensity war and military interventionism, and by the creation of the Caribbean Basin Initiative (CBI), which has been in force since 1984.[2]

This set of policy initiatives represented a project of social, economic and political restructuring of the entire Central American Region and the

Caribbean, characterized by the strong orthodox policies of monetary adjustment and control, the opening-up of economies and the indiscriminate penetration of foreign capital, in addition to the exploitation of the work force and natural resources. It is clear that the CBI contributed to creating an export model in the Caribbean Basin that favoured private investment through three main channels: the support of commerce, investment and bilateral aid.

This combination of an economic crisis and the political changes that took place in the wake of the Sandinista revolution in Nicaragua in the late 1970s mark the stage of exclusion, murder and destruction of the popular sectors of our countries. Edelberto Torres-Rivas (no date) sums up the situation thus:

> The balance of this torment in Central America, which combines the effects of economic stagnation and policies of structural adjustment with the results of widespread fratricide are still not known, let alone appreciated. Three hundred thousand dead, over a hundred thousand orphans, an unknown number of physically incapacitated peoples, and millions of refugees who went north. Negative growth rates in Nicaragua and El Salvador, brutal impoverishment of the rural community, ruralization of the capital cities, a general growth in the grey economy. And along with added misery, severe damage to the emotional well-being of the common man, who has experienced what we have referred to elsewhere as the trivialization of horror.

It is true that the 1990s, with the peace plans (especially the Contadora and Esquipulas II) and the holding of elections in the countries of the region, was a period of transformation, but it is also true that these democratization and pacification processes were carried out in an atmosphere of growing vulnerability due to the processes of regional integration and increased openness through privatization and liberalization policies and the activities of corporate groups, especially in strategic sectors such as finance (Evans, 1998).

With a fledgling institutional structure and a debilitated state in terms of social and economic functions (but not in repressive terms), the imperative at the time was the need to build an economic structure and political citizenship on solid bases that could effectively face the challenges of rebuilding Central American and Caribbean societies. Instead of this transformation, which would have broadened participation and facilitated an inclusive democratization process, we have witnessed tutelary or restrictive democracy. These are democracies that have been drained of citizenship, where democracy is restricted to electoral tournaments and where there is no ideological competition between the political parties. They are democracies bound to the mechanisms of the market and the whims of market research, where people vote but are unable to decide on the direction of policy in their countries.

The era of neoliberalism: commercial liberalization and transnational corporations

Much of the impetus for the implementation of neoliberalism has come through free-trade agreements and investment agreements, both among Central American countries and the Caribbean, and with the blocs of the European Union and the United States and the North American Free Trade Agreement (NAFTA).

Some of the changes that took place in the 1990s entailed centring the commercial policy of the region on three central aspects: 'improving the performance of the product markets, reestablishing the common market and changing policies to anticipate entering GATT and soon after the WTO' (Nowalski, 2002: 60). The result of these measures produced an increase in exports, especially to the United States. For example, exports to the US rose by 44 per cent from 1992 to 1996, compared with the 25 per cent increase in exports to the European Union over the same period. Within Central America and the Caribbean most of the commercial barriers to trade within the region have been torn down. In spite of this, the region has shown little sign of dynamism (ibid.: 67).

Policies of free trade, although leading to a growth in exports in some cases, have not resulted in improved standards of living among the people at large. The policies that are followed in this model of openness and insertion are similar to the previous neoliberal strategies for the integral transformation of Central American societies in a highly polarizing way, creating nuclei of development linked to the transnational corporations. The latter now come to Central America and the Caribbean with services like tourism, banking, electricity, telecommunications and water, whereas previously it was for agro exports.

An example of the type of agreement being pursued here is the proposal launched by the Mexican government and the governments of the Central American Region in 2001, known as the Plan Puebla-Panama, which unites the strategies of development for the transformation and modernization of Central America in the 21st century and for the South-south-east of Mexico, with the aim of encouraging and driving forward (especially in fields such as telecommunications, electricity and the infrastructure of ports, highways and airports) operations and investments from large transnational corporations and local business groups.

The threat to the control of resources and property in the region can be seen, for example, in the Isthmus Mega Project (1997) which proposes the creation of a dry channel connecting the oceans in the isthmus of Tehuantepec, and projects such as the Plan Marcha Hacia el Sur (March Towards the South) premised on the exploitation of the workforce through the establishment of assembly plants throughout the region. Some initiatives, such as the creation of the Mesoamerican Biological Corridor, the plans for the privatization of the regional hydrocarbons (especially oil and gas) and the complete privatization of the electrical industry, are based on the privatization of the biodiversity of the region, which is one of the richest on the planet.

Aguilar (2004: 290) argues that these projects

> cover up the fundamental role of political interference of the international financial organizations, especially the Inter-American Development Bank and the plans for military intervention that are implemented simultaneously to ensure the protection and control of the projects, which include bioprospection banks (robbery of bio-genetical material by the corporations), oil pipelines, gas pipelines and road runners for transporting merchandise from the transnational companies . . . Perhaps the most concrete example is found in the New Horizons Operation that is taking place in many Central American countries (Guatemala, El Salvador and Honduras) that, under the pretext of fighting drug trafficking, favors the military intervention of the US. Also, and more recently, as part of the policy of aggression developed by the US government, military forces from these Central American countries were sent to the occupation of the Middle East, especially Iraq.

The effects that these measures have had at the social and economic levels of the region can be measured by the impact on employment and exclusion. Exclusion is a phenomenon that leads to concentrating part of this problem on particular sectors and social groups, especially women, the young and the elderly, as well as ethnic and cultural minorities such as the Afro-Caribbean, indigenous people and peasants. This socio-economic model, in the context of specific gender, ethnic-cultural and generational issues, leads to a highly polarized pattern that tends to concentrate benefits and leave the burden of costs to those who are in poverty or in a geo-socially vulnerable position. According to data from CEPAL (2004), about

50 per cent of the population in Central America in 2002 lived in poverty, ranging from 71.6 per cent in Honduras (compared with 68.1 per cent in 1980 according to data from IICA/Flacso) to a minimum of 22.9 per cent in Costa Rica (compared with 24.8 per cent in 1980).

These conditions promote inequality and social disadvantage in terms of social, labour and wage conditions. They also lead to xenophobia, racism, violence – Central America today has the highest rates of murder of women in all of Latin America – and the migration of whole groups of people. In turn, the high levels of poverty throw more people onto the job market, especially women and youths. In the 1990s, there were more women and youths on the job market, especially from the more disadvantaged levels of society, but, at the same time, the number of jobs on offer fell, partly because of the reduction in the number of jobs in the public sector following the policies of structural adjustment. Traditionally, the public sector is a significant employer of women. The excessive number of people out of work has a high feminine slant. At the end of the 1990s, the unemployment rate for women in Panama was 18.1 per cent compared with 10.7 per cent for men; in Nicaragua it was 14.8 per cent for women compared with 12.6 per cent for men; and in Costa Rica it was 7.5 per cent for women compared with 4.9 per cent for men. Among youths the bias is even greater. Women under 20 in Panama register an unemployment rate of more than 40 per cent against 27 per cent for men; and in Costa Rica the rate for women is 18 per cent against 11 per cent for men. This not only leads to an increased number of people working informally in the grey market, it also has negative effects on job security and wage levels (Dierckxsens, 2000: 21). For this reason, it comes as no surprise that along with people dropping out of school, in the 1990s poverty among women increased along with violence against women in the region.

The lack of jobs in Central America primarily affects the young who are seeking their first job. The young suffer most with unemployment and the precarious job market. In the 1990s, the youth unemployment rate was five to ten times higher than the unemployment rate among adults aged from 40 to 50. Unemployment rates among young women reached almost double the level of that of men of their age. Jobless rates among the young in the lower socio-economic groups were three times higher than their peers in the upper levels (Dierckxsens, 2000: 44). The high poverty rates oblige young people from poor homes to seek early insertion into the labour force (Nowalski, 2002: 253). To the resulting problem of school drop-out rates must be added the effects of neoliberal policies on the rights of workers, both male and female, in general and the young in particular.

In 2000, of the approximately 14 million workers in Central America, 39.3 per cent were working informally, 30.6 per cent were employed in rural activities (where poverty rates are highest and most concentrated) and only 30.1 per cent were formally employed. With a formal labour market of less than a third of the population, a proportion that shows a downward trend over time, there is a workforce in search of jobs that is twice as high as the number of formal-sector jobs. This floating labour force puts pressure on formal labour. Workers in the 'floating' group have less job stability and exert great pressure on keeping real wage levels down. It also means that trade unions are continually fighting against the current. The policies of free trade find fertile ground here for making the workforce flexible, rewriting the rulebook and the law, and weakening the rights of workers, both male and female. The general climate is one in which conditions are favourable for profit-making but not for wage-making.

Since the late 1990s, the free-market game preached dogmatically through neoliberal ideology has been shown in practice to be increasingly contradictory. The policy of exclusion is associated with the concentration of markets, a reduced number of transnational companies and the bankruptcy and consequent disappearance of local and national companies, resulting in the concentration of wealth in the hands of fewer people. There arises a consumption divide between the well-off who consume more and more products of transnational companies and the less fortunate who consume local products. This changing distribution of income in favour of the former further reduces the relative size of the local economy and the standard of living of those who live by it. Lower income tends to be compensated not only by greater involvement in the informal labour market in the country, but also by increasing migration abroad, especially to the US. Of all the immigrants in the US (who were born overseas) 37 per cent come from Central America and 10 per cent from the Caribbean. Of these immigrants 45 per cent are young adults, aged 25 to 44 (double the size of this cohort in the home countries) and 80 per cent of the 18 to 64 migrant age group are economically active (compared with 60 per cent of this age cohort in the home countries). The remittances of immigrants constitute an important shock absorber for the less-favoured classes of the region. El Salvador is the most dramatic illustration of this situation where remittances is the largest sector of the economy.

The general result of the liberalization programme is that increasingly more exports and imports in Central America and the Caribbean will be from a transnational source. In general, we see a worldwide dynamic where corporations increase their gains and improve their share prices on the stock market whenever they indiscriminately appropriate markets and wealth. Sharing the world market, nevertheless, is finite. The conquest of markets, however, tends to be increasingly difficult. Furthermore, global economic growth has slowed and as economic growth is reduced, the gains for transnationals are increasingly dependent on a greater share of the world market and more intensive exploitation of the work force.

The contradictions of the neoliberal doctrine are more visible when the sharing of the world market does not have enough room for all the transnationals. As a result, we see that disagreements among the main powers have become more frequent. The latest failed efforts to attain a new Washington Consensus and the differences seen at the WTO negotiations and the Summit of the Americas in Buenos Aires (2005) are proof of these growing frictions. It is precisely this growing contradiction and the intensification of competition that subverts the creed of corporate globalization and opens up the political space for social movements to question neoliberal policy. It is in this contradictory atmosphere that different expressions in search of a different world, such as the Mesoamerican and Caribbean Forums and the 'Global Justice Movement' in general, are born.

Reconstitution of social movements and resistance to the corporate agenda

Since the late 20th century, multilateral agreements for sharing the world have failed repeatedly. As a result, the battle for the distribution of the worldwide market has taken a visible and geographic turn. This has been seen with the reaffirmation and accelerated expansion of the various economic blocs. Since the late 1990s, the European Union, instead of consolidating internally, has opted for the rapid annexation of Eastern European countries. At the same time, the US has worked on the rapid confirmation of a macroarea that will allow it to face competition from the European Union. The US seeks complete access not only to Latin American markets through the Free Trade Area of the Americas (FTAA) but also free access to the natural resources of the continent, as was revealed at the summit held in Quebec in 2001 (Tablada and Dierckxsens, 2005: 274–6).

With this growing competition among the blocs of power and among transnational corporations, the policies of commercial liberalization throughout Central America and the Caribbean have produced a true agricultural 'counter-reformation', with the consequent concentration of land and appropriation of natural resources. This has brought with it the, often brutal, total elimination of small farmers and indigenous communities. With the massive exclusion of farmers and indigenous communities, there are no alternatives for them within the neoliberal market. There is no place for the farming world within a neoliberal world marked by the steady development of agribusiness and great plantations of monocultures for export.

The unfettered import of agricultural products and livestock by way of free-trade agreements accelerates the ruin of the production base of, and the national and regional markets for, small- and medium-sized farms. The agreements are the death knell for farming and indigenous economies, as has been shown by the Mexican experience. American farming subsidies are concentrated on products such as maize, rice, beans and sorghum, along with dairy products: precisely those basic products for which the regions' farmers have a certain amount of competitive advantage.

In addition, with neoliberal policies adopted throughout the region, the capacity to replace the labour force increases. In other words, there is a growing flexibility in the labour market and thus economic and social rights tend to be weakened. As a result, growth in wages tends to fall behind inflation, the percentage of people who fall below the poverty line increases, and the workday tends to lengthen. With lack of formal employment and a fall in income, there is more child and female labour, and badly paid at that. Social security deteriorates. Learning opportunities tend to be privatized and suffer in terms of quality. With progressive exclusion, public services may be discontinued for most of the people who live near or below the poverty line, and mostly privatized services remain for the minority with rising incomes. In 1980 Central America had 1.9 hospital beds per 1,000 habitants; in 1997 this figure fell to 1.2 per 1,000. In 1995 in Costa Rica 86 per cent of the population were covered by social insurance; in Panama it was 60 per cent; and in Guatemala, El Salvador, Honduras and Nicaragua it was less than 15 per cent. No new social-security hospitals have been built since. As a consequence of this reduced availability of social-security beds, the average length of stay of patients in social-security hospitals fell, as did the chance to enter such hospitals. The result of this has been the appearance of private hospitals in the whole region.

These policies have spawned resistance. The first wave of privatization was especially resisted by the unions as the workers were the most directly affected. Following this first wave of privatization of public services, and after repeated increases in prices (especially water and electricity rates) often accompanied by worse service (power cuts and water supply interrupted) or total cuts in places with no purchasing power, the majority of the population was affected by the difficulty of securing basic services. The social struggle transcended the limited area of the trade unions and was taken up by consumer movements or associations who were fighting to defend their rights against the transnational corporations.[3]

Over time, the social struggle against privatization moved from the company to the community level. And the struggle went from being about capital accumulation and became one concerned with the reproduction of human life. The context was no longer restricted to male, working-class adults. Now the actors included the community as a whole with strong participation from women, youths, farmers and natives. In other words, movements of the excluded, those who had no chance of improving their lives, were formed, seeking an alternative. In this broader context, all currents that run in favour of the reproduction of life and environment are included.

It is for this reason that since 2001 these excluded people have celebrated, first in Xelajú and Tapachula, what later became known as the 'Mesoamerican Forum'. This constitutes part of the framework of regional organizations such as the Continental Social Alliance and the Continental Campaign against FTAA, but it is especially a part of the Mesoamerican struggle against the Plan Puebla-Panama.

The third version of this initiative, which represents the most important and articulated effort of organized movements and actors from the Mesoamerican region in recent years, was held in Nicaragua in 2002 and was something of a landmark with the significant difference that it included a process of radicalization that challenged neoliberal initiatives and free trade. The Forum made use of the experience built up at other international conventions, such as the World Social Forum in Porto Alegre, and managed to bring together 800 delegates from around 300 different organizations. The aim was to build up a Mesoamerican resistance movement against neoliberal globalization that would search for a popular integration strategy. The later versions of this Forum, the fourth was in Honduras (2003) and the fifth in El Salvador (2004), were aimed at strengthening self-determination and the resistance of the Central American and Mesoamerican peoples in general. The fifth Forum took place in the context of the defeat of the FTAA and with the presence of 700 organizations and over 1,500 participants from Mexico to Panama and extending to Belize.

Likewise, prior to the fifth Forum, organizations of women, young farmers and natives held separate meetings in which they debated the problems and the agendas of each sector. Over 500 women from the region debated the problems of the organized construction of new strategies for fighting for societies without discrimination or inequality of any kind. In their turn, the youth held the first Mesoamerican Youth Forum. Over 160 leaders and rural and indigenous leaderships, in their turn, gathered at the fourth Mesoamerican Farming and Indigenous Meeting, organizing the struggle for the sovereignty of foodstuffs, biodiversity and the conservation of natural resources. At the same time, they fought against genetically modified products, the extinction of species and the patenting of seeds and traditional knowledge.

It is also important to highlight the ecological movements of the region and their fights against oil exploration, the exploitation of minerals and the building of dams. They also defend biodiversity and fight against genetically modified organisms. They have won important victories that indicate their dynamism and significance. In turn, the growth of repression has spurred greater radicalism in social conflicts that often result in a variety of protests, from urban uprisings, prolonged closures of transportation routes, and the occupation of installations and land. From these struggles, a widespread movement for political and social dignity against the interests of business sectors and corporate capital has emerged in the region.

The hope of another world is emerging out of the projects and movements of men and women who seek justice and dignity. In Central America and the Caribbean the celebration of the sixth Mesoamerican Forum and the Caribbean Forum in Martinique are witnesses to this. As long as there are popular movements in the region, there will be hope, struggle and resistance for the other world we dream of.

Notes

1   It is estimated that economic assistance from the USA to the region increased from US$ 210 million in the early 1980s to US$ 939 million in the mid 1980s (Timossi, 1989: 27).
2   In this sense, the military intervention of the USA in Grenada as a policy response by the Reagan Administration to the Sandinista revolution in Nicaragua is a factor that must be taken into account when attempting to understand the CBI proposal in 1982 to the Organization of American States (OAS).
3   This is most clearly seen in specific struggles in countries like Nicaragua against Unión Fenosa and in El Salvador against the privatization of water, for example.

References

Aguilar, C. (2004) 'Mesoamérica en la Hora de la Resistencia Popular', *Observatorio Social de América Latina*, 5, 13: 287–96.
CEPAL (2004) *Social Panorama of Latin America*. Santiago, Chile.
Dierckxsens, W. (2000) *Del Neoliberalismo al Poscapitalismo*. San José: DEI.

Evans, T. (1998) *Liberalización Financiera y Capital Bancario en América Central*. Managua: CRIES.
Nowalski, J. (2002) *Asimetrías Económicas, Laborales y Sociales en Centroamérica: Desafío sy Oportunidades*. San José: OIT/ACDI/FLACSO/CIDH/BID/Fundación Ebert.
Tablada, C. and W. Dierckxsens (2005) *Guerra Global, Resistencia Mundial y Alternativas*. Buenos Aires: Nuestra América.
Timossi, G. (1989) *Centroamérica. Deuda Externa y Ajuste Estructural: Las Transformaciones Económicas de la Crisis*. San José: DEI/CRIES.
Torres-Rivas, E. (1982) 'La Crisis Económica Centroamericana: Una Propuesta de Análisis Histórico-Político', in F. Rojas (ed.), *Centroamérica: Condiciones para su Integración*. San José: FLACSO.

4
The Crisis of Neoliberal Globalization: A Perspective from South America

Paulo Fagundes Vizentini

The globalization process in South America has produced results that in social and economic terms might be considered disastrous. Some of these results can be traced back to, and viewed as the legacy of, military regimes in the Southern Cone (albeit not Brazil), which implemented neoliberal macroeconomic policies, renounced the state-led model of import substitution and engaged in a 'dirty war' against 'subversives' and a policy of repression that disarticulated the forces of opposition and resistance. This situation was worsened by a region-wide debt crisis that hit development processes hard. In addition, the international crisis of the former Soviet Bloc and its collapse spread shockwaves throughout the region and gave a new dimension to the supremacy of the US and its strategic allies.

In this context, the Washington Consensus on 'correct' policy (Williamson, 1990) was adopted throughout Latin America, despite resistance in some countries such as Brazil. In the 1990s, even Brazil, under the presidency of Fernando Henrique Cardoso, together with Argentina, under Carlos Menem, and Peru, under Alberto Fujimori, succumbed to the 'new economic model'. However, Brazil's integration into the globalization process was accompanied by discreet moves towards economic integration with its neighbours, a kind of Plan B at the level of international insertion.[1] Even so, as I will argue in the first section below, the 1990s were the years of triumphant neoliberalism, characterized by a passive form of internationalization, deindustrialization, deteriorating labour conditions – and stagnation, giving the lie to the promise held out by its advocates.

As a result, the neoliberal model throughout the region proved to be economically dysfunctional, sowing conditions of social discontent and political protest that in various contexts produced a crisis of governability. As the governability crisis spread, there were two divergent paradigmatic reactions: the collapse of Argentina and the appearance of a new political project in Venezuela. Neoliberalism began to face resistance even from forces that had enthusiastically supported it. The rise of the World Social Forum in Porto Alegre and the advent of diplomacy of the Lula government became part of the framework for this realignment of forces. In this context, the Free Trade Area of the Americas (FTAA) proposal was temporarily weakened in the regional agenda. On the other hand, the militarization taking place throughout the region, including even the presence of US troops and military bases, was supported by most governments as a means of ending the growing 'governability' crisis. These issues will be discussed in the chapter.

South America is integrated by two great geopolitical realities: Mercosur (Brazil, Argentina, Uruguay and Paraguay) and the Andean Community (Venezuela, Colombia, Ecuador, Peru and Bolivia). In addition, there are the Guianas (with closer ties to the Caribbean) and Chile, which, despite its associated membership of Mercosur, is independent of both groups and has closer links with the United States. Historically, since South America ceased to be a European sphere of influence, it has been incorporated into the US empire, albeit always with a certain margin of autonomy, especially during times of crisis in the world power system. The countries of the region have always kept a distance from each other, 'with a view of the sea and with their backs turned against others', in a context that is defined by the rivalry between Brazil and Argentina. This situation was changed by the rapprochement between Brasilia and Buenos Aires in the 1980s, with the first signs of regional integration in the creation of the Mercosur in 1991.

Supranational integration and social disintegration in South America (1990–9)

The 1980s are known in Latin America as 'the lost decade', characterized by a transition from authoritarian regimes to democracy, and a serious economic and political crisis that shook the structures of the states in the region. During this period, these pressures and the constant marginalizing of the Latin American nations on the international scene led to the attempt to formulate diplomatic solutions to the international challenges. In this context, the axis of Brazilian and Argentinian cooperation was born, led by presidents José Sarney and Raúl Alfonsín. In 1985, the Iguaçu Declaration set up a committee to study integration and, in 1986, the Economic Cooperation and Integration Act was signed for the intensification and diversification of trade. In 1988, the Brazil–Argentina Treaty of Integration, Cooperation and Development was signed, with the goal of establishing a common market between the two countries within ten years. However, the success of these initiatives was not enough to overcome the crisis. In addition, the entire region suffered additional problems with the end of the Cold War in 1989. This event renewed the fear of exclusion and brought the image of an unquestionable victory for the North American superpower. The 1990s would begin with deep neoliberal adjustments for inclusion in this new world and the resolution of local problems.

After a period of rampant hyperinflation, Menem took power in Argentina in 1989 and began a programme of monetary stabilization. The minister of the economy Domingo Cavallo established parity between the peso and the dollar, an informal way of dollarizing the economy, which increased the cost of the country's exports (heavily concentrated in primary products such as meat, wheat and oil) and left the economy extremely vulnerable to the dynamics of the global economy. In addition, the government privatized strategic sectors to foreign investors and dismantled the state. Brazil followed the same path with President Collor: the government drastically reduced its role in the economy, unilaterally promoted the opening of the internal market and privatized the most profitable state-owned industries. In both cases, these measures were justified by the need to reduce the state deficit and encourage the entry of capital. For a brief time, the entry of these resources alleviated the balance of payment deficits owing to the sudden fall in exports and the increase in imports. Chile and Paraguay were pressured by the US to redemocratize, which happened in 1989, but the neoliberal model was maintained. In Chile, the *Concertación* political alliance between the Christian Democrats and Socialists included a pact that the economic model could not be changed.

Similar policies were also adopted by governments of the day in the Andean countries. In Peru, President Alberto Fujimori started the neoliberal shift. The tendency here was towards the re-election of right-of-centre governments, increasing the time necessary for the adjustment, 'pacification' and 'passivism' of the left, which in general terms adhered to the model of the Washington Consensus and the new democratic agenda. Even Bolivia, a country historically plagued by political and financial instability, with countless coups and cycles of hyperinflation, had a series of relatively stable governments and a monetary policy that brought inflation, which had reached 10,000 per cent in the 1980s, under control. Ecuador, despite many conflicts that led to the ousting of several presidents and the fall of several governments during the period, dollarized the economy and adopted the neoliberal model. Colombia, in its turn, wavered between autonomy and aligned subordination to the United States, with internal conflicts and the security agenda dominating the life of the country.

Venezuela was the big surprise. The neoliberal policy of Carlos Andrés Pérez lead to a crisis that opened the doors to Hugo Chávez and an anti-globalization, anti-imperialist agenda in the form of 'the Bolivarian Revolution'.

In the context of the Washington Consensus, notions of a national project, national sovereignty or nationalism were largely abandoned in all these countries in favour of 'globalization' and its promise of inclusion and prosperity in a new world order. Democratically elected governments such as Collor in Brazil and Menem in Argentina were representatives of this unconditional adherence to globalization and the Washington Consensus on the need to structurally adjust national policies to the requirements of the new world. In foreign policy, those neoliberal governments sought a privileged alliance with the US in exchange for benefits, returning to the alignment that was very well symbolized by the expression 'carnal relations', as that used by Argentinian diplomacy. The pressure of victorious rhetoric used by the imperial superpower only accentuated this image. The outcome of this was a reduction of diplomatic activity and the depletion of national resources by means of privatization.

Argentina and Chile were hailed by the media as triumphant models, which would qualify these countries for a privileged economic relationship with Washington. In truth, it was a way to put pressure on Brazil, which was taking its time to adhere to the new agenda. The US needed to correct the commercial deficits that it had with the region, which would happen if the countries opened up and dollarized their economies.[2]

The creation of Mercosur itself has to be seen in the context of these tendencies. In answer to President Bush's Initiative for the Americas (IA), launched in 1990, the cooperation of Brazil and Argentina was transformed by the team of the Brazilian minister of economy Zélia Cardoso de Mello into a form of integration that included Uruguay and Paraguay, countries with very low external tariffs, with the goal of accelerating the reduction of Brazil's own tariffs. In other words, the Brasilia–Buenos Aires axis, which had an autonomist and developmentalist bias in the 1980s, took on a neoliberal hue. In March 1991, the Treaty of Asuncion was signed, which created Mercosur, bringing together Brazil, Argentina, Paraguay and Uruguay. The initial deadline of the Sarney–Alfonsín agreements was reduced almost in half.

Unlike Argentina and other countries that fully adhered to the neoliberal model, intensifying their deindustrialization and socio-economic destructuring, the neoliberal cycle ended up not being completed in Brazil owing to the renouncement, in 1992, of President Collor de Mello, who had inaugurated it. The interregnum of Vice President Itamar Franco froze the privatization processes, defended the importance of sovereignty and highlighted the need for the state to participate in the economy of a developing country like Brazil.

From 1992 to 1994, the new Brazilian diplomacy sought to distance itself from neoliberalism, although the disagreements with the US were kept in low profile. However, Brazil reacted to NAFTA, which was launched in 1994, and to the South American Free Trade Area (ALCSA) initiative, establishing with South American and African countries the Zone of Peace and Cooperation of the South Atlantic (ZoPaCas) in a strategy of concentric circles emanating from Mercosur. The first initiative encouraged other countries such as Venezuela, Chile and Bolivia to join through the negotiation of free-trade agreements, while the second sought to increase South/South cooperation. The definitive institutional structure of Mercosur was established by the Ouro Preto Protocol of 17 October 1994, bringing to a close the transition period and creating the Common External Tariff, which was facilitated by the stability resulting from the implementation of the Real Plan in Brazil the same year, under the responsibility of Fernando Henrique Cardoso, who would soon be elected president.

In the meantime, the Latin American scene had changed: the socio-economic crisis and political instability caused the return of attempted coups in countries like Peru and Venezuela, and popular uprisings in Argentina, Bolivia and Paraguay. In Venezuela, in the wake of several popular uprisings, coups (one led by Chávez), and the election of Rafael Caldera, who had a heterodox economic policy, Venezuelan institutions collapsed.

In its turn, owing to the success of the Real Plan, Brazil fell once again into neoliberalism during the two-term government of Cardoso (1995–2002). Cardoso resumed the project initiated by Collor in a much more articulate fashion, having privatization and economic opening as main goals. In the external arena, his government continued down the road of regional integration, strengthening Mercosur, stimulating the strategy of diversification of partnerships in bilateral relations, negotiating with multilateral economic organizations, especially the WTO, and concentrating efforts on raising the international power position of Brazil, making it a permanent member of the UN Security Council. The focus of the regional policy exchanged the concept of Latin America for South America, with Mercosur as the strategic nucleus.

From 1994 onwards, Mercosur was put under severe pressure by the proposal of the creation of the Free Trade Area of the Americas (FTAA). This situation was exacerbated by the political stance of Argentina during the Menem/Cavallo era, which sought an alignment with the US and adopted an economic model that was deeply neoliberal, as has been described above. In December 1994, Brazil reluctantly agreed to begin negotiations on the basis of the assessment that if it opted to obstruct the process, it would find itself in an isolated position on the continent in direct confrontation with the US. Therefore, the Brazilian position signalled the constant defence of multilateralism in economic and commercial relations and the defence of plans of integration in the region, always attempting to gain time when it came to the FTAA, but without opposing it head on. A virtual consolidation of the FTAA would mean the end of Mercosur in political and economic terms, making the common external tariff impossible.

Meanwhile, the US applied additional pressure on Brazil, opening negotiations between Chile and NAFTA, hailing Chile and Argentina as models of neoliberal success while Brazil was 'half way there'. What mattered was creating an atmosphere in which South American countries could believe that there was an alternative outside of Mercosur. Even so, from 1991–7, intra-zone trade grew rapidly and Mercosur advanced in strategic and political terms to strengthen the mechanisms of conciliation and joint decisions (highlighting the 'democratic clause', decisive in the consolidation of democratic regimes in the region, especially the Paraguayan crises). However, these aspects were not completed, following the crisis of 1999, leading to the end of Mercosur as it had been up to that time.

In social terms, the neoliberal adjustment of the 1990s brought adverse consequences. In less-developed countries, such as the Andean nations, the adoption of adjustment plans led to a contraction of the formal economy and a sharp growth in unemployment and poverty. Although this was in no way a new tendency – it was a characteristic of the sudden changes in economic cycles (for instance, in mineral extraction) – in the 1990s a new factor came with it: growing transnational presence. Overall, privatization meant denationalization. The new owners of these companies were more than exploiters: they were predators, as in the case of the companies that supplied water to Bolivian cities. Furthermore, the old elite of the country lost strength and the middle classes were almost wiped out.

In the Southern Cone countries, at one time considered close to the First World (Uruguay was known as the 'Switzerland of the Americas') and with a broad middle class and an organized workforce with strong trade unions, there was a major downturn. The old Europeanized elite was partly replaced by a new and smaller Americanized one, strongly 'globalized', turned to commerce and financial speculation, and with no commitment to development. Industrialization suffered somewhat. Chile, for example, gave up industrialization as a strategic goal, opting to specialize in primary products or the agri-food business. The middle class was reduced and the working class was strongly diminished. Social exclusion reappeared in these strongly urbanized societies, putting an end to their 'European' character and bringing in its place typical old Latin American poverty and social exclusion. In Brazil, a country strongly dependent on the public sector, similar events took place, with a drop in industrialization, denationalization, increased social exclusion, informal economy enlargement and rising crime.

All over South America, organized crime and government corruption rose. There was a sharp fall in the standards and quality of elementary education. Access to health care also became more precarious and, along with rising crime and unemployment, was seen as one of the most urgent problems needing to be addressed by public policy. But it is worth highlighting that all these problems took place in societies that had become heavily urbanized with gigantic megalopolises, which, although full of problems, are inserted into 'global modernity'. In other words, the new poor generally interact with modernity, generating a new type of contradiction with strong political potential.

The crisis and the alternatives: social and national reactions (1999–2006)

The crisis of the so-called emerging markets had direct repercussions in South America, as the economies were extremely vulnerable and had little to offer for speculative capital. A number of social explosions and national reactions have been outlined since then. The Argentinian *piqueteros* (pickets), who block the roads; the indigenous coca-leaf workers and Bolivian, Peruvian and Ecuadorian workers' movements; the Landless Workers Movement (MST) in Brazil; the urban poor in Venezuela; and many social groups in the popular sectors of civil society in Argentina and Uruguay have all protested violently. Such actions have taken place during the emergence of political and economic crises, with enormous socio-political repercussions. Two Bolivian presidents and an Ecuadorian were removed for adopting neoliberal policies. The Venezuelan president Hugo Chávez was returned to power after the failed coup of 2002 and, obliged to accept a plebiscite on his staying in power, he won, demonstrating his popularity. These are movements that were considered historically outdated but still showed great capacity for action.

The national question, at the core of these popular movements, plays a decisive role in South America given that the privatization process has generally meant denationalization. Therefore, fighting for integration with neighbours does not mean 'playing the game of the multinationals'. In this situation, Mercosur, originally conceived in the late 1980s by neoliberal governments as a regional alliance in the context of the debt crisis, and under the US pressures for the commercial opening of the southern economies, turns out to be seen by the North American government as a barrier to the development of FTAA. Regional integration is regarded in this new context as an attempt to build autonomous South American economies, and, thus, as an obstruction to the projection of North American power in the subcontinent, since it can allow emerging left-wing governments to initiate popular projects within a framework of relative autonomy in the region. The 'politically incorrect' South American governments are denounced by both the right and by liberals for their populist–nationalist stance and the attempt at South American integration is constantly under fire as an irresponsible action by naïve, newcomer leaders whose heads are in the past.

The financial crisis spreading throughout the region severely affected Mercosur. Brazil drastically devalued the real and Chile has adopted controls on the flow of capital. Argentina and Uruguay, which are dollarized economies, have not been able to alter their current policies. The crisis of the real, in its turn, has led to a Mercosur crisis, which has severely affected Argentina. One of the reasons why Mercosur had not grown was the Argentinian position. Not even the election of Fernando De La Rúa, who took over from Menem, made any changes to the neoliberal inclination of the model. This government saw the return of Cavallo to the Ministry of Finance and Economic Development during the progress of the social crisis that he himself had set in motion.

Cavallo sabotaged the common external tariff of Mercosur to facilitate the installation of the FTAA, despite the commercial relationship between the US and Argentina not being favourable or complementary (only eight per cent of Argentinian exports are for the US market and compete with North American products in other countries). However, the logic showed that the model would not endure. A long recession, the bankruptcy of banks and clearly forgetting the plight of the people, culminated in the social backlash in December 2001, coupled with the resignation of De La Rúa, which led to many power struggles and the collapse of the economy.

The only reason that the crisis was not worse or did not occur earlier was that Argentina had easy access to the Brazilian market, which maintained a budget surplus. However, when Brazil faced the consequences of its own model in 1998–9, with currency devaluation in the wake of the re-election of Cardoso to the presidency, the situation could no longer be sustained for this Mercosur partner (the time of easy gains with integration had also run out). The deficiencies of the Real Plan, which led to this devaluation, such as fixed currency exchange rates, increased deficit, low growth and unemployment, along with the crises of capitalism (like those in Asia in 1997 and Russia in 1998), forced the government to review its agenda. The worldwide situation in which the government had based its international policy had begun to come apart: the discourse concerning subordinated adhesion to neoliberal globalization was substituted with criticism of 'asymmetric globalization'.

Although Chávez in Venezuela had already used similar rhetoric, the articulation of South American initiatives only began to solidify with Brazilian leadership under Luis Inácio Lula da Silva's government. It should be remembered that Brazil had already played a role in the reorganization of left-wing thought, promoting in January 2001 in Porto Alegre the World Social Forum, which has been an important landmark in the search for an alternative model.

With these initiatives and pressured by the same realities, the other countries of South America joined their policies to the Brazilian proposals, culminating in the Brasilia Summit, held on 31 August and 1 September 2000. Given the local economic crisis, the pressures of negotiations of the FTAA and the difficulties of commercial advancement in the region, the focus of the meeting was the integration of transport, energy and communications infrastructure (connecting roads, railroads, hydroroads – newly built rivers – oil and gas pipelines, and energy and telecommunications networks). These negotiations in South America have advanced positively, despite the difficulties, and have retained an element of continuity between the governments of Cardoso and Lula, giving place to the Initiative for the Integration of the Regional Infrastructure in South America (IIRSA). In 2004, the agreement between Mercosur and the Andean Pact was formalized and, in 2005, the first meeting of the South American Community of Nations (CASA) was held. The FTAA process has been put on hold, especially following 9/11.

In one scenario that is still unfavourable to them, the nations of the region attempt to overcome their vulnerabilities and renew their insertion into the international community with the creation of this alternative agenda. An important part of this process in recent years has been the election of governments that are more left-wing, such as Lula in Brazil, Nestor Kirchner in Argentina, Lucio Gutiérrez in Ecuador (later removed from power), Tabaré Vázquez in Uruguay, Evo Morales in Bolivia and Michelle Bachelet in Chile, not to mention President Chávez in Venezuela. Furthermore, the Toledo government in Peru has also altered its policy and headed in the same direction following numerous popular protests, which was also the case in Bolivia in the wake of the fall of neoliberal president Sánchez de Lozada.

The election of Lula caused a great deal of apprehension, as many people expected his international policy to be based on the ideology of an unprepared president. But what took place was a strategic and tactical diplomacy, with a long-term view, which symbolized and coordinated a resistance movement in search of an alternative to globalization in South America and which reaches worldwide dimensions. The Cardoso government's virtual withdrawal in terms of foreign policy was averted, and Lula's high-profile diplomacy salvaged the central nature of the national question.

Although President Kirchner revealed Argentina's will to change its economic policy, abandoning neoliberalism and returning to a model based on public investments and combating poverty, the tensions with Brazil were not all eliminated. From 2003–5, there was a certain resistance to Brazilian leadership, although initially the government had expressed a desire to establish a strategic alliance with Mercosur, actively cooperate with the integration of South America and establish an attitude of equidistance with the US. Suffering pressure from trade unions and domestic industry, Kirchner imposed protectionist measures on some Brazilian products vis-à-vis Mercosur.

Argentina's ambivalence towards Brazil and the distance kept by Chile towards other South American countries and its policy of attracting the US market weakened, but did not eliminate, these attempts at autonomy. Besides aiming for integration, the region, also with Brazil at the spearhead of the process, has established strategic partnerships with other continents that have been facing similar challenges, such as Africa, Asia and the Middle East, strengthening the deepening relations with China, Russia, South Africa and India. The defence of this social agenda, the establishment of a multi-polar international system and the principle of democratization of international relations are explicitly invoked.

These initiatives that unite South America to these other axes of power have been consolidated in diplomatic contacts at the highest level, like the First Summit of Arab Countries and South America, and by the strengthening of alliances of variable geometry both between nations in the South and between nations of the North and South. The North–South partnership refers more specifically to the G4 alliance between Brazil, India, Japan and Germany, which seeks to reform the UN Security Council. However, it is in terms of the South–South alliances that these countries stick out with the initiatives of the G3, also known as IBSA, a coalition between India, Brazil and South Africa and the G20 (or G Plus).

The G3 will promote trilateral cooperation, reciprocated commercial liberalization and the unification and strengthening of positions at multilateral forums. Negotiations will involve Mercosur, the SACU (Southern African Customs Union) and possibly SAARC (South Asian Association for Regional Cooperation).[3] Brazil, South Africa and India have equally shown the desire to attract Russia and China into the group and become the G5, which would join almost half the world's population and a considerable part of production, which would significantly influence multilateral negotiations. The G20 was articulated by Brazilian diplomacy as a network of developing countries affected by protectionism and by agricultural subsidies in developed countries, making their voice heard at the WTO meeting in Cancun in 2003, and which continues to be heard at other meetings and on the commercial circuit.

Despite the success of the G20 and its ties to the G90 and other groups, countries and institutions, the alliance has met many challenges due to the pressures of developed countries. In 2004, Uruguay did not back the G20, preferring to support the Cairns Group, launching its own candidate for the position of director general of the WTO, Pérez del Castillo. As a response, Brazil put forward a candidate, the diplomat Luiz Felipe Seixas Corrêa. The level of conflict was only reduced by the election of reformist candidate Tabaré Vásquez, but, at the WTO, both were defeated, and Pascal Lamy was elected.

All in all, these events had an impact on the FTAA negotiations. The positions of Brazil and the US were unchanged. There was no convergence of agendas and the battle lines of the WTO confrontation were drawn once again. While Brazil and its allies wished to negotiate protectionism and agricultural subsidies and protection to backward industries in the US, the North Americans wished to discuss the liberalization of the service industry, investment, government acquisitions and intellectual property issues. As for the arrangement, the matter of compatibility of pre-existing agreements and FTAA (Brazil's position) or their dilution (the US position) is still under discussion.

As no agreement was reached in 2005, negotiations go on without a clear prospect of a solution in the short term. The reactivation of the Brazilian and American economies seems to be the immediate goal, as a way of making trade easier. The major problem is that without the support of Brazil, the FTAA will not be implemented, as the US already has access to the economies of the other countries, which are smaller than Brazil's. The new Brazilian diplomacy and the profile of international South American relations have reinforced the local capacity for resistance and even the bilateral approach of the two countries.

Therefore, what we see is the return of South America to diplomacy and the process of integration, with the parallel statement of internal agendas and social and economic development. Furthermore, diplomatic action in South America is not only on a regional scale but also on a worldwide scale. However, the internal situation is not stable, for socio-economic conditions have seriously deteriorated and, worse, there is no formation of a new hegemony in proportion to the neoliberal wear and tear. The political dispute in Bolivia, the growing regional protagonism of the Chávez government and the exhaustion of the Chilean model have signalled political polarization in South America.

The South American situation at present is still somewhat in turmoil. In April 2006 in Havana, Fidel Castro, Hugo Chávez and Evo Morales signed the Trade Agreement of the People, giving consistency to ALBA (the Bolivarian counterpoint of the FTAA). This initiative was, to a certain extent, an answer to the North American initiatives of establishing free-trade agreements with Andean countries such as Columbia, Ecuador and Peru and possibly Tabaré Vásquez's Uruguay.

In this sense, the Andean Community of Nations is literally divided, while Brazil is in a position halfway between the two blocs. In early May 2006, Bolivia nationalized petroleum and gas, which directly affected Brazil, given the huge investments made by the Brazilian company Petrobras in that country. Obviously, the fact was nothing really new, given that Evo Morales saw this as a matter of principle and strategic necessity. There will be no social policies in the impoverished Andean country without an effect on the contracts forced on previous governments who had little commitment to national interests.

What is not clear is what the reaction of the popular masses will be in the light of this diffuse context, since power of action of the left-wing governments is limited and the expectations of the population are high. Stuck with international pressures and regional contradictions, these governments have very limited room for manoeuvre, running the risk of being abandoned by their supporters. In this light, not all is as it seems: Lula, despite his apparent acceptance of neoliberalism and international moderation, is indispensable to assuring the maintenance of the other left-wing governments and a collective project. His disappearance would mean favourable conditions for instability for every one of these governments. On the other hand, Kirchner represents provincialism and populism, willing to sacrifice regional integration and even neighbours like Uruguay.

In this context, another factor must be considered: the militarization taking place in South America with the support of North American (i.e. US) troops. Plan Colombia is already well known, with North American resources and advisers militarizing the conflict that tortures Colombian society and leading it to a warlike outcome. At the same time, a military tension ends up involving Colombia and its neighbours Venezuela (owing to the character of its regime) and Ecuador (owing to incidents with refugees). Furthermore, there are North American advisers who help the Andean governments to combat drug trafficking. Washington insists that the countries of the region accept the term 'narcoterrorism', which Brazil rejects. Finally, since the installation of the large American base in Manta, Ecuador, a group of guard posts have been installed in the countries of the region, especially along the Brazilian border. The latest initiative in this sense was the installation of a North American guard of 400 soldiers in Paraguay, near the huge Itaipu hydroelectric power plant belonging to Brazil and Paraguay, which has greatly upset the Lula government.

Conclusion

South America must be viewed as a region which has its own dynamic when it comes to pressure from North America. The financial and economic crises have produced explosive social and political situations in the region, affecting Argentina, Paraguay, Bolivia, Ecuador, Colombia and Venezuela, while in Uruguay and Peru there has been an expressive change of direction. The pressures to undo the viability of the actions of the governments of Brazil and Venezuela, for instance, demonstrate that there has been a certain amount of loss of control and a reduced attractiveness of the neoliberal model. The association between the Andean Pact and Mercosur with the Initiative for the Integration of the Regional Infrastructure in South America (IIRSA) paved a new way, albeit fragile. The opposition of neoliberals and the US to the projects for the building of oil and gas pipelines, as well as the fusion of South American state-owned industries in the field of energy and tele-communications, has been forceful.

The building of the infrastructure would allow the implementation of a public works programme that would attract investment and generate a significant number of jobs, reducing unemployment. This is a Keynesian type of policy meant to trigger economic growth and regional cooperation.

The election of Alain Garcia in Peru with only a slight majority made this president of diminished prestige seek support in the South American integration proposed by Brazil as a way of neutralizing his opponent, Humala, an ally of Chávez, and to stave off American pressures. The easy re-election of the conservative Uribe in Colombia, although it may be the advent of an anti-South American model (pro-US), may yet come with surprises, depending on the future relationship of the country with

Venezuela. But all of this arrangement depends on the re-election of Lula in Brazil and a more social profile for an eventual second term, since many of the weaknesses inherited from the neoliberal period have been resolved, at least partially.

There is a clear weakening of the allies of the neoliberal project, but the left has not succeeded in occupying the political space that it finds in dispute. In their turn, the Andean countries seem to be the new protagonists in the political game in South America, and the efforts of Brazil to become an integral part of the region and push forward for development will be decisive. Although many may be pessimistic about the future, it is important to recognize that South America has turned up not a few surprises for those who put stock in the neoliberal thesis of the 'end of history'. There may be other surprises in the coming years.

Notes

1   Owing to the distance of the region from the big geopolitical and geoeconomic centres, the industrial capitalism built in Brazil during the Vargas years (1930–45), the populist and the military regimes had certain regional room for manoeuvre.
2   Petras and Veltmeyer (2005) have argued that Latin America overall sustained a commercial deficit with the US for much of the 1980s and 1990s. The US, they argue, has turned to Latin America in an attempt to use its commercial surplus as a means of compensating for the enormous deficits it has with other parts of the world.
3   SACU is an economic bloc comprising South Africa, Namibia, Botswana, Lesotho and Swaziland that is negotiating an agreement with Mercosur. SAARC is an economic bloc comprising India, Pakistan, Nepal, Bhutan, Bangladesh, Sri Lanka and Maldives. Brazil, South Africa and India were associated with the G3 or IBSA during Lula's government.

References

Petras, J. and H. Veltmeyer (2005) *Empire with Imperialism*. London and Halifax: Zed Books and Fernwood Books.
Williamson, J. (1990) 'What Washington Means by Policy Reforms', in *Latin American Adjustment: How Much Has Happened?*. Washington, DC: Institute for International Economics.

5
Negotiating the Limits of the Possible: A Perspective from Western Europe[1]

Andreas Antoniades

In a seminal text in foreign policy analysis Graham Allison (1971: 176) argued that 'where you stand depends on where you sit'. Following this principle, the examination of a Western European perspective on globalization will start with an analysis of where Western Europe has been 'sitting' in relation to globalization. Western Europe is conceptualized as the politico-economic area covered by the European Union before its eastward expansion (i.e. the EU15).[2]

The main argument of this chapter is that a Western European perspective on globalization is formed by the interplay between two competing discourses/projects. The first proclaims that Europe, instead of participating in or contributing to an international 'race to the bottom' in economic, social and environmental terms, must intervene in (and humanize) globalization by standing by and defending its social model, values and standards of living and working. The second proclaims that globalization is not something that can be resisted. The only way for Europe to maintain a strong voice in world politics and to secure its values and living and working standards is by improving its international competitiveness. The antagonism between these two views has translated into a Western European identity crisis. The question 'what is globalization?' has led to the (existential) questions 'what is European?' and 'what is possible?'. Here a long list of adjectives (e.g. Anglo-Saxon, Continental, Germanic, Nordic/Scandinavian, Mediterranean) and actors (e.g. political parties, business associations, labour unions, civil society organization, religious leaders) blend and struggle with each other, trying to communicate or enforce their own views on Europe and globalization. It is indeed interesting that a region that for centuries was trying to change the world in 'its own image' is now trying to find its own image and essence.

Western Europe's place in globalization

Western Europe maintains a very strong position in international political economy. Five out of the ten largest economies of the world, in terms of GDP, are in Western Europe (Germany, UK, France, Italy and Spain). The region is also represented by four members in the G7 (Germany, UK, France and Italy). Furthermore, 48 out of the largest 100 corporations (in terms of revenues) in 2005 were based in West European countries (*Fortune* magazine's 2005 ranking of the world's largest corporations). Similarly, 32 out of the first 50 corporations, ranked by foreign assets, in 2003 were also based in Western Europe (UNCTAD's 2003 list of the world's top non-financial transnational corporations). The strong position of Western Europe in the world economy is also evident in foreign direct investment (FDI) with the EU15 accounting for half of the world's outward FDI, compared to 29 per cent for North America. Similarly the EU15 is the largest recipient of FDI, receiving 40 per cent of the global FDI pie, well ahead of North America that receives 22 per cent.[3] Western Europe is also the world's leading exporter and the second largest importer of goods and services (see Figures 5.1 and 5.2).

Considering Western Europe's central place in the global economy it seems impossible for globalization to have taken place without its endorsement and promotion by Western Europe. Yet the most important politico-economic project in the region for the last few decades has been that of European integration. Is then Western European integration to be understood as a feature of globalization? If not, what is the relationship between these two processes?

European integration and globalization

A key event for conceptualizing the relationship between European integration and globalization is the signature of the Single European Act (SEA) of 1986. In many respects, the SEA was born out of the unsatisfactory progress towards completing the common market of goods agreed with the Treaty of Rome in 1957. With SEA, Western European states set as their target the transformation of their region, by December 1992, from an incomplete common market of goods to a single market, that is, an area where capital, goods, services and labour would enjoy free movement. To meet this target the participating member states carried out a huge politico-economic programme of market and capital account liberalization. This programme involved a far-reaching deregulation process at the national level, combined with a re-regulation process at the EU level (Tsoukalis, 2003).

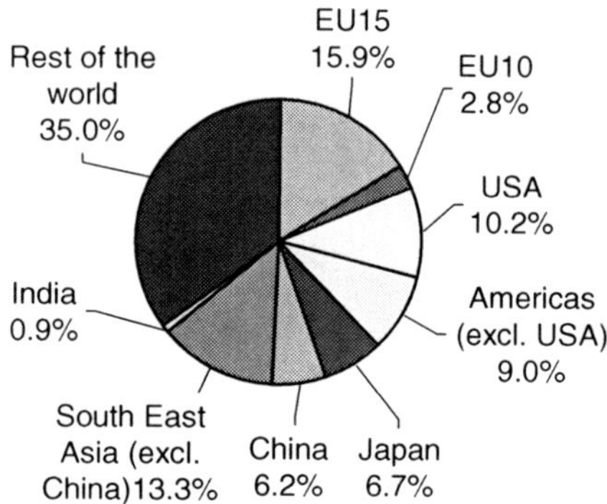

Figure 5.1   Regional shares of world exports, 2003
Sources: UN Comtrade and European Commission.

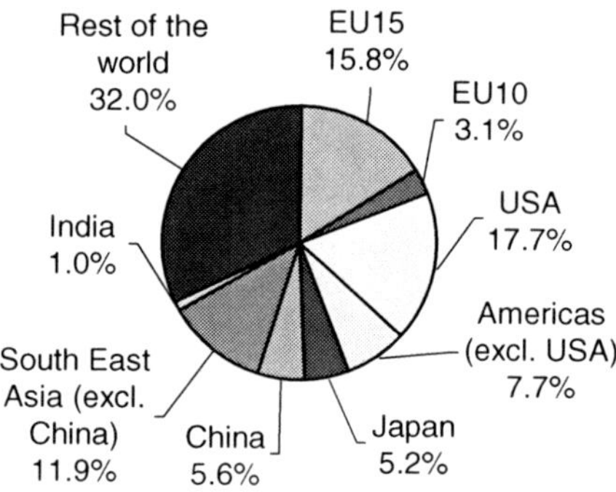

Figure 5.2   Regional shares of world imports, 2003
Sources: UN Comtrade and European Commission.

The single market project was then pushed forward with the Treaty of Maastricht, signed at the beginning of the 1990s, that set as its target the establishment of an Economic and Monetary Union (EMU) with a single currency, the 'euro'.[4] Taking into consideration these developments it can be argued that European integration was a 'globalization project'. Indeed, the integration of Western European financial markets, along with the promotion of a neoliberal politico-economic agenda, involving conservative fiscal policies, the reduction of state intervention in the economy, the reduction of the state sector, and the liberalization and deregulation of national economic frameworks contributed a great deal to the global integration of financial markets and the transformation of international political economy in terms of (neoliberal) globalization.

Interestingly, however, much of the rationale and justification for the single market and the EMU was predicated on the need to deal with (what we call today) globalization (the term globalization entered the EU lexicon only at the end of the 1980s). The main argument was that an integrated Europe would be better positioned to survive and prosper in an era of relentless international competition. A bigger market would allow the European companies to increase their competitiveness and efficiency; and increased competition and efficiency along with new, optimum, economies of scale would speed up growth rates and thus would generate jobs, wealth and prosperity.

What were the forces that were driving the above dynamics? National governments had the first say in these changes and controlled the driving wheel throughout the integration process. The important role of the European Commission and the European Court of Justice in keeping integration on track must also be underlined (Dashwood, 1983). In addition, the role of big European business, although hard to discern and prove, has also been instrumental for the direction of European integration. In this regard, Tsoukalis (2003: 48) argues that 'big business in Europe came to perceive the fragmentation of the European market, caused by persisting government intervention and various forms of non-tariff barriers, as the main reasons for the lack of competitiveness in international markets'. The single market project seems to have been a response to these concerns. Thus, the big European businesses and employers, either through their institutional mechanisms (mainly the European Round Table of Industrialists (ERT) and the Union of Industrial and Employers' Confederation of Europe (UNICE)) or outside them, must be considered as a critical force behind regional integration in Western Europe (Cowles, 1995; Rosamond, 2002; Bieler, 2003). Finally, the economic hardship which followed the oil shocks was also an important factor in the direction of the integration project, for it created a crisis (and a sense of crisis related to the perceived failure of Keynesian policies) that opened the policy window to new ideas, represented by monetarism and supply-side economics.

Yet Western European integration cannot be boiled down to 'neoliberal globalization'. The Single European Act and EMU did not only introduce neoliberalism in the EU. They also set as their aim the 'economic and social cohesion' of the EU and created the Structural Funds and Cohesion Fund to support and secure this aim through (unprecedented) redistribution provisions. In this manner, redistribution became a defining part of Western European 'globalization policies'. Some analysts would treat this development as evidence of a distinctive European, social model of capitalism; others, as a way of buying support and creating consent in Western Europe in favour of the single market and EMU (Tsoukalis, 2003: 19, 50–3; European Commission, 2005a; Allen, 2005).

To conclude, the Western European integration process could and should be seen as an important feature of the phenomenon of globalization. Yet it has been distinctively 'European' in nature in two ways. First, it took place as a response to globalization. Thus although the integration process accelerated cross-border assets acquisition, through the integration of financial markets and in general the spread of neoliberal economic norms, policies and practices, it was conceived and designed by West Europeans as a means of dealing with increased global competition and globalization. In this regard, the phenomenon of globalization was instrumental in the definition of Western European integration (for a similar process in the case of NAFTA, see Chapter 2). Second, in Western Europe 'liberalisation . . . [became] directly linked to redistribution' (Tsoukalis, 2003: 19). Thus, European economic integration was not only conceived by the *majority* of Western European states and populations as a response to globalization but also as a project that served the vision of a politically united Europe, as well as a project that followed a distinctively European tradition of political economy, often referred to as the 'social model'.

Having explored Western Europe's place in the global political economy, it is now time to examine its stance towards globalization. These two issues, of course, are closely interrelated, and as evidenced below inform one another. The main claim of the following section is that a Western European perspective on globalization should be understood as an interplay between two antagonistic discourses: the Continental and the Anglo-Saxon. These discourses are based on a different understanding of what is European and what Europe should do in the era of globalization. In the Continental discourse, globalization emerges as a zone of contestation and as a process that needs to be controlled, if not resisted. In the Anglo-Saxon discourse it emerges as a new challenge that requires a new 'ideology' and a new set of policies in order to be met. It should be stressed, however, that these two antagonistic discourses, as used here, do not correspond to specific geographical areas, but are embedded in broader transnational discursive fields. Thus, Anglo-Saxon attitudes may be held by specific groups/actors in Continental Europe and vice versa.

Perspectives in Western Europe on globalization

The question 'what is globalization?' seems to have been translated in Western Europe in the 1990s into the questions, 'what is European?' and 'what is the European model of capitalism?'. Here, if the concept 'Western Europe' is to retain any analytical relevance then it needs to be broken down into its constituent units. Different Western European states and peoples, based on different conceptualizations of globalization, had different answers to these questions. What follows is an attempt to refer to these national pieces that constitute the broader jigsaw of a Western European perspective on globalization.

By the end of the 1990s globalization had acquired a negative connotation in many Continental Western European states. In 2005, in a Eurobarometer survey, globalization conjured up negative images for 46 per cent of the EU15 respondents (54 per cent in Germany, 61 per cent in France (Eurobarometer, 2005)). The origins of this negative connotation are multiple and include:

- the failure of the structural adjustment programmes of the IMF and the World Bank to achieve development (and through this the real or perceived failure of the Washington Consensus);
- the international financial crises of the 1990s;
- the use of globalization by national elites as a reason or scapegoat for painful domestic reforms or for European integration (see Hay and Rosamond, 2002);
- the competitive pressures on domestic production exercised by the internationalization of production;
- the negative impact on domestic employment produced by the relocation of large European enterprises to low-cost countries, that is, delocalization (Eurobarometer, 2005; Schmidt, 2006a);
- the increasing power (real or perceived as such) of big business to enforce their will on governments and set the rules of the international game;
- the debates about an emerging harmful tax-competition regarding corporate tax regimes;
- the debates about a 'race to the bottom' regarding workers' rights and living standards;
- the ever-increasing flexibility in domestic labour markets;
- the pressures on traditional welfare policies and provisions;
- and the discourse about the end of the welfare state.

Within the above context, globalization came to be conceptualized as a direct threat to the traditional '*European* social model'. There are therefore two critical moments that define the emergence of globalization discourse in Western Europe: the emergence of the contradiction between globalization and the European social model, and the association of globalization with a/the (Anglo-Saxon) model of capitalism that was considered to be foreign to and non-compatible with the (Continental) European tradition. The conflict between the two 'models' (Anglo-Saxon vs Continental) was not of course new. However, it gained unprecedented publicity, popularity and momentum after the mid 1990s. The following paragraphs attempt to offer a snapshot of how this dichotomy informed the conceptualization of globalization in Western Europe during the last decade. To do so, three large and two smaller West European states are examined (France, Germany, the United Kingdom, Greece and Ireland). It should be mentioned here that the United Kingdom and Ireland are considered to be the main (if not the only) representatives of the Anglo-Saxon tradition in Western Europe; Germany is the case par excellence of the Continental model (often referred to as the Germanic); whereas France and Greece are treated as cases of the Mediterranean model, which is considered a subcategory of the Continental model.

In French public discourse, globalization (*mondialisation*) acquired from the early 1990s a very strong negative connotation. It was construed as a predatory force that prioritized the interests of the markets and big business over those of society and the environment, and thus put in danger the post-war model of social welfare (see Hanley, 2001; Hay and Rosamond, 2002; Clift, 2005; Ivaldi, 2006). In this discourse globalization is an aggressive and regressive neoliberal project of deregulation, liberalization and privatization of national economies and societies. The main thesis is that, if left unconstrained, globalization would strip citizens and workers of their rights and powers, and states and public authorities of their power to play the role they ought to play, that is, take care of the welfare of their citizens. Thus uncontrolled globalization has the potential to destroy the European social model. Furthermore, it is related to concerns over cultural homogenization and/or Americanization, and US hegemony. Yet (neoliberal) globalization is not conceived as inevitable, but as something that should be resisted. The way to do so, and the only way to guarantee the survival of the European social model, is, it is claimed, through the EU and (further) European economic integration (Hanley, 2001; Clift, 2005). The main stake in the French public discourse on globalization therefore has been the need to defend the European social model against neoliberal globalization. Many times, the latter is related to the Anglo-Saxon model of political economy, and specifically to Britain (this was especially the case during the referendum for the EU Constitution). For instance, Jacques Chirac (2005) has argued: 'I don't believe the British model is one we should envy or copy. Admittedly, unemployment there is lower than ours, significantly so, but if you take the important things in life in society – health policy, the fight against poverty – you see that we are nevertheless in a far better position than the British.'

The role of civil-society organizations and intellectuals must be stressed separately here. *Le Monde Diplomatique*, ATTAC, the Confédération Paysanne, and intellectuals such as Pierre Bourdieu were crucial in the articulation of globalization discourse in France (see for instance Waters, 2004). Furthermore, French civil society and intellectuals are very influential in many Western European countries, and therefore French public discourse is a significant indicator of trends, tendencies, ideas and attitudes found in Western Europe. This is also evident in the study of globalization discourse in Greece.

As in France, the concept of globalization in Greece has been related to fears over uncontrolled markets and the domination of market over society; developments that have the potential to lead to a 'new barbarism' in Europe and the world (see PASOK, 1996). Along these lines globalization was seen as serving the interests of the markets and big business rather than those of the citizens. Furthermore, as in France, globalization is associated with cultural homogenization and US hegemony. It is indicative that in a Eurobarometer survey on European attitudes towards globalization in 2003, Greece had the highest percentage of opposition to globalization (51 per cent), followed by Austria (40 per cent) and France (33 per cent), while the EU15 average was 29 per cent (the question in the survey was: 'Are you personally in favour/opposed to the development of globalization' (Eurobarometer, 2003)). Moreover, in the question, 'In your opinion, if globalization intensifies in the future, would you say that overall this would be more or less advantageous for you and your family', France and Greece were at the top of the negative responses (with 47 per cent and 46 per cent respectively, while the EU15 average was 32 per cent). Interestingly, this negative attitude towards globalization in the two countries is combined with a high 'awareness' of globalization. In the question 'Have you ever heard of globalization', Greece and France were in the third (88 per cent) and fifth (86 per cent) places respectively, well above the EU15 average (77 per cent).

German attitudes complicate the above (Continental) picture on globalization. The impact of the reunification process and the peculiar bond between the German and the European identity are important factors here (Hay and Rosamond, 2002; Menz, 2005; Schmidt, 2006b). Thus, whereas in France the dominant political forces, both at the left and the right, are united in their opposition to neoliberalism and their support of European integration as a counterweight to globalization, German elites, from the early 1990s, seemed to have adopted the necessity for a 'neoliberal turn' in the economy. German unification was instrumental in this change (Menz, 2005).

Thus, Helmut Kohl and the Christian Democrats (CDU/CSU), in power from 1983 to 1998 (in coalition with the FDP), used the concept of globalization to justify unpopular domestic reforms (see Banchoff, 1999; Hay and Rosamond, 2002: 160). Furthermore, domestic resistance to neoliberal policies that targeted the German 'social market' model were circumvented after the 'transferring' of the economic reform game from the national to the European level (with SEA and the Treaty of Maastricht) (Menz, 2005: 40–2; see also Schmidt, 2006b: 29–30).

The coming to power of Gerhard Schröder and the SPD in 1998 gave rise to contradictory tendencies (Hay and Rosamond, 2002). On the one hand, Schröder adopted Blair's 'third way' rhetoric (see below), co-authoring with him the *The Third Way/Die Neue Mitte*, a manifesto/policy paper, which endorsed several neoliberal economic prescriptions (Blair and Schröder, 1999). On the other hand, Schröder developed a discourse that was closer to the French approach, that is, in favour of the 'European social model', and based on a conceptualization of the EU as a bulwark against neoliberal globalization. In his last participation as Chancellor in an EU summit, and with regard to a European Commission's directive concerning the liberalization of services, Schröder argued: 'We are confronted with a fundamental conflict. Should we elevate the market and never-ending liberalization at the heart of our political action, or do we Europeans stick to our basic beliefs' (*Financial Times*, 28 October 2005).

All in all it can be said that the perspective on globalization from Germany was more positive and optimistic compared to that from France. It is indicative that in the aforementioned Eurobarometer survey regarding the public support of globalization, Germany and Ireland occupied the second place (both 71 per cent), after the Netherlands (78 per cent), and well above the EU15 average (63 per cent). Similarly, the percentage of the German respondents that believed that further intensification of globalization would have a positive impact on them and their families was the fourth highest (60 per cent), very close to that of the UK (61 per cent), and again well above the EU15 average (52 per cent). Notwithstanding this positive view, the tension between the Anglo-Saxon and the European social model seems to remain integral in the German reading of globalization. Along these lines, the European Union is construed as a means 'to reclaim at a European level much of the political capacity and influence lost at the national level' (Hay and Rosamond, 2002). It is interesting that in the question 'Would you say that the European Union is too liberal or too protectionist?', Germany and France had the highest percentage of respondents believing that the EU is too liberal (both 34 per cent), followed at some distance by Greece and Belgium (28 per cent), while the EU15 average was 26 per cent (Eurobarometer, 2003).

In the above question, the United Kingdom was at the opposite end of the spectrum. It had the second highest percentage of respondents regarding the EU as too protectionist (31 per cent) (after the Netherlands with 44 per cent, while the EU15 average was 22 per cent). The United Kingdom has traditionally been the most proactive advocate of neoliberal economic policies and globalization in Western Europe. After the election of Tony Blair's New Labour in 1997, the concept of globalization dominated the British public discourse as a non-negotiable external economic constraint that required a series of specific (neoliberal) policy reforms. Thus, for this discourse, the prosperity of Britain, and any country, in the new global environment required the endorsement of the imperatives of globalization (Watson and Hay, 2003; Hay and Smith, 2005). This approach to globalization was intrinsically related to the discourse of the 'third way' that became the political doctrine of Tony Blair and New Labour (ibid.).[5] Interestingly, the 'non-negotiable external constraint' discourse in the UK did not lead to a politicization of the concept of globalization, as happened in Germany (Hay and Rosamond, 2002). On the contrary, the discourse of globalization moved in the opposite direction. Globalization came to be conceptualized as an unprecedented positive challenge for national and international development, and therefore as a process that (even though inevitable) should be defended (Hay and Smith, 2005).

As a response to the Continental critics of the Anglo-Saxon model, a counter-European social model discourse has also emerged in the UK. In this regard, Tony Blair (2005) has claimed: 'Some have suggested I want to abandon Europe's social model . . . But tell me: what type of social model is it that has 20 million unemployed in Europe, productivity rates falling behind those of the United States; that is allowing more science graduates to be produced by India than by Europe'. The bottom line of this discourse is that an economic model that follows the flexible characteristics and open nature of British political economy is much better positioned to face the challenge of globalization, and therefore the member states of the European Union have to move towards this (Anglo-Saxon) direction. The old European model of high unemployment and low productivity should be modified or abandoned. For, if Europe is to keep its living standards and its leading position in world politics, then efficiency and competitiveness have to take precedence over all other targets (Hay and

Smith, 2005). Ireland is usually used as an instructive model and best example in this regard (for instance, see European Commission, 2005b).

As in the UK, globalization in Ireland has been conceptualized as an inexorable external constraint and a positive challenge and opportunity. Most importantly, however, globalization is intrinsically related in Irish public discourse to the Irish economic miracle of the 1990s and the concept of 'Celtic Tiger' (Smith, 2005; Antoniades, 2007). Ireland has indeed been the fastest growing economy in Western Europe for over 15 years and one of the most dynamic and globalized economies in the world (among others see Foreign Policy, 2004). This economic miracle can explain why the Irish are the most enthusiastic and warmest advocates of globalization and its imperatives in the EU15 (in the Eurobarometer's 2003 survey on globalization, Ireland had the highest percentage of respondents (66 per cent) stating that the intensification of globalization would have a beneficial impact on them – the EU15 average was 52 per cent).

It is worth mentioning here that the conditions of endorsement of the imperatives of globalization in Ireland and the UK have been very different. In Ireland, the rise of neoliberalism and globalization was combined with the rise of a strong, well-functioning and ever-inclusive social partnership (a defining characteristic of the Continental model of political economy). This consociational nature of the Irish economy secured and enhanced significantly the positive conceptualization of globalization in Irish public discourse. Thus, the perspective on globalization from Ireland is that of a historical opportunity for development and a unique means for the prosperity of smaller and peripheral states that used to be at the margins of industrial capitalism.

From states to societies and transnational actors

In attempting to offer a Western European perspective on globalization this chapter has focused on national public discourses. This framing of the topic is not the only one and certainly is not without its limitations. Instead of adopting a state-centric, vertical approach one could adopt a horizontal approach focusing on and contrasting specific social actors (e.g. workers and employers) across Western European countries. Unfortunately, the literature in this regard remains underdeveloped. Before concluding this chapter, however, I would like to attempt a combining of the above vertical analysis with some horizontal insights. To do so, I briefly examine the attitudes of social actors in the two countries that define the opposite ends of Eurobarometer's survey on globalization (2003): Greece and Ireland.

The first conclusion to draw from this different angle of analysis is that the national context does matter. The overall impact that globalization has on a country (e.g. whether growth rates increased and/or unemployment decreased) does seem to relate positively to the attitude towards globalization that dominates in the public discourse. Thus, the fact that Ireland managed to escape from economic underdevelopment and its population experienced an unprecedented rise in its living standards constitutes a reasonable explanation for the positive attitude of the Irish population towards globalization. These positive developments also explain why globalization and neoliberal economic policies remained uncontested for a long period of time by actors that one would expect to challenge neoliberal policies, such as workers' unions and the Labour Party.

The influence, however, of the 'position' of a state in globalization on the attitudes of domestic social actors seems to be only a temporal effect. Thus, after the end of the 1990s, globalization and neoliberal economic policies did start to be politicized in Ireland (Antoniades, 2007). The Irish Congress of Trade Unions (ICTU) did develop a discourse in favour of the European social model (see for instance the motion, 'Economic Strategy: Nearer to Brussels than Boston' in ICTU, 2001), even if this development appears overdue in comparison to Greek or other Western European trade unions. Along similar lines the Irish Labour Party did endorse a mainstream European left discourse on globalization (see for instance Labour Party, 2002), even if this happened four to five years after similar policy and discursive shifts had taken place in Greek left parties. Interestingly, the church in the two countries (i.e. the Catholic Church in Ireland and the Orthodox Church in Greece) adopted from the mid 1990s a very proactive discourse against globalization, relating the latter to cultural homogenization and unchecked capital markets (Antoniades, 2006). On the other hand, and as one would expect, the main employer associations in the two countries (the Irish Business and Employers Confederation and the Federation of Greek Industries) adopted from the late 1980s a very proactive stance in favour of policies related to economic globalization (such as liberalization, privatization, deregulation, etc.).

The analysis of the above actors points towards broader and transnational/Europeanized trends, interactions and processes. Thus, the discourses of Greek and Irish workers and employers were informed by the respective European-wide associations the European Trade Union Confederation (ETUC) and The Confederation of European Business (UNICE). The same can be said, although to a lesser extent, about the participation of political parties in broader coalitions in the European Parliament (for instance the participation of the Irish Labour Party in the 'Party of European

Socialists' group). The point to be made here is that, in addition to the vertical/state-centric dimension, a Western European perspective on globalization has also a horizontal/transnational dimension. Through the angle of the latter, what matters more in the understanding of globalization is not the national origin of the social actors under examination, but their position in their political and economic systems. With regard to the latter, the size of business and/or the sector of the economy examined are of particular importance. Furthermore, in this horizontal dimension, one should pay particular attention to the role of transnational civil society organizations such as ATTAC or the European Social Forum.

The above analysis suggests that national and transnational stances and attitudes towards globalization seem to overlap in multiple ways in Western Europe. In this complex game, the national context is crucial in understanding short-term behaviours and orientations. Yet, if one is to understand the dynamics that define a longer Western European perspective on globalization (or indeed anything), then the focus of the analysis should shift from the aggregate public discourse level to specific domestic institutional actors, as well as to transnational European actors, coalitions and interactions. This change of focus may not change significantly our findings from the study of aggregate national public discourses. Indeed the above brief comparison between Greece and Ireland did not seem to redefine what a Western European perspective on globalization might be. Yet it offers us a more accurate picture of the dynamics and forces that led and governed a Western European perspective on globalization.

Conclusion

The analysis in this chapter leads to the conclusion that a Western European perspective on globalization should be understood as a zone of competition and antagonism among different perspectives coming from different national and transnational points of the politico-economic region of Western Europe. A closer look at this zone of antagonism seems to reveal a bipolar logic and system of organization.

The two approaches of this bipolar system share a common normative (European) view of rights, modernity and the world, but they adopt a different ontological position with regard to the questions, 'what is globalization?' and 'what is possible in (the context of) globalization?'. The first perspective suggests that globalization is what is produced through states' policies and practices. Thus, by defending for instance European working standards in an ever-interdependent world, a more humane globalization process will be secured. This approach suggests that Western Europe's orientation in globalization should be based on and guided by the European values and rights on which the European social model has been based. It furthermore suggests that to take neoliberal globalization for granted and try to adapt to it is a strategy for producing neoliberal globalization. Europe, therefore, must work to produce another globalization that is based on the principles of its social model. Reversing Graham Allison's principle with which we started this chapter, advocates of this approach would argue that Europe's position in the world demands a different role and stance by Europeans in world political economy. The second perspective suggests that the globalization of production and finance and the revolution in technologies and communications have unleashed forces that are beyond (European) control. This process carries with it a great promise for growth, welfare and prosperity nationally and globally. Yet to take advantage of it, and to secure the welfare and prosperity of its citizens, Europe must adapt to globalization. For this approach, the alternative to globalization is isolation. Therefore it is suggested that Western Europe's orientation in globalization should be based on and guided by competitiveness. The study of these two perspectives points to two competing mantras: 'no competition or development without social standards' vs 'no social standards and development without competition'. Of course, the two perspectives do not ignore each other. Those that advocate that Europe needs to 'defend' its social model do not ignore that competitiveness is a decisive factor for survival in today's world; and those that advocate that Europe needs above all to be 'competitive' do not ignore the importance of maintaining certain elements of the Continental social model. Yet the two approaches set different priorities, have different criteria for assessing success and most importantly are based on a different understanding of globalization and the 'possible'.

It is important to stress here that the aforementioned two 'poles' do not exhaust a Western European perspective on globalization but they rather delineate a broader field of antagonism that define such a perspective. This broader field should not be construed as limited to the realm of economic policies. As was mentioned above, globalization has forced Western Europeans to reflect on who they are and where they want to go. The formation of the above two poles should therefore be understood as a process that is embedded in a broader field of antagonism that is more transnational than international in its nature and organization, and where what is at stake is the nature of the European identity itself.

Notes

1   The author would like to thank Paul Bowles, Henry Veltmeyer and Dermot Hodson for their constructive comments.
2   The EU15 does not exhaust the politico-economic area of Western Europe. The debates, however, in the remaining Western European states (e.g. Norway and Switzerland) mirror, to a great extent, the debates that are taking place within the EU15. The latter includes: Austria, Belgium, Denmark, Finland, France, Germany, Greece, Ireland, Italy, Luxembourg, the Netherlands, Portugal, Spain, Sweden and the United Kingdom.
3   Source: UNCTAD, quoted in European Commission (2005b). The data refer to 2003 and are not adjusted for intra-EU FDI.
4   EMU was then followed by the Lisbon Strategy which was launched in 2000 with a view to making the European Union 'the most competitive and dynamic knowledge based economy in the world by 2010' (Lisbon European Council, March 2000).
5   The political philosophy of the 'third way' has been inspired by the writings of the sociologist Anthony Giddens (1998). Towards the end of the 1990s the 'third way' emerged as a new vision for social democracy in the 21st century. High-profile meetings in Europe and the US, including Tony Blair, Bill Clinton, Gerhard Schröder, Lionel Jospin and Massimo D'Alema, had been instrumental in generating a discourse on globalization as both a fact of life and a contingent but positive challenge. Yet this common line soon gave its place to diverse perspectives on what is globalization and 'what should be done'.

References

Allen, D. (2005) 'Cohesion and the Structural Funds', in H. Wallace, W. Wallace and M. Pollack (eds), *Policy-making in the European Union* (5th edn). Oxford: Oxford University Press.

Allison, G. (1971) *Essence of Decision: Explaining the Cuban Missile Crisis*, Boston: Little, Brown.

Antoniades, A. (2007) 'Examining Facets of the Hegemonic: the Globalisation Discourse in Greece and Ireland', *Review of International Political Economy*, forthcoming.

Banchoff, T. (1999) 'Narratives of Globalization and Social Policy in Germany and the United States', paper presented at the University of Wisconsin–Madison, 22–24 April.

Bieler, A. (2003) 'European Integration and Eastward Enlargement: The Widening and Deepening of Neo-liberal Restructuring in Europe', *Queen's Papers on Europeanisation*, 8.

Blair, T. (2005) Speech to the European Parliament on 23 June, available at http://www.pm.gov.uk/output/Page7714,asp.

Blair, T. and G. Schröder (1999) 'The Third Way/Die Neue Mitte', available at: http://www.conscience-politique.org/international/thirdway.htm.

Chirac, J. (2005) Televised interview given on 14 July, Paris, available at: http://www.elysee.fr/elysee/elysee.fr/anglais/speeches_and_documents/2005.

Clift, B. (2005) *French Socialism in a Global Era*. London: Continuum.

Cowles, M. (1995) 'Setting the Agenda for a New Europe: The ERT and EC 1992', *Journal of Common Market Studies*, 33(4): 501–26.

Dashwood, A. (1983) 'Hastening Slowly: The Communities' Path towards Harmonisation', in H. Wallace, W. Wallace and C. Webb (eds), *Policy-Making in the European Community*. 2nd edition, Chichester: Wiley.

Eurobarometer (2003) *Globalization*. Flash Eurobarometer 151b, November. Brussels: European Commission.

Eurobarometer (2005) *Public Opinion in the European Union*, Standard Eurobarometer, 63, Spring, Brussels: European Commission.

European Commission (2005a) *European Values in the Globalised World*. Brussels: European Commission.

European Commission (2005b) *The EU Economy 2005 Review*. Brussels: European Commission.

Foreign Policy (2004) 'Measuring Globalization', March/April: 54–69.

Giddens, A. (1998) *The Third Way: The Renewal of Social Democracy*. Cambridge: Polity Press.

Hanley, D. (2001) 'French Political Parties, Globalization and Europe', *Modern and Contemporary France*, 9(3): 301–12.

Hay, C. and B. Rosamond (2002) 'Globalization, European Integration and the Discursive Construction of Economic Imperatives', *Journal of European Public Policy*, 9(2): 147–67.

Hay, C. and N. Smith (2005) 'Horses for Courses? The Political Discourse of Globalization and European Integration in the UK and Ireland', *West European Politics*, 28(1): 124–58.

ICTU (2001) *Report of Proceedings: Fifth Biennial Delegate Conference*, Bundoran, 2001. Dublin: ICTU.

Ivaldi, G. (2006) 'Party Elite Discursive Repertoires of Globalisation, Europeanisation and Immigration in France', paper presented at the ECPR Joint Sessions, Nicosia.

Labour Party (2002) *Our Values, Our Pledges*. Dublin: Labour Party.

Menz, G. (2005) 'Auf Wierdersehen, Rhineland Model: Embedding Neoliberalism in Germany', in S. Soederberg G. Menz and P. Cerny, (eds), *Internalizing Globalization*. Basingstoke: Palgrave.

PASOK (1996) *Strong and Modern Greece*. Athens: PASOK.

Rosamond, B. (2002) 'Imagining the European Economy: "Competitiveness" and the Social Construction of "Europe" as an Economic Space', *New Political Economy*, 7(2): 157–77.

Schmidt, V. (2006a) 'Social Contracts under Siege: National Responses to Globalised and Europianised Production in Europe', paper presented at the Center for Global Initiatives, available at: http://www.mtholyoke.edu/acad/programs/global.

Schmidt, V. (2006b) 'Adapting to Europe: Is it Harder for Britain?', *British Journal of Politics and International Relations*, 8: 15–33.

Smith, N. (2005) *Showcasing Globalization: The Political Economy of the Irish Republic*. Manchester: Manchester University Press.

Tsoukalis, L. (2003) *What Kind of Europe?* Oxford: Oxford University Press.

UNCTAD (2002) *World Investment Report 2002*. New York: United Nations.

Waters, S. (2004) 'Mobilising against Globalisation: ATTAC and the French Intellectuals', *West European Politics*, 27(5): 854–74.

Watson, M. and C. Hay (2003) 'The discourse of Globalization and the Logic of No Alternative', *Policy & Politics*, 31(3): 289–305.

6
Globalization in Disguise: A Perspective from Central Europe

Jacek Kochanowicz

It is increasingly clear, that the concept of globalization – however elusive – is relevant for understanding what has been happening in the countries which after 1989 abandoned state socialism. What has occurred could hardly be understood in terms of an endogenous process of isolated social units. The realization of the relevance of globalization, however, has come rather late. The concept most often used for explaining the complex processes unfolding in countries abandoning state socialism was that of 'transformation' – from planned economy to the market, and from undemocratic to democratic political system. But it may be argued that the collapse of state socialism itself was a result – and a part of – globalization. This transformation may in turn be understood in a narrow sense to denote processes that started after the final political collapse of communism, in 1989 in Central Europe, and somewhat later in the Soviet Union. But it can also be interpreted in a broader sense, namely, as including also a process of decomposition of state socialism which led to its demise.

No easy answer can be given to the question as to how to date the beginning of this decomposition, as various economic and political crises were present in state socialism, or more precisely the Central European satellite countries, from as early as the 1950s.[1] Still, as late as the 1970s, state socialism had been regarded – inside the Soviet bloc as well as outside of it – not only as a viable system, but also as a possibly attractive solution for the less-developed countries. At the same time, convergence theorists in the West were arguing that Soviet communism and Western capitalist mixed economies were just varieties of industrial society, which might have become more alike if only the East would introduce some democracy and a bit of the market, and the West more planning and income redistribution.

It is in the 1970s that these perceptions – of Western mixed economies as well as Eastern state socialism – started to change, and this because of various trends and developments in the Western world. It is in this period that one should look for the visible beginnings of the last wave of globalization, of the crisis in state socialism, and – perhaps – of the beginnings of 'postmodernity'. The West went through the oil shock and stagflation, the Bretton Woods system had been dismantled, the welfare state came to be regarded more as a problem than a solution, neoliberal ideas replaced Keynesianism, the developmental economics tailored for the Third World were put to rest, and the newly industrializing countries of the Far East became new players in the world economy. And, increasingly, new tendencies crystallized the field of technology and economic organization, with 'flexible specialization' replacing Fordism (Piore and Sabel,1984), the rich countries de-industrializing, and transnational corporations playing an increasing role. State socialism proved unable to adapt to these tendencies, and in this way its decomposition and final demise has been a part of globalization. Its ultimate collapse came in a moment of the triumph of globalization, and the economic, social, political and cultural reconstruction that followed has been unfolding as a part of the globalization processes. Transformation and globalization cannot be separated.

This chapter focuses on the meaning of globalization for part of the post-communist world: that of Central Europe. The processes of the decomposition of state socialism started in this region earlier than elsewhere, and the adaptation to the new world is the most advanced there, as witnessed by the accession of these countries to the European Union. The chapter starts with a review of the long-term evolution of the location of this region in a wider, European context. Then it addresses the issue of the relations between state socialism (communism) and globalization, and then it turns attention to the most recent period when the agents of pro-globalization changes in the region are discussed, along with the experience of globalization by Central European societies and the responses of these societies to the challenges that globalization brings.

What is Central Europe?

Between the end of World War II and the collapse of communism in 1989, in the eastern part of Europe, there were six satellite states of the USSR (Bulgaria, Czechoslovakia, the German Democratic Republic, Hungary, Poland and Romania) and two communist countries outside the Soviet influence (Albania and Yugoslavia). Now, in the same region, there are

18 states, which often are classified into the four following groups: the Baltic countries (Estonia, Latvia and Lithuania), Central Europe (Czechoslovakia, later split into the Czech Republic and Slovakia, Hungary and Poland), Eastern Europe (Belarus, Moldova and Ukraine), and South Eastern Europe (Albania, Bosnia Herzegovina, Bulgaria, Croatia, Macedonia, Romania, Serbia and Montenegro, and Slovenia).

The concept of Central Europe in its present meaning emerged only during the 1970s, when intellectuals from the region tried to show that – while trapped in the Soviet political sphere of influence – these societies in fact have strong affiliations to the West (Szűcs,1983). Indeed, Christianity had come from the West and the legal concepts in case law were those of Germanic and Roman law. With settlers from Germany and other Western lands came agricultural know-how, architectural design and construction technologies. Universities – founded in Prague in 1348 and in Kraków in 1364 – were patterned on the Italian model; the Habsburgs ruled over substantial parts of these territories in the modern era; and French culture had influenced the elite.

But, despite the cultural impact of the West, these lands had economic and social histories different from that of the western part of continent, but at the same time were very much marked by trade relations with it, particularly by the agricultural exports to Western Europe and which intensified in the 16th century and lasted until the mid-20th century. Because of its relations with Western Europe, Central Europe is often said to be located on its 'periphery'. Wallerstein's (1974) idea of the 'world-system' may be said to prefigure theories of globalization. In the second half of the 19th century, the periphery of Europe was affected by the industrial pull of Western Europe through the further rise of the demand for primary and agricultural products (Berend and Ránky, 1982). In the region itself, some industrialization occurred, but the gap – in terms of per capita income – between the region and the West has been increasing all the time up to the present (Janos, 2000).

If the second half of the 19th century was the first wave of globalization (O'Rourke and Williamson, 1999), the period between 1914 and World War II was marked by the collapse of the world economy and its disintegration into smaller, semi-autarkic fragments, with many countries attempting to isolate themselves from the international economy. In Central Europe these tendencies were strengthened by the nationalist ideology (Kofman, 1997) as nation building had become the highest priority for those countries which had emerged from the dissolution of the Ottoman and Habsburg empires. Economic policies were to a significant degree subjected to these wider political goals as most of these states attempted to develop economies that would support national independ-ence. This they did through tariff protection, industrial policies, and often through developing state-owned industrial firms, particularly in arma-ments. World War II brought this region a tragic discontinuity – but state socialism, which came afterwards, while turning everything upside down, turned at the same time to be a repetition of the autarkic tendency. At least, up to a point.

Communism and globalization

Communism in its own, distorted way was an attempt at radical modern-ization, thus realizing the Enlightenment ideas of reason and progress. Among its many ambiguities, one was that the communist elite tried to construct something radically different from the West, but also – at the same time – to imitate the West, particularly in terms of technological and economic development. The key pillar of the communist project was industrialization. The pattern had been set by the Soviet five year plans of the 1930s, focusing on heavy industries and forcing mobilization of rural labour as well as shifting agricultural surpluses to the cities. The plan-ners wanted to make the socialist economy self-sufficient and independent of the vagaries of international markets. This model of industrialization – achieved at enormous human costs due to mass terror – had been relatively successful as long as it was based upon the Fordist pattern of the mass factory production of relatively simple goods by a low-skilled labour force. It proved, however, totally unsuited to post-Fordist flexible specialization and to the information economy of the last decades of the 20th century. While the gap between the Soviet economy and the West was closing during the period of the 1930s to the 1960s, afterwards it began to broaden.

Despite all attempts, the Soviets never managed to de-link themselves from the world economy, either under the Fordist model or what came afterwards. They invested heavily in military R&D, but were hardly able to develop advanced technologies of the day and were dependent upon either importing or copying them from the West, paying first in gold, then in oil and increasingly in natural gas (Castells, 1998; Kotkin, 2001). The Soviets were also short of grain. While collectivization enabled a mass transfer of food to the cities to finance the industrialization of the 1930s, in the long-term perspective it was a failure. Since the Khrushchev era, the Soviets were importing grain from the West: American bumper crops prevented potential political unrest in the Soviet world.

In the 1940s and 1950s, the Soviet model had been imposed on Central Europe. The reasons for including Central Europe into the Soviet political sphere were not economic, but geopolitical: to extend further the buffer zone between the Soviet Union and the West, as well as to secure the communication routes to East Germany, the Soviet prize trophy of the war and the military frontier of the empire. During the 1950s, all satellite countries underwent a programme of massive industrialization, which was a replica of the Soviet pattern. However, the weaknesses of the Soviet model showed in Central European countries as well. They too were unable to mastermind the high technologies of the day or to deliver consumption goods to their respective societies. In the 1970s, Poland and Hungary, trying to import investment goods from the West, and unable – as the Soviet Union could – to cover costs by exports, got heavily into foreign debt.

Czechoslovakia, Hungary and Poland, being frontier countries of the Soviet bloc, and having long-lasting traditions of contacts with the West, were the least closed to Western cultural and political influence, although things became more difficult for Czechoslovakia after the failure of the Prague Spring of 1968 and the Warsaw Pact invasion in August of that year. The products of Western culture were finding their ways into the region. Western 'open Marxism' fuelled the critique of the system, and 'market socialism' was expected to replace the command economy. In the 1970s, Marxism was gradually losing its appeal among the critics of the regime, being replaced by the idea of human rights. In a parallel way, the younger generation of economists was increasingly doubtful as to the feasibility of market socialism and were attracted to the new, neoliberal ideas coming from the West.

Thus, while a sudden final collapse of state socialism in Central Europe in 1989 was a result of a coincidence of several factors of a particular character, it was a collapse of a structure which was in an advanced stage of decomposition anyway, and the process of this decomposition was in turn affected significantly by the processes of interaction of the communist system with the outside world.

Agents of change

Ideas, coming mostly from the West, had already played enormously important roles in the process of change before 1989 as well as after. Concomitantly, a large role had been played by the carriers of these ideas, the East European intellectuals of the former opposition (Falk, 2002). But, in a paradoxical way, some members of the ruling establishment – particularly the managers and technocrats – also worked towards a certain reconnecting of Central Europe with the West. These were people who realized very well the technological gap dividing state socialism from the West and who were responsible for developing the hard currency exports, for importing new technologies, for arranging foreign credits, and so on. The younger among them were indifferent (and sometimes hostile) to the Marxist ideology, and it was evident for them that the patterns for modernization could be taken only from the West. No surprise that so many of them changed, after 1989, into successful capitalists.

With the demise of state socialism, it was natural to the intellectuals of the former opposition that the rule of law and democracy should replace the hitherto existing political regime. In their attempts to promote these views among their societies, they were aided by Western governments and non-government organizations, such as the Open Society Institute (OSI), set up by American financier and philanthropist of Hungarian origin, George Soros. The OSI helped to establish all over Eastern Europe a network of foundations, active in promoting grass-roots democracy. Through a wave of constitutional and legal reforms, these ideas were gradually turned into laws. Introducing democratic reforms had been strengthened by the foreign-policy agenda. After the dissolution of the Soviet Bloc, the elites of Central Europe – for symbolical as much as for practical reasons – wanted to reorientate radically their political allegiances. Joining NATO and the European Union – at the beginning of the 'transformation' only vaguely mentioned as possible long-term goals – gradually, since the middle of the 1990s, crystallized into agendas and projects. Obviously, keeping the standards of democracy and human rights became a necessary prerequisite of such plans.

Another idea was that of market economy. It came to Central Europe in a quite dramatic way and in a radical form, since it happened in the heyday of neoliberalism. That does not mean, however, that market radicalism was new for the Central European economists. Quite the contrary. They were eager to embrace 'the market', being disillusioned with more than three decades of attempts to reform state-socialist economies through selective decentralization, partial introduction of the market and employee participation in management.[2] Since these remedies evidently proved unable to reverse the process of economic crisis and decay, already in the 1980s in Poland and Hungary, economists – attracted by the then developing theory of property rights – started to argue that perhaps more radical medicine was needed (Kornai, 1986, Winiecki, 1991). Price liberalization and the reintroduction of private property had been mentioned as necessary for achieving economic efficiency.

With the fall of state socialism, these ideas started to be put into practice in the most radical way in Poland, as a so-called 'shock therapy'. What is characteristic of these early views on transformation is their close affinity to neoliberalism and what had been called the Washington Consensus, a set of ideas developed out of the experience with the economic crises in the less-developed countries, and arguing for price liberalization, deregulation, opening economies for trade, privatization, ending subsidies, and so on. Many Western economists, who gained experience in the Less Developed Countries (LDCs) – as was the case with Harvard's Jeffrey Sachs – came to advise the post-communist world. Among the local economists they found eager listeners, as the inefficient economies and state overspending seemed to present a challenge of a similar sort.

By necessity, these countries were also receptive to the pressure coming from the international financial institutions, particularly the IMF and the World Bank. Poland and Hungary had very high foreign currency debts, accumulated since the 1970s, and it was crucial for them to get a clean bill of health from these institutions in order to maintain a secure position in the international financial markets. Thus, they drafted and redrafted stabilization plans, necessary to start all kinds of international financial projects. In terms of political economy, the local economists – particularly those of a younger generation – increasingly came to serve as ambassadors of the ideas propagated by the international institutions, working as experts for the World Bank, or finding employment there, which was one of the best professional careers possible.

Experiencing globalization/transformation

How have the post-communist societies experienced globalization? It is hardly possible to generalize, and only with a warning of simplification could it be argued that there are certain similarities within each of the group of countries singled out at the beginning of this chapter. In the institutional sense, as well as in terms of standard measures of success (particularly, the rate of growth), the Central European countries, the Baltic countries, and Slovenia (the richest of all of them) are more successful than the rest in terms of the GDP statistics as well as in social costs. While they (Poland in particular) suffered from initial, so-called transformational recession, all of them managed to resume growth within two to three years and to attain reasonable rates of growth (see Figure 6.1). Recession in Eastern Europe and the Balkans was deeper and took longer to recover (see Figure 6.2). The situation of a number of successor states of the former Yugoslavia is specific because of the legacies of war and of the acute ethnic conflict. Belarus is another special case because of the authoritarian regime and lack of reforms there. On the other hand, neglecting or postponing reforms in a country (Ukraine may be the case in point) does not make

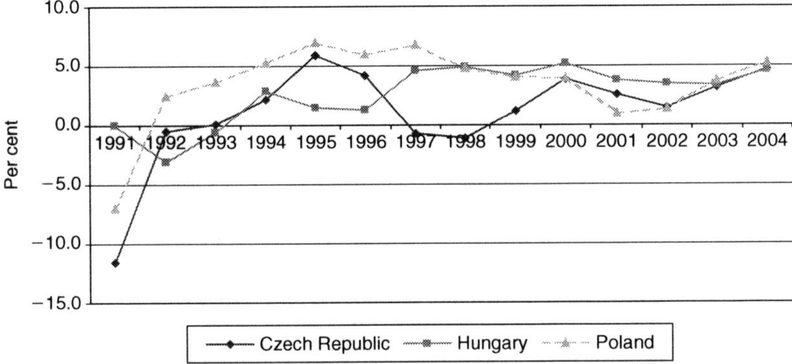

Figure 6.1   Annual growth rate – Czech Republic, Hungary and Poland
Source: OECD Factbook 2006: Economic, Environmental and Social Statistics,
http://titania.sourceoecd.org/.

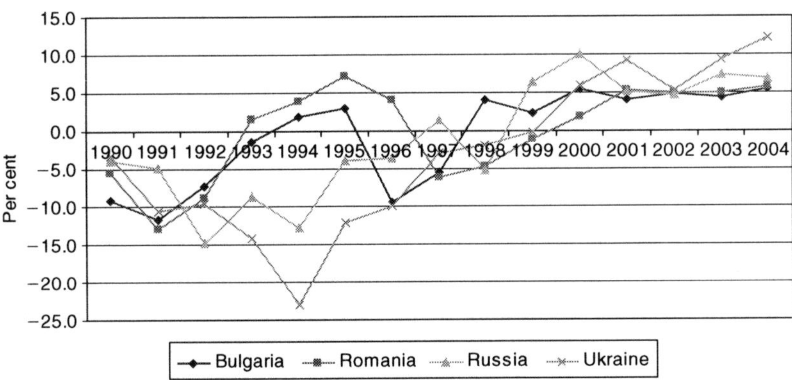

Figure 6.2   Annual growth rate – Bulgaria, Romania, Russia and Ukraine
Source: Author's computation from real GDP growth index (1 TransMonEE 2005 database,
http://www.unicef-icdc.org/resources/transmonee.html).

it immune from some of the various plights often attributed to globalization, such as poverty, income differences, corruption and AIDS.

Focusing on the four countries singled out for this chapter, the most
important element of the influence of globalization has been the change
of the economic system, and it is practically impossible to separate the
effects of globalization from the results of the systemic change. At the time
when the changes were introduced, they were rarely (if at all) treated as
elements of globalization. 'Transition' or 'transformation' were terms used,

and – later on – 'modernization' (Ziółkowski, 1998). But, with the benefit of a hindsight, it is possible to say that the 'transformation project' – the idea of bringing democratic capitalism to Central Europe through a set of institutional changes – was clearly a part of a globalization process, as the leading model was that of the flexible, American-type, laissez-faire variety of capitalism – in rhetoric at least, if not in practice.

Transformation consisted of whole sets of legal (institutional) changes, which – for the sake of simplicity – are usually clustered into macro-economic adjustment, economic liberalization (allowing private enterprise, abolishing state monopoly in foreign trade) and privatization. While macroeconomic adjustment (price liberalization, balancing budgets) and liberalization/opening were, in a sense, technically easy one-time moves, privatization has been a long-term process, not yet finished. In the longer run, the embedding of a market economy required many institutional reforms such as rewriting property laws, commercial codes, banking laws, creating stock exchanges, and so on. All these triggered off changes in behaviour of various social and economic actors, both foreign and domestic.

If any one single issue is to be put into the fore of these institutional changes, it is privatization of state-owned enterprises, and a parallel process of creation of new private property. While privatization has been a feature of economic changes all over the world for the last 30 or so years – from the Britain of Margaret Thatcher to many LDCs – the ones that have been taking place in the post-communist world have had a particular character. Both in the highly developed and in LDCs, privatization meant a quanti-tative change – expansion of already existing private ownership into certain areas which were directly managed by the state. In the post-communist world it was a qualitative change of a revolutionary character. In these countries, almost all economic activity, from mining to manufacturing to retail trade, had been in the state's hand. With exceptions, like Polish agriculture, property in land was severely restricted. Without much simpli-fication it may be said that the state was the only owner, the only employer, and the only retailer in town. From a technical point of view, privatization in the post-communist countries employed means similar to those in other places: the sale of assets or shares and managerial buyouts, with perhaps the exception of voucher schemes – a post-communism invention – in Russia, Czechoslovakia and Poland. From a sociological, cultural and polit-ical point of view, however, privatization meant vast change. Firstly, it triggered a wide-ranging transfer of wealth. Secondly, it remapped all sets of meanings, symbols and cognitive patterns – the meanings of wealth, property, work, one's social position and one's relation to others. Thirdly, it influenced the formation of new patterns of political behaviour.

Summarizing all the different aspects of the privatization processes unfolding in several countries is not possible here, so – on the risk of repeating commonplaces – only a few points can be made. Thus, because of the lack of local capital, an important and increasing role has been played by foreign capital, particularly by foreign direct investment (see Table 6.1). By and large, the coming of foreign firms and capital has been welcomed, as they have been perceived as a hope for jobs and technological change. In some sectors – as is the case of banking in Poland, and even more in Hungary – foreign capital plays a much bigger role than in the highly developed countries of Western Europe. In Central Europe, efforts have also been made to make foreign investors somehow sensitive to such concerns as the environment and the labour market, obviously because it was feared that doing otherwise is asking for political trouble. Critics point out that, while the modernizing role of foreign firms is visible, it should not be overestimated, as these firms tend to be of an assembly-plant kind, using still relatively cheap labour and adding little to bringing the Central European economies closer to the technological frontiers of the knowledge economy.

An important consequence of privatization has been a far-reaching restructuring of the economies at large and of enterprises. State socialism was not so much underdeveloped, as misdeveloped, with too much of traditional, heavy, sunset industries having little chance of survival in the modern open economy. Many of those factories had to be closed down. On a microlevel, restructuring has meant first of all an increase of efficiency. State-owned enterprises under communism operated under soft budget constraints and were overmanned, while the productivity of labour was low and product quality neglected. Restructuring meant a change in enterprise strategies, of products, of technologies, and of managerial practices. For the employees, restructuring meant the loss of various social services, hitherto provided by the enterprise (health clinics, resort houses, housing programmes) and, most of all, the loss of job security and the end of full employment. Unemployment, hitherto unknown in the region, appeared on a mass scale (see Table 6.2). Differences in the unemployment rate are a matter of debate, with one of the reasons being different long-term demographic patterns.

The rise of capitalism resulted in the emergence of new business and a managerial elite. The group which seems to profit from the emergence of the private sector are some members of the former communist establishment, who proved capable of converting their social and political capital, acquired under state socialism, into economic capital important in the new system (Eyal *et al.*, 1998). Many of them – particularly former

Table 6.1 Inflows of foreign direct investment (millions of US dollars)

Country	1991	1992	1993	1994	1995	1996	1997	1998	1999	2000	2001	2002	2003	2004
Czech Republic	n.a.	n.a.	0.65	0.87	2.56	1.43	1.30	3.72	6.33	4.98	5.64	8.48	2.11	4.46
Hungary	1.47	1.48	2.45	1.14	5.10	3.30	4.17	3.34	3.31	2.76	3.94	2.99	2.16	4.17
Poland	0.36	0.68	1.72	1.88	3.66	4.50	4.91	6.37	7.27	9.34	5.71	4.13	4.12	6.16

Source: OECD Factbook 2006: Economic, Environmental and Social Statistics, http://titania.sourceoecd.org/vl=672761/cl=15/nw=1/rpsv/factbook/
11-02-01.htm

Table 6.2 Unemployment rate (%)

Country	1992	1993	1994	1995	1996	1997	1998	1999	2000	2001	2002	2003	2004
Czech Republic[a]	n.a.	4.3	4.3	4.0	3.9	4.8	6.5	8.7	8.8	8.1	7.3	7.8	8.3
Hungary[a]	9.8	11.9	10.7	10.2	9.9	8.7	7.8	7.0	6.4	5.7	5.8	5.9	6.0
Poland[b]	13.7	14.9	13.9	13.1	11.5	10.2	10.6	15.3	16.0	18.5	19.7	19.3	18.8

Notes: [a] Annual average per cent of labour force.
[b] Data as of November/IV quarter.
Sources: TransMonEE 2005 database. http://www.unicef-icdc.org/resources/transmonee.html, 2004 – OECD Factbook 2006: Economic, Environmental
and Social Statistics, http://titania.sourceoecd.org/vl=672761/cl=15/nw=1/rpsv/factbook/05-02-01.htm

managers of the state-owned enterprises – acquired assets through privileged insider buyouts of state property, many others found themselves useful for the new Western companies. The extreme case of this is the emergence of the 'oligarchs' in Russia – amazingly rich new businessmen, who acquired their wealth mostly through the shrewd acquisition of state assets via a legally dubious process. In Central Europe, however, such processes have not taken place. Changes in social structure, related to the new forms of business activity, were not restricted to the elite, as the emergence of small-and medium-sized businesses have led to the rise of a more numerous middle class of self-employed businessmen and professionals and white collar employees of private firms.

How have these changes been experienced by individuals, by the 'common people'? They were dramatic. From the point of a (prospective) consumer, the rise of the market economy meant a jump from the world of greyness, uniformity and persistent shortages to a world of abundance of goods and services, of full shops, and of quickly rising supermarkets and shopping malls, all of which foreign capital was ready to provide at the speed of light. This was a specific experience of the post-communist world, as even in the Third World the problem was not a shortage of goods, but of money. Central Europeans were learning the consumer paradise the hard way, however, as parallel to that they had to take a crash course on what was the flexible labour market as well as that shiny goods in shops came with prices several times higher than it was the case under the previous system.

These experiences have to be related to different social groups. Transformation brought a rise of social differences, as well as of poverty and social exclusion. One of the measures of social differences is distribution of income (Table 6.3). While its standard measure, the Gini coefficient, increased visibly with the transformation, the new levels are by no means dramatic, as they are now similar to those of Western Europe. The measurement of income distribution captures but one aspect of new social differences, which are also reflected by changing life styles, consumerism, including the conspicuous consumption of the newly rich, bringing in turn some resentment of those less lucky. Another outcome of transformation was the rise of poverty (see Table 6.4). Interpretation of the statistical data on poverty is by no means easy because of an arbitrary character of poverty lines and problems of measurement, but there is no doubt about the tendency. Detailed research suggests that particularly hard hit by poverty are (not surprisingly) the unemployed, the families with large numbers of children, and people locked in places where former socialist industries had collapsed. At the same time, the poverty – even

Table 6.3   Distribution of income: Gini coefficient

Country	1989	1995	2000	2003
Czech Republic	0.198	0.216	0.231	0.246
Hungary	0.225	0.242	0.259	0.268
Poland	0.275	0.321	0.345	0.356

Source: TransMonEE 2005 database. http://www.unicef-icdc.org/
resources/transmonee.html

Table 6.4   Poverty rates (%)

Country	1992	1993	1994	1995	1996	1997	2001	2002	2003
Czech Republic[a]	2.4	n.a.			5.9	n.a.	7.8		n.a.
Hungary[b]	13.8	11.5	12.3	12.6	13.2	14.7	n.a.		13.2
Poland[c]	n.a.	12.0			14.0	n.a.	17.1	17.0	18.4

Notes: [a] Based on incomes from microcensus data. Poverty line reflects European concept (60% median equivalent incomes, OECD scales).
[b] Based on incomes from TARKI Panel (HHP Survey). Poverty line equals 50% of mean equivalent income (local scales).
[c] Based on expenditures from household budget survey conducted by Central Statistical Office. Poverty line is set at, 50% of mean equivalent expenditure (OECD scales).
Sources: Czech Republic 2003: Tomas Sirovatka (2005) 'Poverty in the Czech Republic and the Policies to Combat it', in S. Golinowska, E. Tarkowska and I. Topińska (2005) *Ubóstwo i wyklucznie spoleczne. Badania. Metody. Wyniki*, pp. 252–71: Czech Republic 1992, 1996: Tomas Sirovatka (2004) 'Social Assistance. Czech Republic', report prepared for IWM project *Comparative Institutional Reform in Social Policy. East-Central Europe in a European Context* (unpublished); Hungary 1992–7: *Hungary Long-Term Poverty, Social Protection, and the Labor Market, World Bank, 2001*, vol. 2, table A1-4. http://www.worldbank.org/; Hungary 2003: András Gábos and Péter Szivós (2005) 'Poverty in Hungary on the Eve of Entry to the EU', TÁRKI Social Report Reprint Series No. 4, table A3. http://www.tarki.hu/

if extensive – is not very deep, and in this sense it does not resemble the acute poverty of the Third World.

While generalization may be somewhat risky, it is possible to summarize these social changes, following the often-used metaphor of 'winners' and 'losers' of the transformation process. To the winners belong those who are better educated, live in great urban centres, and those members of the former establishment, who proved capable of converting their political capital into economic capital. To the losers belong many blue-collar workers of the former state-owned enterprises, people stuck in villages and small provincial townships, women blue-collar workers, semi-skilled white-collar workers, peasant smallholders and, in particular, the workers of the former state-owned large farms all over the region, or Roma, which are prevalent especially in Hungary and Slovakia. In assessing the social costs of transformation, though, one should beware of idealizing state socialism, despite the lower social stratification and the higher social security. State socialism not so much liquidated social and cultural differences within a society as glossed over them through the job security and a primitive, albeit comprehensive, 'welfare state'. Once these were gone, all kinds of historically accumulated social and cultural differences re-emerged.

If culture is a set of meanings, and if experience is perception, then transformation/globalization has been first and foremost a cultural experience, and this was an experience of a revolutionary character. 'One morning' – writes a historian about the Hungarians, but it is as true for all the people in the region – 'they woke up unsuspecting and found themselves in a brand new world, with all their certainties disappearing' (Rév, 2005). Apart from the vast changes of meanings related to everyday economics (working, shopping, thinking about one's life strategy), and apart from the exposure to the hitherto unknown, aggressive, commercial mass culture coming from the West, Central Europeans had to cope with a complete reorientation of their historical and political spaces. For years, they had been officially taught the superiority of socialism over capitalism and about their eternal alliance with the Soviet Union, while unofficially (within family and friendship circles, Church communities, dissident groups) they were talking of different stories – sometimes of human rights, but sometimes of Jewish conspiracies, of the glorious past of their nation, of the mass death of their parents' generation in Siberia. With the system change, the official history was gone, but also part of the unofficial, in as much as it was not politically correct in the multicultural world nor in view of a prospective accession to the European Union.

In the realm of politics, one of the experiences of transformation is democracy, which replaced the authoritarianism of the late phase of communism. Much longed for, it had barely been known in the region when, with the demise of the old order, it had to be learned from scratch. In a certain way, it succeeded, as basic conditions of democracy, such as free elections leading to change of governments, free media, basic civil rights, are respected. In another sense, democracy is weak and not well socially embedded, as – particularly in Poland – electoral participation is low and various polls show lack of trust in democratic institutions. Also, the idea of the rule of law in its basic, Hayekian sense of a predominance of abstract, procedural rules protecting freedoms (sometimes those of disliked minorities) over substantive particular interests and ideologies seems often to be poorly understood.

Another political experience is that of a change of political and military alliances. The Central European countries, after regaining their sovereignty, managed to join NATO (in a moment, some would say, when the purpose of this alliance ceased to be clear) and (without much of the enthusiasm of the wealthy countries of Western Europe) the European Union. This all looked like unequivocal success of the foreign policy of the local elites, as well as a case in point of national consensus. When the moment of truth came with September 11 and the growing rift between Europe and the United States, Central European governments (much less so their societies) supported the US when the war with Iraq started.

Responses

The collapse of state socialism posed enormous challenges to the societies of Central Europe. Under the incomplete modernization of the defaulted system, they had not shed their agrarian past completely, and the experience with the inefficient Fordist modernization hardly prepared them for a life in the post-industrial world. Most people in these countries led under communism a very modest life, constantly in search for scarce goods and constantly staying in line. At the same time, their lives, with job security and access to social services (whatever their quality), were basically secure. All this ended with the fall of communism, and now they had to respond to the new challenges.

Many responded in a positive, active way. Establishing a private business was one such way, and in Poland alone over two million small businesses were registered during the first couple of years. However, many of these had little to do with the spirit of capitalism; rather they were witness to the desperate fight for survival in the conditions of a dramatically shrinking labour market. No doubt, more serious local business also emerged, although economists agree that the share of small-and medium-sized enterprises in the region is still too small, if compared with more developed and mature countries. Another active response has been a spontaneous rush for education, when it was realized that this is a necessary (albeit not a sufficient) condition for personal success. Yet another response, which showed on a larger scale after the accession of Central Europe into the EU, is job migration to the West. Numbers are difficult to ascertain, but from Poland it took place on a massive scale.

These active responses keep Central Europe developing and modernizing. The question remains as to whether the pace of this modernization is fast enough, and whether the region is on a convergent trajectory with the core countries. In order to reduce the distance it must grow faster; in the post-industrial era it must attune itself to the trends of the knowledge economy. However, for this it seems not to be innovative enough. Poland, in fact, scored a last place in Europe in 2005 in terms of the societal attitudes to innovation (European Innovation Scoreboard, 2005).

There is also resentment by those who can't cope effectively with the challenges posed by globalization. To the dissatisfied belong people locked in rural communities and small towns, those who are less educated and older, those who are psychologically not flexible enough to adapt to fast social changes. Their inherent potential for a possible political mobilization is limited. The trade unions diminished in importance with the process of privatization, the rise of small business and, more generally, deindustrialization. However, several times the disaffection with the transformation process has been capitalized by political parties – on the one hand by the post-communists reinvented as social democrats, and on the other by more diverse political parties of self-styled rights. 'Left' and 'right' are misleading concepts for understanding Central European politics, particularly when referring to the economic realm, and they refer to collective identities rather than to ideological content. Thus, the left usually means ex-communists, while the right-wing parties oppose them and stress national and religious values. In Hungary, a clear case in point is Fidesz, a party of self styled 'young democrats', who, at the beginning of the nineties, redefined themselves as national conservatives. In Poland, it is now the Law and Justice Party, which has won both parliamentary and presidential elections in 2005. This party, supported by the poorer, older and less-educated electorate, accuses its opponents of corruption, stresses national and religious values, and is distrustful of the European Union.

The fact that particular parties capitalize on resentment does not lead necessarily to specific economic policies, however. By and large, during the last several years whatever the populist rhetoric, governments in Central Europe usually tried to pursue policies that would not bring an economic disaster. Now they have another check – Brussels. But also, due to European funds, they have more money to keep their electorates happy.

Concluding remarks

For centuries, Central Europe was a periphery of Western Europe, culturally close, but poorer and with a different economic and social structure. In the 20th century, the distance from the West increased because of wars and communism. With the collapse of state socialism, Central Europe became swiftly reintegrated into the international economy and the

Western cultural sphere, to a degree unprecedented in the past, as this reintegration has proceeded in the context of an overall globalization.

There are three points that can be offered as conclusions to this chapter. Firstly, for the post-communist world, globalization has indeed been a force that came not from within, but from without. Already during the 1970s it became clear that the world of state socialism was out of tune with the technological, economic and cultural changes unfolding in the outside world. The process of transformation to a market economy and democracy after 1989 – institutionalized in legal reforms and developing through the spontaneous actions of the social actors – has been, too a large degree, influenced, designed and implemented according to ideas and blueprints coming from the centres of the developed world, 'the West'. In this sense, the post-communist transformation was a part of the wider globalization process.

Secondly, alongside the Baltic countries and Slovenia, Central Europe has been the most successful in this process. The way the globalizing trends operated in the various parts of the post-communist world depended upon the local context, first and foremost upon the cultural context, a product of the history of a given community, forming sensitivities, mindsets, value systems and cognitive patterns of their members. Within the Soviet bloc, the societies of Central Europe were the closest to the West in the geographical as much as the cultural sense; thus they were the first where the cracks in the old system showed, and also the most successful in the process of adaptation to the new demands. An important reason for that was the openness of Central European elites to the ideas coming from the West. It should not be forgotten that globalization has been as much a technology-driven process as a process of changes of perceptions and ideas on how 'things work' and how they should be reorganized to work better. Somewhere around the 1970s there was a rift in these perceptions, a philosophical revolution, related first and foremost to how economies should be institutionalized – a revolution often summarized by the term 'neoliberalism'. Many intellectuals, politicians and managers from Central Europe, tired of state socialism, were embracing these ideas enthusiastically.

Thirdly, the success of Central Europe is, obviously, relative. It shows when these countries are compared with Eastern Europe and South-east Europe. On the other hand, the gaps in measurable indices of performances-such as GDP per capita-between the Central European countries and those of Western Europe reflect the level of social and cultural capacity of the former to take part in the game of modern economic life. This social and cultural capacity is, moreover, very unevenly distributed among the members of Central European societies. Rising income differences, high levels of poverty and social exclusion suggest that there is a considerable

danger of a crystallization of dual societies, in which only a part of the
population will be able to take advantage of the processes of modernization.
It also remains to be seen what place these countries will secure for themselves in the medium-to-long run within the larger context of the European
and global economies – will they move closer to the core, or will they
become stuck on the periphery?

Notes

1   The most dramatic political crises occurred in the GDR in 1953, in Hungary
    and Poland in 1956, in Czechoslovakia in 1968 and in Poland in 1970, 1976
    and 1980/81.
2   That was the case with such later prominent reformers such as Poland's Leszek
    Balcerowicz, Hungary's Lajos Bokros and Czechoslovakia's Valcav Klaus.

References

Berend, I. and G. Ránki (1982) *The European Periphery and Industrialization*. Budapest:
    Akademiai Kiado.
Castells, M. (1998) *The Information Age: Economy, Society and Culture, Vol. I: The Rise
    of the Network Society*. Oxford: Blackwell.
European Innovation Scoreboard (2005) *European Innovation Scoreboard 2005*.
    http://trendchart.cordis.europa.eu/scoreboards/scoreboard2005/index.cfm.
Eyal, G., I. Szelényi and E. Townsley (1998) *Making Capitalism without Capitalists:
    The New Ruling Elites in Eastern Europe*. London: Verso.
Falk, B. (2002) *The Dilemmas of Dissidence in East-Central Europe: Citizen Intellectuals
    and Philosopher Kings*. Budapest: CEU Press.
Janos, A. (2000) *East Central Europe in the Modern World: The Politics of the
    Borderlands from Pre- to Postcommunism*. Stanford: Stanford University Press.
Kofman, J. (1997) *Economic Nationalism and Development: Central and Eastern Europe
    Between the Two World Wars*. Boulder, CO: Westview Press.
Kornai, J. (1986) 'The Hungarian Reform Process: Visions, Hopes, and Reality,' *The
    Journal of Economic Literature*, 19(4): 1687–1737.
Kotkin, S. (2001) *Armageddon Averted: The Soviet Collapse, 1970–2000*. Oxford: Oxford
    University Press.
O'Rourke, K. and J. Williamson (1999) *Globalization and History: The Evolution of
    a Nineteenth-Century Atlantic Economy*. Cambridge, MA: MIT Press.
Piore, M. and C. Sabel (1984) *The Second Industrial Divide*. New York: Basic Books.
Rév, I. (2005) *Retroactive Justice: Prehistory of Post-Communism*. Stanford, CA: Stanford
    University Press.
Szűcs, J. (1983) 'The Three Historical Regions of Europe', *Acta Historica Academiae
    Scientiarium Hungaricae*, 29(2–3): 131–84.
Wallerstein, I. (1974) *The Modern World-System I: Capitalist Agriculture and the Origins
    of the European World-Economy in the Sixteenth Century*. New York: Academic Press.
Winiecki, J. (1991) *Resistance to Change in the Soviet Economic System: A Property
    Rights Approach*. London: Routledge.
Ziółkowski, M. (1998) 'Miejsce społeczeństwa polskiego wświatowym systemie
    kapitalistycznym. Dylematy teoretyczne i praktyczne' (The Place of Polish Society
    in the World Capitalist System), *Kultura i Społeczeństwo*, 4.

7

Cultural Encounters of the Uneven Kind: A Perspective from the Arab World

Galal Amin

Although the use of the term 'globalization' to describe what is happening in the world is new, the phenomenon itself is very old. If understood to mean the rapid shrinking of distances separating human communities, whether with regard to the movement of goods, people, capital, information, ideas and values, globalization appears to be almost as old as human civilization. Something not dissimilar to our present strong consciousness of globalization must have been experienced by the first person to go into space, 50 years ago, who must have also seen the world as a 'global village'. Long before this, however, the first European colonizers of America 500 years ago must have also been struck by the degree to which distances had shrunk. Both great excitement and great apprehension about globalization can also be traced far back in history, wherever awareness of it has been acute. Peter the Great, for example, caused great enthusiasm as well as great opposition when he decided that Russia should go 'global' 300 years ago. The arguments for and against colonialism, old and new, could also be seen as the result of similar concerns.

At the very centre of these concerns – and of how we should interpret and understand globalization – is the possible impact of globalization on poverty and on culture. Opponents of the 'opening-up' of their countries were afraid that such openness would not only threaten their cultural identity but also 'marginalize' a good section, or perhaps the majority, of the population. On the other hand, enthusiasts for globalization were too impressed by the power of new technologies, or too tied up with certain economic interests, to bother about the impact of globalization on such vague and elusive aspects of the life of society as 'cultural identity' (especially the cultural identity of other races) or to bother about its impact on the non-privileged groups of their own or other populations.

With the shift of the centre of human civilization from one geographical area to another, the centre from which the force of globalization was to emanate also shifted from one region of the world to another. The Arab World[1] has been such a region more than once in human history, but since the rise of the modern West, it has been mainly a passive recipient of the impact of globalization.

The year 1998 marked the 200th anniversary of the beginning of contact between the Arab World and the modern West. In 1798, Egypt was introduced to the modern world by the French campaign; a few years later, Mohamed Ali ushered the integration of the Egyptian economy into the world economy, mainly through the exportation of cotton. In the remainder of the 19th century, one Arab country after another came to be integrated through British or French occupation.

It would have been inconceivable for such a process of globalization to have not exerted a profound impact on various aspects of economic and social life. It is easy, however, to tell the story of this impact both in highly positive terms as well as in very negative ones. This chapter provides a very brief review of both types of impact of globalization in the Arab World over the past 200 years, followed by an examination of the period since the 1970s, which can be seen as a period of accelerated globalization. The final section considers the post-September 11 situation which, in many ways, brings us full circle as the 'globalization through oil' of the contemporary period resembles the 'globalization through colonization' which occurred in earlier periods.

Two hundred years of globalization

It is largely due to globalization that almost everything in the Arab World today is bigger and moving faster than it was 200 years ago. This is hardly surprising. Two hundred years ago, Europe was just starting its Industrial Revolution that caused virtually everything in Europe to become bigger and to move faster, whether it was population, agricultural or manufactured output, cities, trade, transport or finance. It was hardly possible for the Arabs to become tied to Europe at that time without everything in the Arab World also getting bigger and moving faster.

At the time of the French invasion of Egypt, the entire Arab population could not have exceeded 20 million. Thus, in 200 years, the Arab population multiplied at least 15 times, which would have been inconceivable had the Arabs not learnt from the West how to reduce the death rate. To reduce the death rate by such magnitude, many important things had to grow rapidly as well: cultivated land, agricultural output (particularly food) and means of transportation to transfer food from one place to another, as well as the power of the state to establish law and order and to enforce the introduction of modern hygiene. All this had to be – and actually was – learnt from the West.

It was highly unlikely that cultivated land and food production would have grown exactly at the required rate to match the growth of population. The Malthusian law worked very well with regard to the rate of growth of population surpassing the growth of food production, but it did not work at all well with regard to Malthus's positive or negative checks. As for positive checks, the Arabs learned very quickly from the West how to put an end to them (by learning how to eliminate epidemics and famines), but they refused to learn to apply the negative checks (methods of birth control), and the result was, of course, the population explosion. This must have been what Lord Cromer meant when he said, referring to British rule in Egypt, 'Whatever impoverishment has taken place, is much more due to good than to bad government' (Issawi, 1982: 13). He meant of course that it was good government that led to the decline in the death rate, although people consequently became poorer.

Another inevitable consequence of population increasing faster than food production was the very rapid rate of urbanization, since the surplus rural population had to find something else to do other than agriculture. Arab urbanization has been proceeding at a rate faster than any ever experienced in the West. This rate was also the result of Arab contact with the West, for both the push and pull factors in Arab urbanization were due either to Western technology, Western hygiene, Western consumption habits, the influx of Westerners, or the growth of a Westernized Arab elite.

But it would be unfair to describe the impact of the West on the Arab economy as constituting only the growth of population, of cultivated land, of agricultural output, of trade, of means of transport and of urban centres, and so on. There has also been genuine progress in some aspects of human development, the most obvious aspect being the rise of life expectancy. The first estimate ever made of life expectancy in the Arab World was for Egypt in the 1930s, when life expectancy at birth for Egyptian males was 31 years, roughly equal to the life expectancy of an Englishman in the late-13th century (Owen, 1981: 25). Today, life expectancy at birth in Egypt has more than doubled (to 64 years). Life expectancy is higher still in all the other Arab countries (except Sudan and Yemen). The decline in the death rate has meant a real decline in misery. In the hundred years before the French campaign, the inhabitants of Cairo, Damascus or Aleppo hardly 'had time to recover from one attack (of the plague) before another struck' (Owen, 1981: 4). There were five attacks of the plague in Cairo during the 18th century, which killed between a third and a half of Cairo's population. There were five attacks of the plague in Aleppo over a period of 40 years and four attacks in a period of similar length in Damascus (Owen, 1981: 4–7). When the French came to Egypt, they found that one in every three Egyptians had sight in only one eye, and one in ten were totally blind (Owen, 1981: 25).

The rate of literacy in the Arab World in 1800 must have been well below 5 per cent. When Mohamed Ali embarked on his programme of modernization, he was unable to find a single Egyptian who knew a European language (Issawi, 1982: 110). Today, there are more than 50 million students in the Arab World (Arab League, 1996: 24), and whatever one may say about the quality of the education they get, most of them must, by the end, acquire some knowledge of a European language.

The net result of it all was the growth in per capita income. We do not have estimates of per capita income over a sufficient length of time to say with certainty how much income has grown in each country of the Arab World over the entire period of 200 years. One could make a very rough estimate for Egypt, where the increase in income falls in the middle range – neither as great an increase as in the Arab Gulf States, which started from a lower point 200 years ago and ended much higher than Egypt, nor as small an increase as that of Yemen or the Sudan, both of which initiated close contact with the West much later than Egypt. This rough estimate indicates that real per capita income in Egypt has increased by a factor of about eight over the past 200 years. This is an impressive achievement, especially since it was associated with a 20-fold increase in the population.

However, globalization also had some significant negative impacts. After all, the West did not come to the Arab World to develop it, but to develop itself, and hence the positive impact on human welfare must have been more by accident than by design. More land was indeed cultivated, but not to feed more people or to feed them better. The main aim was to grow more cash crops for export to Western manufacturers or consumers. When cereals competed with vineyards, as in North Africa, wine production was increased at the expense of cereals. When cotton competed with food, as in Egypt or Sudan, cotton was preferred, and education was expanded only to the extent that it served the requirements of colonial administration. In Algeria for example, just before independence, and after 130 years of French rule, the literacy rate among Algerian Muslims was no more than 15 per cent (Issawi, 1965: 507). This was roughly the literacy rate among Egyptians in the early 1950s after 70 years of British rule. When the Italians left Libya during World War II, there were exactly two Libyans with university degrees (Issawi, 1982: 112).

Even with regard to the least controversial benefit of the Arab–Western encounter, that of access to modern medicine and hygiene, this was also done within limits drawn by the requirements of the safety of Europeans. When Western interests dictated otherwise, a policy of depopulation was applied. Thus, the French invasion of 1830 cost so many Algerian lives that it took the Muslim population about 40 years to regain its 1830 level. Libya's Bedouin population was reduced by one-half to two-thirds during the first 20 years of Italian rule, through either death or emigration.[2]

The impact on income distribution of opening-up to the outside world has most probably been negative over the past 200 years. While it is impossible to belittle the importance of indigenous causes of inequality of income, wealth and power, which existed in the Arab World before its contact with the West, rapid growth, resulting from this contact, must itself have been a new cause for inequality. Beneficiaries of such contact have always constituted a small proportion of the total population; even if the standard of living for the rest of the population did not deteriorate as a result of contact with the West, inequality must have tended to grow.

One may go further and hypothesize that, the greater the gap between the dominant and the dominated economies, the greater is likely to be the difference in value between what the dominant economy wants to sell and what the people of the dominated economies can afford to buy; hence the greater is the degree of inequality that is in the interest of the dominant power to maintain. In other words, the degree of inequality that is required in an Arab country to market an American Cadillac is likely to be greater than the degree of inequality that is required to market a piece of English cloth, however luxurious it may be. If this is true, then one should expect income distribution in the Arab World to have tended to become more unequal, for this reason alone, over the 200 years of contact with the West.

In the early decades of the 19th century, the ratio between the per capita income of England (the richest country at the time) and the Arab countries was probably not more than 3:1; now, the ratio between the average per capita income of developed countries and that of the Arab countries as a whole is closer to 15:1. The difference between the richest and the poorest Arab countries is much greater now than it ever was, but the gap between levels of income within any one Arab country is also almost certainly larger now than it was 100 or 200 years ago. Consider, for instance, income disparities within, say, Saudi Arabia before and after the discovery of oil.

Accelerated globalization since the 1970s

Arab countries have varied greatly among themselves with regard to the degree of openness to the outside world. Taken as a whole, the degree of their collective integration in the world economy has also fluctuated heavily during the past 200 years. These fluctuations have largely followed the same pattern experienced by other regions of the world, with less integration in the world economy during periods of world wars or depression, and greater integration during more peaceful and prosperous times.

During the two decades following World War II, however, major world developments led the Arab World to take two very different paths with regard to integration in the world economy. While the cold war between East and West encouraged some Arab countries (notably Egypt, Syria and Iraq) to follow highly protective policies, taking one form or another of 'Arab Socialism', the unprecedented growth rates in the West led other Arab countries (particularly the oil rich countries, but including also Lebanon and Jordan) to become more integrated than ever in the world economy. In the following three decades (1965–95), the process of globalization swept over virtually the whole of the Arab World, with those countries with open economies becoming even more open, and those with relatively protected economies rapidly dismantling their systems of state control. This process has accelerated further since 1990: many Arab countries have adopted economic stabilization and structural-adjustment programmes; many have signed new international trade agreements; and some have entered into free trade agreements with the European Union and forms of economic cooperation with each other (such as the Gulf Cooperation Council).

Measured by the ratio of external trade to gross domestic product (GDP), the degree of openness today varies greatly from one country to another – from 38 per cent for Egypt to 146 per cent in Bahrain (World Bank, 2006). Regionwide, the average ratio is as high as 70 per cent, mainly because of the weight of oil exports. The share of the Arab World in world trade is still only about one-fifth of the share of developing countries in Asia, or about the same as that of Latin America, and twice that of sub-Saharan Africa (IMF, 1996a: 5). The degree of dependence of the Arab World on international trade is particularly high in the export of oil and the import of food. Oil accounts for about three-quarters of total Arab exports; for the major Arab oil exporters, an insignificant percentage of output is used domestically. Almost all Arab countries are net food importers, and this dependence has increased significantly over the last three decades.

The significant differences between Arab countries is the extent to which they have been economically integrated with the rest of the world are also evident from the data on capital flows. The net inflow of capital in recent decades has been much higher in the Arab *Mashreq* (eastern) countries than in the Arab *Maghreb* (western) countries (17 per cent and 3.5 per cent of GDP, respectively, during the period 1970–90), with some of the former countries relying more on this capital inflow as a source of foreign exchange than on exports of goods and services (Diwan et al., 1993: 1). The result was a heavy burden of external debt, reaching 76 per cent of the combined gross national product (GNP) of five countries in the *Mashreq*, namely Egypt, Jordan, Syria, Yemen and Lebanon, and 69 per cent of GNP for the three countries of the *Maghreb* (Algeria, Morocco and Tunisia) in the early 1990s (see ibid.: Annex 2: 12).

The inflow of capital has been predominantly in the form of borrowing from abroad rather than of direct foreign investment (FDI). Thus, since the mid 1980s, total FDI flows to the Arab World fluctuated between 0.5 per cent and 0.75 per cent of GDP, well below FDI flows to Asia and Latin America (El-Erian and Sheybani, 1996: 14). FDI in the Arab World has also been heavily concentrated with regard to areas of investment and to host countries. Most of it went to the energy sector, while about 80 per cent of total net FDI in the Arab World in 1996 went to only three countries, namely Egypt, Morocco and Tunisia (Economic Research Forum, 1997: 6). Some countries, such as Yemen, Syria, Algeria and Sudan, have been receiving very insignificant amounts of FDI (Economic Research Forum, 1996: 47). Technology transfer has similarly been highly concentrated in a few economic sectors, mainly energy and defence.

Contrary to the IMF conclusion that the 'bold reformers' – meaning those Middle Eastern countries which went further in opening up their economy to the outside world, namely Jordan, Morocco and Tunisia – 'have enjoyed higher per capita real growth and have performed better in terms of employment creation, lower inflation and faster poverty alleviation than countries that have reformed more slowly or are only beginning to implement outward-oriented policies' (IMF, 1996b: 56), the economic experience during the last three decades in the Arab World tends to support a sceptical view about the impact of globalization on growth, and especially about its impact on poverty alleviation. Looking at the Arab World as a whole, the rapid economic growth in the 1970s and the first half of the 1980s (during which an average annual real growth of about 5 per cent was achieved) was followed by a GDP growth rate that was nearly halved during the following decade (1985–95), when it fell below the rate of population growth. Per capita real income for the Arab World as a whole is estimated to have fallen by about 40 per cent between 1980 and 1997 (Economic Research Forum, 1997: 4). The main cause for the rapid rise and fall of growth rates was the violent fluctuations in oil prices and oil revenues and hence in labour remittances and investment rates. This has very little, if anything, to do with the change in the degree of openness of Arab economies.

Some aspects of human development have almost certainly benefited from greater openness of Arab economies to the external world during the last three decades, as they have benefited over the larger time span discussed in the earlier part of this chapter. Thus, those Arab countries which started to benefit from their contact with the West, some time in the last century, in reducing infant mortality and lengthening life expectancy, continued to do so during the last three decades, while others, which started their contact with Western medicine and sanitation measures relatively recently, made even more rapid progress in this respect. For the Arab countries as a whole, a child born in 1990 could expect to live 13 years longer than the previous generation (World Bank, 1995b: 33). Average life expectancy at birth is now about 65 years, which is close to the world average. Infant mortality was reduced by more than half during the last 30 years and is now only marginally higher than the world average. Even countries that initiated contact with the West relatively early, such as Egypt, made rapid progress in life expectancy at birth (about 10 years in the case of Egypt, from 52.1 to 61.6 years between 1970–5 and 1990–5) (ESCWA, 1997: 55).

Increased contact with the West could also be given part of the credit for the reduction in the gender gap in the rates of enrolment in schools at different levels of education as well as for the increase in the rate of female participation in the labour force. Although there is still a wide gap between male and female school enrolment in all Arab countries, some Gulf countries have higher rates of enrolment in higher education for women than for men (Economic Research Forum, 1996: 97).

Apart from the obvious benefits reaped through greater access to modern medical facilities and exposure to a greater variety of cultures and ways of life, there is hardly a channel through which globalization takes place that is not a mixed blessing. The Arab World provides ample evidence of this. For example, increased participation in international trade may lead to the growth of total output by widening the market and allowing a greater division of labour, but it does not always leave the distribution of income intact and may increase the incidence of poverty. Resources may be directed away from the production of goods that constitute an important part of the consumption of the poorer classes, and towards the production of items for export. Examples from the 19th century highlight the impact of a shift from production of foodstuffs to export items due to colonialism in North Africa, or of the introduction of cotton cultivation in Egypt. In both cases, this shift in the pattern of cultivation led to a change in the distribution of land ownership. The poor seem to have suffered less in the case of Egypt, but merely because of differences in policy orientation between the colonial administration in French North Africa and that of an enlightened despot in Egypt. One may, of course, on purely theoretical grounds, argue that in such cases what is to blame for worsening distribution is not participation in foreign trade but other government policies. Nevertheless, one cannot help noticing that powerful practical factors often tie an open-door policy with a particular choice of distribution policy. Egypt's shift to more liberal trade policies since the mid 1970s, for example, seems to suggest the existence of a close relationship between these policies and the relaxation of the more egalitarian policies that had been introduced in the 1950s and 1960s. Indeed, taking a longer 200-year view, it is evident that in periods during which the government pursued more open policies to the external world, it also tended to abandon several of its responsibilities for the protection of the less-privileged groups of the population.

In the 1990s, the number of Arab migrant workers reached a peak of more than five million workers in the Gulf states, and about half as many migrant workers went from the *Maghreb* countries to Europe. This amounted to as much as 10 per cent of the labour force of the labour-exporting countries on average, but much more than this percentage for Jordan, Lebanon, the West Bank and Gaza, and Yemen. Remittances constituted significant percentages of GNP: 10 per cent in Morocco, 12 per cent in Egypt, 18 per cent in Jordan, 22 per cent in Yemen and 30 per cent in West Bank and Gaza (World Bank, 1995a: 6).

The period of accelerated globalization has been accompanied by a period of accelerated intra-regional migration with the Arab World divided between oil-exporting, labour-importing countries and non-oil exporting, labour-exporting countries. This has led to social and political tensions in both sets of countries and has added to the growth of social dualism which almost all Arab countries have experienced as a result of opening their doors to foreign capital. The effects on the poor have been particularly acute since the accelerated globalization of the 1970s has been accompanied by a reduction in the role of the state. This retrenchment of the role of the state, widely observed throughout the Third World, can be seen as an essential part of the process of contemporary globalization; the growth of external debt may have served only as an opportunity or pretext for such retrenchment rather than having precipitated the retrenchment per se. Accelerated privatization of public enterprises and the withdrawal of the state from many of its long-established responsibilities may be seen as the necessary price for having accumulated a large external debt, but alternatively it could be the result of forces of globalization that led to both the growth of debt *and* the reduction in the role of the state.

In the Arab World, the impact of the retrenchment of the role of the state can be seen perhaps more clearly than in many other regions of the world, simply because the state has traditionally played a much more prominent role in this part of the world. Of all the Arab countries, the Egyptian experience demonstrates, perhaps more than any other, the sharp contrast between the impact of a large government on human welfare and the impact of the rapid decline of this role.

Finally, globalization can have a significant impact through the growth of cultural contact and of the transmission of information, ideas and value systems. A more open society may be expected to be a more dynamic society with greater potential for innovation. However, this is by no means the only possible impact of increased cultural contact and greater infiltration of foreign ideas. The net impact must vary with the degree of exposure to foreign influences, whether this exposure is sudden or gradual, and of course with the nature of the invading and invaded cultures. Too much or too sudden exposure to foreign influences could create very disruptive influences, hampering rather than enhancing creativity. It could also create too great a tension between social classes, which may threaten social and political stability. Such an exposure to foreign ways of life could also lead to deterioration in the role of local institutions that had contributed positively to social welfare, but for which no 'modern' substitute could compensate. Yemen provides a clear example from the Arab World of the negative cultural impacts in these respects where the traditional Islamic social institutions of *Zakat* and *Waqf* have greatly declined in importance with greater integration with the modern world.

One certainly cannot generalize about whether the net impact of closer cultural contact is good or bad, not only because this may vary greatly from one case to another, but also because a large dose of value judgement and personal preference is involved. For the Arab World, 200 years of contact with Western cultures have produced immense transformations in ways of life, general outlook and value systems, which must have had a great impact on human welfare. Nor has this drama of cultural encounter been of a constant nature during the whole period. For almost 150 years, the encounter was mainly between the Arabs and Europe; however, for about 50 years now, the main source of change has been the United States. The process of Westernization has turned from Europeanization to Americanization, and the difference is very great. The differences can be seen in the rate of change, in the mechanism of change, even in the goals that motivate the change, and hence, of course, in the ultimate results. This will be discussed further below in the final section on the post-September 11 situation. Different persons may have different assessments of the net result of these contacts, but it cannot be denied that both varieties of cultural encounter have had a very profound impact on the Arab World.

To conclude this section, it is worth pointing out that in its experience with globalization the Arab World shows at least three special features. First, as already indicated, in probably no other region of the world (outside the socialist bloc before 1990) has the state played, over the last 50 years, a more important role in the economy than in the Arab World. This could be explained partly by historical traditions going back to ancient times, as in the case of Egypt, and partly by the nature of the resource endowment of societies that rely heavily either on river irrigation or on oil mining. With the inevitable retrenchment of the state as a result of the accelerated globalization of trade, capital movements and communication, traditional measures of protection provided by the state for the underprivileged groups of the population have been greatly reduced.

Second, one strategic commodity, namely oil, has played an enormously important role in the economic development of the region. For many Arab countries (Kuwait, Qatar, Bahrain, UAE, Oman, Saudi Arabia and Libya), the very beginning of 'globalization' was through the discovery and export of oil, and their history of contact with the outside world is almost identical with the history of their export of this one commodity.

Third, it was largely because of the crucially important role of oil that the Arab World has experienced a rate of intra-regional migration that is rarely surpassed in any other region of the world. This has led the impact of 'oil wealth' to spread far beyond the boundaries of the oil-rich countries themselves. Thus, almost all the Arab World has become involved in the process of 'globalization through oil', and both the positive and negative impacts of this process have been strongly felt throughout the region. However, this involvement in 'globalization through oil' has taken quite a dramatic turn, with far-reaching consequences at the very beginning of the 21st century.

Globalizing the Arab World after 11 September 2001

From the 11th September 2001 onwards, the Arab World has been suddenly brought into the limelight as a result of its being accused of causing a serious disruption to the world order and presenting a serious threat to global peace and security. The attacks on the twin towers of the World Trade Center in New York and on the Pentagon in Washington, DC, were attributed to Islamic fanatics; but these were all said to be citizens either of Saudi Arabia or of Egypt. The leader of the organization responsible for planning the attack is said to be originally Saudi, and his main assistance to be Egyptian, though both were believed to be living and running the organization from Afghanistan. 'A War on Terror' was declared, leading to the occupation of Iraq, and more attacks are promised either on Iran or Syria or both.

Meanwhile, the whole of the Arab World has been suddenly brought under a very critical light, with heavy emphasis in the international media on various shortcomings of Arab regimes, with hardly any exception, related to the lack of democracy, economic inefficiencies, defective educational systems, discrimination against women, as well as to the poor observance of human rights generally. A United Nations agency (UNDP) published three reports, in the three successive years following the events of September 11, pouring very harsh criticism against almost every aspect of Arab economic, social and political life, implying no doubt that the occupation of Iraq, and maybe future attacks on other Arab countries as well, could very well be justified, since in this way, democracy, economic development and greater respect for the rights of women and other human rights could be brought about.

All these developments are glowing examples of 'globalization', from the very attacks in New York and Washington, DC, by terrorists coming from a distant point of the globe, to the American attack on Afghanistan, to the American/British occupation of Iraq, which are bringing back the old type of globalization through colonization. Even the United Nations' severe critique of the Arab World, which launched an unfamiliar kind of involvement in the affairs of sovereign nations, using a language quite unknown in other UN reports, was another instance of a new campaign to 'globalize the Arab World'.

It seems foolish, however, not to be able to see through the rhetoric accompanying the present wave of globalization, which is engulfing the Arab World. After such a long history of a great variety of colonial experiences and foreign domination, from outright military occupation to manipulation through foreign aid, the Arabs should be immune from believing the current rhetoric of 'war on terror', 'bringing democracy to the Arab World', 'granting more freedoms to women', and so on. Many Arabs rightly suspect that behind all these modern slogans lie such goals as having greater control of the oil wealth of the Arab World and Iran, or establishing easier access to the oil wealth of Central Asia, in a world that is about to witness a new period of fierce competition among economic blocs, old and new, for securing the sources of energy.

Egyptians still remember how the British occupation of their country was originally justified by the need to restore law and order following a small skirmish between a humble Egyptian and a Maltese subject of Great Britain, over the right price that had to be paid for a donkey ride. The result was a military occupation that lasted for 74 years, during which much more important things were settled than the price of a donkey ride, including the right policy for the cultivation of Egyptian cotton to be shipped to British textile factories, the right tariff that guaranteed the flow of British cloth to the Egyptian market, as well as the most suitable system of education in Egypt that could not obstruct such policies.

The Americans and the British are doing very similar things now in Iraq, while using very similar rhetoric, even though some 120 years separate the beginnings of the two occupations. There are of course important differences. One of the most important of these differences has to do with the cultural impact. For it seems that controlling the oil wealth of another nation, at the beginning of the 21st century, requires a very different cultural policy from that which was required a century ago for forcing a country to export its cotton to another and to import from it ready-made cloth. Globalization now has a very different flavour, involves many more people and evokes much deeper emotions that touch some of the most intimate beliefs. One important difference between the two types of globalization, which must produce important differences in the cultural impact, is the difference in the nature of the goods which are searching for markets. Marketing useless, or virtually useless soft drinks, requires a deeper change in attitudes than that required for marketing foreign cloth. There is also an important difference stemming from the size and nature of the social classes involved in the process of globalization. A much deeper social change is required to effect a change in the tastes and attitudes of a large middle class, which is now being tempted to join the 'consumer society', than was required to tempt a small elite at the top, as was the case with the earlier case of 'European' globalization, a hundred or more years ago. The economic and political damage that may be brought about by today's globalization may not be difficult to repair with time. What is much more difficult, and may prove impossible to repair, is the damage that is bound to occur to the culture of those who happen to stand in the way.

Notes

1   The 'Arab World' in this chapter is understood to include 21 countries: seven in North Africa (Morocco, Algeria, Tunisia, Mauritania, Libya, Egypt and Sudan), two in East Africa (Somalia and Djibouti), five in the eastern Mediterranean (Syria, Lebanon, Palestine (Gaza and the West Bank), Jordan and Iraq), and seven on the Arabian peninsula (Kuwait, Qatar, United Arab Emirates, Bahrain, Oman, Saudi Arabia and Yemen). Their total population is about 300 million, or about 5 per cent of the world population, but they produce just 2 per cent of world gross domestic product (GDP). It is a region of sharp contrasts; it includes some countries of less than a million people, such as Bahrain and Qatar, as well as a country of 70 million people (Egypt). It has some of the poorest countries in the world, such as Mauritania, Somalia and Sudan, but also some of the richest, including the United Arab Emirates (UAE), Kuwait and Qatar.
2   See Issawi (1982), pp. 93–4, although for Algeria he mentions that there were also causes other than the French invasion.

References

Arab League, The Arab Fund for Economic and Social Development, Arab Monetary Fund and OAPEC (1996) *The Unified Arab Economic Report* (in Arabic), Cairo.

Diwan, I., L. Savire and J. Underwood (1993) *External Finance in the Middle East.* Cairo: Economic Research Forum.

Economic Research Forum (1996) *Economic Trends in the MENA Region.* Cairo: Economic Research Forum.

Economic Research Forum (1997), *Forum.* Cairo.

El-Erian, M. and S. Sheybani (1996) 'Private Capital Flows in the Development of the Arab Countries', Paper submitted to the Cairo Papers Sixth Annual Symposium, American University in Cairo, November.

Economic and Social Commission for Western Asia (ESCWA) (1997) *Selected Social Trends in the ESCWA Region.* New York: ESCWA.

International Monetary Fund (IMF) (1996a) *Growth and Stability in the Middle East and North Africa.* Washington, DC: IMF.

International Monetary Fund (IMF) (1996b) *Building on Progress: Reform and Growth in the Middle East and North Africa.* Washington, DC: IMF.

Issawi, C. (1965) 'The Arab World's Heavy Legacy', *Foreign Affairs*, XL111, 3: 501–12.

Issawi, C. (1982) *An Economic History of the Middle East and North Africa.* London: Methuen.

Owen, R. (1981) *The Middle East in the World Economy*, London: Methuen.

World Bank (1995a) *Will Arab Workers Prosper or Be Left Out of the Twenty-First Century?* Washington, DC: World Bank.

World Bank (1995b) *Claiming the Future: Choosing Prosperity in the Middle East and North Africa.* Washington, DC: World Bank.

World Bank (2006) *World Development Indicators 2006.* Washington, DC: World Bank.

8

A Force for Integration or Marginalization? A Perspective from West Africa

Amadu Sesay and Kehinde Olayode

If globalization implies at one level that world trade and financial markets are becoming more integrated, how far have developing countries been involved in this integration process? This chapter examines the extent to which West Africa has participated in the global economy in an era of globalization and questions some of the assumptions underlying the unbridled optimism about the capacity of unregulated markets to sustain economic growth and address problems of poverty and inequality, especially in the West African subregion. In other words, it attempts to provide answers to these important questions: Do developing countries have the opportunity, interest or ability to actualize the benefits promised by globalization and reduce the restrictions and losses that accompany it? How are the issues of globalization and equity played out in West Africa? Will further integration of West Africa into international capitalism help countries in the subregion to create the internal socio-political, economic and ideological conditions, which will enable them to satisfy the needs, demands and exigencies of nation building and development? Clearly, there are no ready-made and conclusive answers to these important questions, especially since globalization even as a purely economic phenomenon is a highly complex process. Our argument is that under the existing international trade and finance rules, globalization is marginalizing many countries in the subregion and threatens the livelihoods and welfare of its vulnerable communities. This is because in spite of its abundant natural resources, the level of poverty in West Africa is the worst in the world. The subregion has also not been able to participate effectively in the global economy because of endemic corruption, political instability, structural vulnerability, a crippling debt burden and over dependence on raw material exports.

Globalization, characterized by liberalization, competition and free-market policies, undermines West Africa's fragile political systems and economies and creates phenomenal developmental challenges for the entire region. Driven by the explosive growth of information, communications and other forms of technological changes, the interrelated processes of globalization, marginalization and integration profoundly influence West Africa's development needs, challenges and opportunities. Keeping pace with the processes of globalization demands a high degree of literacy and technical ability – skills the majority of Africans do not yet posses. The combined effects of globalization and economic liberalization have thus intensified West African countries' needs for external aid and development assistance. The subregion's increasingly peripheral roles in the global economy, is dramatized in two main areas – its declining share of official development assistance (ODA) and its shrinking share of foreign direct investment (FDI). For example, West Africa's share of world FDI decreased from 2.5 per cent in 2002 to 1.8 per cent in 2004 (UNCTAD, 2005). In contrast with all other developing regions, West Africa has remained aid dependent, with FDI generally lagging behind official development assistance. Between 1970 and 2003, FDI accounted for just one-fifth of all capital flows to the subregion.

The factors responsible for West Africa's marginalization are varied. However, the most popular reasons relate to the liberalization of Eastern European economies, which now provide new investment opportunities for Europe and America (Callaghy, 1990), along with the intractable civil conflicts that have made West Africa unattractive for investment. The assertion that West Africa is marginalized in the global economy, however, is an increasingly contentious one. It is clear that through its heavy dependence on external aid and the dominant international financial institutions, such as the World Bank and the IMF, the subregion is being tightly incorporated into the global economy. Furthermore, by adopting the IMF/World Bank's structural adjustment programmes (SAPs), which epitomize the economic dogma of neoliberalism, West Africa has been grafted into the global political economy. This phenomenon of simultaneous marginalization and integration underscores the region's ambivalent, if not uncertain, posture in the global economy in particular and globalization processes in general.

West Africa: a geopolitical and socio-economic survey

West Africa refers to the 15 states that constitute the Economic Community of West African States (ECOWAS). They are: Benin, Burkina Faso, Cape

Verde, Côte d'Ivoire, The Gambia, Ghana, Guinea, Guinea-Bissau, Liberia, Mali, Niger, Nigeria, Senegal, Sierra Leone and Togo.[1] Surely there are ethno-cultural and economic similarities between West African countries which are far more remarkable than the differences. Cross-border trading and the free movement of people under the Protocol on Free Movement, currently in its third phase, enhance these similarities. It must be pointed out, however, that the Protocol does not in practice make much sense to the majority of citizens of the subregion, who either do not recognize the artificial borders or are not in a position to take advantage of it. Apart from the common colonial legacies, particularly among Anglophone countries on the one hand and Francophone on the other, West African countries also share similar experiences of long-standing political instability, ethnic conflicts, civil wars, debt burden and peripheral participation in the international economic system. The subregion is also unique in that the United Nations Conference on Trade and Development (UNCTAD) currently designates 13 out of its 15 countries as Least Developed Countries (LDCs). In addition, 14 West African countries are also classified as Heavily Indebted Poor Countries (HIPC), which are eligible for debt relief (World Bank, 2005b).

According to the World Bank's *Doing Business in 2006*, West African countries impose the most regulatory obstacles on entrepreneurs and are slower than any other region in implementing reforms to ease constraints on doing business. Private investment in the region averaged below 14 per cent of GDP in the six-year period from 1998 to 2004 while foreign direct investment averaged 2.8 per cent of GDP during the same period. It is also noteworthy that the informal sector represents 72 per cent of trade in the ECOWAS countries (*World Bank*, 2005a). The value of West Africa's export trade between 2000 and 2004 was approximately 1.5 per cent of total world exports, whereas the value of Asia's exports (excluding China) within the same period was 29 per cent (UNCTAD, 2005). From 1995 to 2002, the average electrification rate for the region improved to 27 per cent – a gain of five percentage points but still remained the lowest in Africa. An estimated 34 per cent of the total population has access to safe water and only 32 per cent to improved sanitation, and although the number of telephone subscribers has tripled, less than 5 per cent of households have phones (World Bank, 2006). Data in *World Development Indicators 2006* show a remarkable growth in some West African states since 2000. The recent surge in oil exports and the boom in the price of oil have pushed up the growth rate in Nigeria. However, in spite of the recent recovery in some countries, the region's poverty rate remains the world's highest. About 44 per cent of the total population lives on less than $1 a day. This is in sharp contrast to East Asia, where the number of extremely poor people fell by 580 million to 12 per cent of the total population. Current projections are that in 2015, West Africa's poverty rate will remain at over 48 per cent – far above the 22.3 per cent target set by the Millennium Development Goals (MDGs) – (World Bank, 2006).

West Africa's population growth rate presents both risks and opportunities. A large, youthful population – 44 per cent below the age of 18 – could result in increased capacity for growth and poverty reduction, if they are healthy and adequately trained. But to seize this opportunity will require increased investment in education. However, recent data from child labour surveys show that in many of the poorer countries, such as Chad, Togo, Burkina Faso, and Sierra Leone, over 65 per cent of children aged between seven and fourteen years are working, while more than half do not go to school at all (World Bank 2006). Primary education completion rates are only 42 per cent. The gains in education have been uneven, with tremendous progress in a country like Mali where primary school completion rate quadrupled from 11 to 44 per cent between 1991 and 2004. However, other countries such as Guinea Bissau and Niger have primary school completion rates of less than 30 per cent (World Bank, 2006).

A massive effort is needed in the subregion to provide infrastructure that will reduce transport costs and improve power supply. Only 30 per cent of the region's rural population has access to all-season roads – the lowest level in the entire developing world. And while West Africa has benefited from the global expansion of the telecommunications sector, coverage is still small in comparison with other regions. In terms of water availability and food security, the West African subregion is the world's most vulnerable, and could be severely affected by global climatic changes. Finally, changes in rainfall patterns could have a serious impact on areas dependent on hydroelectricity, and could increase the risk of droughts, crop failure, livestock losses, malnutrition and disease (UNDP, 2005).

The impact of globalization on West Africa

The planetary phenomenon of globalization portends a new order of marginalization for the West African subregion. Globalization – the universalization of communication, mass production, market exchanges and redistribution – rather than engendering new ideas and developmental orientations in West Africa, tends to increasingly subvert the region's autonomy and self-determination. Globalization has enlivened the venomous potency of mass poverty and its accompanying multi-dimensional depravation of the citizenry; and it has significantly disarticulated the industrial sector of most, if not all of the states in West Africa. This phenomenon has been particularly evident in the costs of production, which have become uncomfortably high in most countries of the subregion. Relative lack of government incentives to encourage local production, subversion of local products by the unrestricted importation of cheap but superior quality goods, have exacerbated the situation under WTO agreements, currency devaluation and depletion of foreign reserves.

Furthermore, the neoliberal assumption that market reforms would promote liberalization at the social and political levels has not been borne out by evidence from the West African experience. The policies that are touted for preparing the subregion for a more rewarding integration into the world system come in the form of stabilization and Structural Adjustment Programmes (SAPs). But the implementation of SAPs and the privatization of the state only increased social appropriation and accumulation by the political elites, and led to the abdication by the state of its social responsibilities. It is also argued that SAPs threatened nation building and democratization by exacerbating social conflict, weakening the capacity of the state to respond to the many demands on it, and riding roughshod over public opinion without due respect for democratic processes (Joseph, 1999: 120–1).

In Nigeria, for example, the broad objectives of SAP were to achieve fiscal balance by altering and restructuring the production and consumption patterns of the economy, eliminate price distortions, reduce heavy dependence on crude oil exports and consumer goods imports, and finally enhance the non-oil export base and to achieve sustainable growth (Olukoshi, 1991). Other goals of the policy were to rationalize the role of the public sector and accelerate the growth potential of the private sector (Olukoshi, 1993). The key policy elements through which Nigeria sought to achieve these goals include:

(a)   the adoption of a market-determined exchange rate for the Naira, the local currency;
(b)   deregulation of external trade and payment arrangements (i.e. trade liberalization);
(c)   deregulation of interest rates;
(d)   monetary and physical restraints;
(e)   relaxation of administrative controls;

(f)   adoption of a new pricing policy – elimination of subsidies;
(g)   divestment of the state from the economy through privatization and commercialization;
(h)   external debt management (Adejumobi and Momoh, 1994; Sesay and Akinrinade, 1998).

However, except for a small number of beneficiaries – foreign exchange dealers and the new finance houses – that emerged to reap huge profits from high interest rates, the vast majority of ordinary Nigerians lost out considerably under SAP. The rural farmers who were supposed to be the major beneficiaries from the high produce prices made little gain, with the probable exception of cocoa farmers who enjoyed an initial boom due to the curb on over-invoicing practices of middlemen and produce exporters (mostly Lebanese). But, whatever the gains that cocoa farmers made were easily wiped out by galloping inflation and the attendant high production costs. In his study of the adjustment policies in Nigeria, Fadaunsi (1993) concluded that the major beneficiaries of the gains of SAP were not the rural dwellers or the urban poor, as the advocates of the policy had envisaged, because

> Once the inflationary consequences of devaluation started to catch-up with the cost of farm inputs and labour, in a context of subsidy withdrawal on tractor hiring, seeds, and fertilizers, the farmers began to experience diminishing incomes. The costs of other non-farm goods and services also turned the terms of trade against the rural farmers.
>
> (Fadaunsi, 1993: 45)

The removal of subsidies on petroleum products, and massive currency devaluations, also raised the cost of food, rent, transport, electricity, healthcare, education and other social goods and services beyond the reach of many average Nigerian families, while unemployment remained high with continual lay-offs in the public sector. Fashoyin (1993) estimated that about one million workers lost their jobs in the public sector between 1984 and 1989, in addition to the large number of unemployed graduates, school leavers and workers who were made redundant in the private sector, especially by the manufacturing companies that operated at less than one-third of installed capacities.

Côte d'Ivoire is an example of a country that was relatively prosperous and stable until its engagement with the World Bank and IMF in 1989 (World Bank, 2002). Significantly, liberalization coincided with a drastic decline in the world cocoa price, and the farmers were the worst hit.

Unfortunately, the government was unable to intervene as its role in the cocoa industry had been terminated with the introduction of SAP. The standard of living of farmers and rural dwellers dramatically declined following the unprecedented cuts on the education and health budgets, which made health and education services inaccessible to the ordinary Ivoirean. Things were made much worse when the CFA (official currency in West African Francophone countries) was devalued by 50 per cent in 1994 to make exports cheaper and more competitive in the world market (World Bank, 2002). As would be expected, the move significantly affected the poor as their savings and purchasing power shrunk overnight. Côte d'Ivoire's debt burden was also worsened by the devaluation of the local currency. As would be expected, its external debt grew from $7.4 billion to $17.7 billion between 1980 and 1990, making it one of the Heavily Indebted Poor Countries. The increasing debt burden had negative social consequences as repayments and debt servicing were done at the expenses of vital social services. Expectedly, from 1988 to 1995, the incidence and intensity of poverty in Côte d'Ivoire doubled from 17.8 to 37 per cent of total population (World Bank, 2002). To fight back and ease the pain of liberalization, cocoa-producing countries in West Africa formed a cartel to control the price of cocoa beans by restricting the supply of their commodities through negotiations with Western buyers. Unfortunately, the cartel could not make a significant impact on the international cocoa market and price for a number of reasons. First was the lack of consensus among its members on the terms of engagement with Western buyers. Second was their inability to influence the price of the commodity, which seriously undermined the credibility of the group. Finally, unlike crude oil, which could be left underground and is also easy to store, cocoa is a highly perishable commodity. Thus in the absence of effective storage facilities, West African producers were compelled to sell the commodity at the existing market price.

Ghana, another West African country, launched its Structural Adjustment Programme in 1983 in the form of an Economic Recovery Programme (ERP). In the late 1980s, the IMF and the World Bank hailed the programme as 'the model' (Fontana, 1994). Today, the IMF and the World Bank are very reluctant to refer to Ghana as their 'model'. The government of John Jerry Rawlings turned to the two agencies in 1983 and accepted their fiscal and monetary recommendations in exchange for assistance packages to ease the country's difficult economic and social transformation. Foremost among the changes put in place were the retrenchment of the government's activist role and the encouragement of free-market forces to promote the efficient and productive development of local resources. The reforms cut government budgets, privatized state enterprises, devalued the currency, and tried to rebuild the country's battered industrial infrastructure through foreign-assistance programmes. As in other countries of Africa in the 1980s, government was identified as the problem, and free-market forces were seen as the solution. By the 1990s, however, the effects of the structural adjustment programme in Ghana were being assessed with mixed feelings. According to the World Bank and other Western financial institutions, the economy had become much more stable and production was on a more solid footing than it had been a decade earlier (World Bank, 1996). Many Ghanaians, however, wondered if the structural adjustment programme benefited all citizens or just a few sectors of the economy. Critics of the World Bank claimed that the reforms concentrated on infrastructure such as airports, roads and other macroeconomic projects that did little to improve the lives of ordinary people. Although under the sway of free-market forces production increased in Ghana's traditionally strong sectors of cocoa and gold, a more broadly based economy did not develop. In addition, substantial loans were obtained by the government to rebuild the infrastructure, but only at the expense of recurrent budget expenditures on health and education. Although the government claimed that its finances were much healthier in the 1990s than they were in the 1980s, the long-term economic and social impacts of structural adjustment remained uncertain. More importantly, under the ERP, the civil service was reduced by 5 per cent, which resulted in about 150,000 civil servants being laid off each year from 1986 to 1989 (Baden, 1995).

Another prescription of the structural adjustment programme in Ghana was the removal of subsidies, which increased the cost of production as well as the prices of essential goods, causing high inflation rates, averaging 30 per cent in the 1990s, while wages lagged behind, thus reducing the purchasing power of wage earners. Market liberalization, which SAPs often demand, also resulted in very high interest rates. The lending rates in Ghana averaged 36 per cent p.a. between 1998 and 2000, making the cost of borrowed capital expensive. This situation discouraged local manufacturers from borrowing, thereby forcing many small-scale industries to close down. SAPs also left a huge debt overhang in Ghana as foreign debt rose from US$1 billion in 1983 to almost US$6 billion in 2000 (IMF, 2001).

In almost all of the ECOWAS countries, the 'economic reforms' imposed on them by globalization, such as deregulation, privatization and minimal governmental intervention in the economic sectors gave rise to a resurgence of diseases such as tuberculosis, typhoid and cholera that were almost wiped out in the late 1970s. This was in addition to the debilitating HIV/AIDS scourge. In 2003 alone, 2.6 million people in West Africa became newly infected with HIV (UNAIDS, 2004). Treatment coverage remains low in the subregion and only 3 per cent of an estimated 4.4 million in need received antiretroviral therapy in 2003 (WHO, 2004). In early May 2006, the Global Fund suspended funding assistance to Nigeria because the actual number of people on antiretroviral treatment was much lower than the number initially submitted by the National Action Committee on AIDS (NACA). Households affected by AIDS in the subregion are more likely to suffer severe poverty than HIV/AIDS-free households. AIDS is also intensifying chronic food shortages by causing farm labour losses and depleting family income that would normally be used to purchase seeds and food. In addition, the epidemic has contributed to rapid health-sector deterioration by increasing the burden on already strapped health facilities (Cheru, 2002).

The challenges of globalization for West African states

Among the immediate challenges facing West African states is resolving the many diversionary and divisive conflicts in the subregion. The negative impacts of these conflicts and violence on human, social and economic activities are enormous. Nigeria and indeed the entire West African subregion have thus far devoted considerable human, material, political and diplomatic resources to the prevention, management and resolution of the conflicts, starting with Liberia, then Sierra Leone and Guinea-Bissau. Similar initiatives are being deployed with equal vigour and commitment in other parts of the subregion, especially Côte d'Ivoire, to bring the warring parties to the negotiating table.

Closely related to the absence of peace is the appalling level of poverty in the subregion. Since 1996, the last ten countries on the global list of the Least Developed Countries have consistently been ECOWAS states (Hertz, 2004). Fighting poverty thus remains a daunting challenge for the subregion. With regard to the Millennium Development Goals, the subregion is unlikely to meet the goal of halving poverty by 2015 (UNDP, 2003). According to the UNDP, at current levels it will take Nigeria, the subregional super power, 40 years to achieve the MDGs. Furthermore, Nigeria and the Democratic Republic of Congo have the highest child mortality rates on the continent (UNDP, 2005). Poverty, underdevelopment and a fragile infrastructure create fertile conditions for violent conflicts and new security threats, including easy access to, and arbitrary use of, small arms and light weapons, unrestricted movement of mercenaries (i.e., ex-child soldiers, especially those left out in the rehabilitation projects in countries like Sierra-Leone and Liberia), armed militia groups, human trafficking and terrorism (Sesay, 2003; Sesay and Simbine, 2006).

Finally, globalization is increasingly polarizing West African societies in the same way that the unequal gains of the 19th-century Industrial Revolution gave rise to social discontent, which arguably paved the way for communism in many countries much later. The uneven spread of economic opportunities within West African countries as a result of globalization is increasing discontent, especially among the youths, the poor and other disadvantaged groups. The result is an increase in crime rates and social upheavals, which in some countries resulted in rebellion against the governments or interethnic rivalries and even outright wars (Sesay, 2003). The rise of interethnic violence has been particularly frightening in Nigeria, a country of about 250 different ethnic groups and nationalities. Many of the ethnic groups individually and collectively complain of marginalization by either the federal, state or local governments, and have called for a Sovereign National Conference to discuss and determine the basis of continued association in a loosely governed Nigeria, and to agree on a formula for sharing the huge oil wealth of the country (Sesay *et al.*, 2003). But so far the federal government has refused to hold a Sovereign National Conference fearing that it would lead to the breakup of the country.

Responses to the challenges of globalization

While globalization is accelerating interdependence on a worldwide scale, regionalism attempts to harness the pressures of globalization through enhanced collaboration among states, most notably in Europe through the European Union, in North America through NAFTA, the Asia Pacific Economic Cooperation (APEC) in Asia and in West Africa, through the Economic Community of West Africa States (ECOWAS). The challenges of globalization have given governments a strong justification for undertaking collective action in pursuit of regional cooperation. The institutional opportunities presented by such a collective approach to problem solving allow countries to undertake regional cooperation schemes, which are seen as important elements in the globalization processes. Accordingly, a major question that is relevant to the focus of this chapter is whether regional integration has been an appropriate response by West African countries to the challenges of globalization. There is no doubt that regional integration offers opportunities for the subregion to overcome the scourge of marginalization as well as other negative impacts of globalization. There is no doubt that in theory closer trade links between ECOWAS partner states would strengthen their capacity to participate in world trade. With 15 relatively small, low-cost economies, regional integration would harmonize national policies and create larger markets. The benefits of economies of scale in production and distribution, particularly, lower transaction costs and increased reliability will enhance the efficiency and competitiveness of domestic producers and enhance trade with the rest of the world.

To enhance their competitive position in the global economy, West African leaders are at the forefront fostering regional economic integration. They know that the region's problems cannot be contained within national borders, because political instability in one country tends to spill over to others, uncontrolled infectious diseases spread across national borders, while poor transport and communication infrastructure links between countries raise the cost of doing business and reduce market sizes. For the ECOWAS leaders then, an important intermediate step towards profitable and effective integration into the world economy is through the promotion of regional integration at home. Regional cooperation in key structural areas – such as tariff reduction and harmonization, legal and regulatory reforms, payment systems rationalization, financial sector reorganization, investment incentives, tax systems harmonization, and labour market reforms – enables participating countries to pool their human and institutional resources in order to attain greater technical and administrative competence than they could on their own. In addition, the possibility of shared energy, power, telecommunications and transportation systems is not only cost effective but would also help bring the 15 countries closer together as they set common regional policies and goals. Finally, it is assumed that a collective regional approach in critical areas of economic and social development will in turn allow the partner countries to protect and promote their interests more effectively in the international arena.

In order to facilitate the free movement of goods, ECOWAS launched a Trade Liberalization Scheme (TLS) in 1990, which aimed at systematically reducing and eliminating tariff and non-tariff barriers among member states, leading to the formation of a free trade area. The scheme covered three groups of products: traditional handicrafts, unprocessed goods and industrial products. The removal of tariff and non-tariff barriers therefore remains a major preoccupation of ECOWAS to realize the objectives of the TLS (World Bank, 1998).

After decades of limited success in promoting economic integration, and faced with debilitating conflicts in some member states, the leadership of ECOWAS quickly responded by revising the Original Treaty in 1993 to re-energize the integration process. ECOWAS also adopted a fast-track policy in 1999/2000 to deepen and accelerate the pace of regional integration and enhance its conflict management capability. As part of the integration process, member states adopted a Protocol on the Free Movement of People, which among other things, abolished visas for citizens travelling in the subregion. Under the third phase of the protocol, an ECOWAS citizen is free to enter, reside and settle in any member country. There is also now an ECOWAS passport, although many countries in the subregion are yet to start issuing it to their citizens.

In the area of monetary cooperation, the ECOWAS Monetary Cooperation Programme (EMCP) was introduced in 1987 to promote financial and monetary cooperation among the member states with the ultimate objective of achieving a single currency area after complying with a set of macroeconomic convergence criteria. The EMCP is expected to lead to the establishment of a monetary union, a regional central bank and a single currency policy. To accelerate monetary union, the ECOWAS authority initiated a second monetary zone, the West African Monetary Zone (WAMZ), among Nigeria, Ghana, Gambia, Sierra Leone, Liberia and Guinea within a fast-track framework. The aim of the WAMZ is to provide a platform for achieving a single monetary zone by floating a second currency and then merging it with the West African Economic and Monetary Union (UEMOA), or the CFA zone, to create a single West Africa-wide currency (Magbagbeola, 2003). Nevertheless, the 2005 deadline for the merger of the WAMZ with UEMOA to form the West African Monetary Union (WAMU) failed to materialize, as none of the five participating countries was able to fully satisfy the macroeconomic convergence criteria. Other problems frustrating the monetary union include the low level of intra-regional trade; the presence of parallel and competing monetary arrangements consisting of the franc, the dollar and other national currencies; the underdeveloped subregional capital markets; and lack of political will by member countries to implement agreements jointly reached by them (Sesay, 2005).

Against the background of these efforts, the World Bank in 2001 adopted a Regional Integration Assistance Strategy (RIAS) for West Africa to promote a much more focused approach to integration in the subregion within the framework of a Regional Poverty Reduction Strategy Paper (RPRSP) in order to provide the basis for a comprehensive review of the regional dimension of poverty and map out a collective strategy for fighting the scourge in ways that are well beyond the scope of national efforts (World Bank, 2002). What is worthy of note here, however, is that encouraged by the decision to fast track their regional integration process, the ECOWAS authority organized a summit in Yamoussoukro, Côte d'Ivoire, in May 2002, on the implementation of the New Partnership for Africa's Development (NEPAD) in West Africa. Since 2003, the executive secretariat has focused on creating the necessary synergy between NEPAD and ECOWAS programmes, and the region has embarked on the implementation of NEPAD programmes and projects in the areas of energy, road transport, telecommunications, monetary and fiscal policies, agriculture and food security, intra-regional trade development, and strengthening good governance, democracy, regional peace and security. Finally, in 2001, the ECOWAS authority adopted a Protocol on Democracy and Good Governance to encourage subregion-wide convergence, with emphasis on zero tolerance of unconstitutional changes in government (Sesay, 2005).

In spite of these determined efforts, it is evident that regional integration is painfully slow and that not much is being done to put in place the requisite physical infrastructure to promote greater intra-regional trade and make the region more competitive vis-à-vis the rest of the world. It is also obvious that integration has not had much visible impact on economic development of member states because of the low level of implementation of Community Acts and Decisions. More importantly, due to constant threats to peace and security in the region, ECOWAS has been compelled to reposition itself to deal with the violent conflicts that erupted in some member states and which threatened to destabilize the entire region (Adekeye, 2002; Sesay *et al.*, 2003).

This development necessitated the creation of ad hoc mechanisms, at least initially, and thereafter, on a more permanent basis, to address both the nature and dynamics of conflicts in the subregion that were propelled mainly by internal factors such as poverty, gross violations of human rights, exclusion and corruption. A lot of attention has accordingly shifted to conflict management, sometimes leaving little time to concentrate on the original economic agenda in key areas such as trade and economic development. Understandably, the biggest constraint to the integration project in West Africa in the last 15 years has been, and remains the elusiveness of peace and stability in the subregion.

Conclusion

As far back as 1975, and long before globalization became the buzzword of contemporary international economic relations, West African states had established the Economic Community Of West Africa States to integrate their economies and exploit economies of scale. The integration efforts were intensified after the end of the cold war and the greater marginalization of weak regions and states that characterized the ensuing globalization processes. From such a standpoint, then, regional integration is perceived as the platform that would end their marginalization and facilitate effective participation in the global economy and politics.

However, several years of SAPs left state capacity seriously eroded while the social sector and infrastructure collapsed. Under such circumstances, regional integration projects suffered a serious setback as each member state struggled to remain afloat. The growing potency of the IMF and the World Bank as well as other global financial institutions made it impossible for West African states to effectively control the parameters with which they could chart the fortunes of their economies. Presented with a fait accompli on major financial and economic issues by international agencies such as the World Bank, the IMF and the World Trade Organization, there was great tension between national policies on the one hand and subregional goals under the auspices of ECOWAS on the other, hindering progress towards subregional integration. For instance, starved of funds, ECOWAS became increasingly dependent on donor funds for most of its programmes and projects. The declining economic fortunes of West African states, which were exacerbated by an excruciating debt burden, limited access to new technology; and even the lack of skilled manpower considerably slowed down the pace of integration in the subregion, further accentuating their marginalization in the global economy.

In addition, the long years of civil strife, civil wars and state collapse among member states of ECOWAS resulted in the impoverishment of their citizens and the consequent withdrawal of citizens from the public space into informal sector enterprises. Not surprisingly, it has been estimated that informal trade currently accounts for more than 70 per cent of trade transactions within the West African subregion. Coupled with the unwillingness of the Western trade partners to open up their markets to goods from the subregion, West African states have not been able to fully benefit from trade liberalization under the current globalization processes. The cumulative result is that the majority of West African states have continued to suffer social, political and economic regression and instability. Unable to protect themselves against the unbridled onslaught of globalization processes such as free trade, deregulation and privatization, economic and political development in all the West Africa countries has deteriorated considerably since the 1980s, making the subregion one of the most underdeveloped in the world.

Our analysis, therefore, leads to the conclusion that it is unlikely that the regional integration initiatives of West African states would mitigate the negative impacts of globalization as manifested in their marginalization and inability to fully integrate into the global economy, at least in the short run. Indeed, the intensification of the forces of globalization may further increase their peripheral status in both the global economy and politics, thereby worsening their crisis of legitimacy, which could ultimately result in political instability and perhaps even state collapse in the subregion.

Note

1   It should be noted that Mauritania, the sixteenth state in West Africa, withdrew its membership from ECOWAS in 2000.

References

Adejumobi, S., and A. Momoh (1994) *The Political Economy of Nigeria Under Military Role 1993–94*. Harare, Zimbabwe: Sapes Books.

Adekeye, A. (2002) *Building Peace in West Africa: Liberia, Sierra Leone and Guinea Bissau*. Boulder, CO: Lynne Rienner.

Baden, S. (1995) 'Gender and Adjustment in Sub-Saharan African Agriculture', unpublished MA dissertation, University of Manchester.

Callaghy, T. (1990) 'Africa and the World Economy: Caught Between a Rock and a Hard Place', in J. Harbeson and D. Rothchild (eds), *Africa in World Politics*. Boulder, CO: Westview Press.

Cheru, F. (2002) *African Renaissance: Roadmaps to the Challenges of Globalization*. London: Zed Books.

Fadaunsi, A. (1993) 'Devaluation: Implications for Employment, Inflation, Growth and Development', in A. Olukoshi (ed.), *The Politics of Structural Adjustment in Nigeria*. London: James Currey.

Fashoyin, T. (1993) 'Consequences of Unemployment', in A. Adepoju (ed.), *The Impact of Structural Adjustment on the Population of Africa*. London: Heinemann.

Fontana, M. (1994) 'Trade Liberalisation and Income Distribution in Developing Countries: The Case of Ghana and Sri Lanka', unpublished M.Phil. dissertation, IDS, University of Sussex.

Hertz, N. (2004) *The Silent Takeover: Global Capitalism and the Death of Democracy*. London: Arrow Books.

IMF (2001) *Ghana: Enhanced Heavily Indebted Poor Countries (HIPC) Initiative*, available at http://www.imf.org/external/np/hipc/2001/gha/ghapd.pdf

Joseph, R. (1999) *State, Conflict, and Democracy in Africa*. Boulder, CO: Lynne Rienner.

Magbagbeola, N. (2003) 'The Quest for a West African Monetary Union: Implementation Issues, Progress and Prospects', paper presented at the CODESRIA's West Africa Sub-Regional Conference, Cotonou (Benin), 6–7 September.

Olukoshi, A. (1991) *Crisis and Adjustment in Nigerian Economy*. Lagos: Jad.

Olukoshi, A. (ed.) (1993) *The Politics of Structural Adjustment in Nigeria*. London: James Currey.

Sesay, A. (ed.) (2003) *Civil Wars, Child Soldiers and Post Conflict Peace Building in West Africa*. Ibadan, Nigeria: College Press.

Sesay, A. (2005) 'Can ECOWAS Re-Invent the Nationalist Dream'?, in A. Fawole, and C. Ukeje (eds), *The Crisis of the State and Regionalism in West Africa: Citizenship, Identity and Conflict in West Africa*. Dakar, Senegal: CODESRIA.

Sesay, A., and S. Akínrìnádé (1998) *The Impact of the Structural Adjustment Programme on the Structure of Nigeria's International Economic Relations*. Ibadan, Nigeria: NISER/SSCN National Research Network on Liberalization Policies in Nigeria.

Sesay, A. and A. Simbine (eds) (2006) *Small Arms Proliferation and Collection in Nigeria's Niger Delta*. Ibadan, Nigeria: College Press.

Sesay, A., C. Ukeje, O. Aina and A. Odebiyi (eds) (2003) *Ethnic Militias and the Future of Democracy in Nigeria*. Ile-Ife, Nigeria: University Press.

UNAIDS (2004) *World AIDS Reports*. Washington, DC: UNAIDS.

UNCTAD (2005) *The Handbook of Statistics*. Geneva: UNCTAD.

United Nations Development Programme (UNDP) (2003) *Human Development Report*. New York: UNDP.

United Nations Development Programme (UNDP) (2005) *Human Development Report*. New York: UNDP.

World Bank (1996) *Global Finance*. Washington, DC: The World Bank.

World Bank (1998) *World Development Report 1998/99*. Washington, DC: World Bank.

World Bank (2002) *World Development Report*. Washington, DC: The World Bank.

World Bank (2005a) *World Development Report: Equity and Development*. Washington, DC: The World Bank.

World Bank (2005b) *World Development Indicators*. Washington, DC: The World Bank.

World Bank (2006) *World Development Indicators*. Washington, DC: The World Bank.

World Health Organization (WHO) (2004) *World Health Report 2004 – Changing History*. Geneva: WHO.

9
The Contradictions between Globalization and Development? A Perspective from Southern Africa

Lisa Thompson

> The first public protest against NEPAD occurred at the July 2002 World Economic Forum regional meeting in Durban, where anti-apartheid poet Dennis Brutus, acting secretary of Jubilee South Africa, led more than a hundred demonstrators into horse-charging policemen. Brutus held up a sign for national television viewers: No Kneepad! . . . [The NEPAD document's] core premise is that poverty in Africa can be cured, if only the world's elite gives the continent a chance: 'The continued marginalization of Africa from the globalization process and the social exclusion of the vast majority of its peoples constitute a serious threat to global stability.'
>
> (Bond, 2002a: 369)

In this chapter Southern Africa is used mainly to refer to the members of the Southern Africa Development Community (SADC), the regional organization that was founded in 1980 and reformed in 1992. Member states include Angola, Botswana, the Democratic Republic of Congo (DRC), Lesotho, Madagascar, Malawi, Mauritius, Mozambique, Namibia, South Africa, Swaziland, Tanzania, Zambia and Zimbabwe. Apart from geographical proximity, many of the 14 members share common colonial experiences and similar societal and political features. While there are some important factors of differentiation (such as recent experiences of warfare and distinctive paths of political transition in countries such as the DRC, Mozambique and South Africa) membership of the organization in some regards provides cohesiveness to economic and other policy objectives, an aspect that is particularly significant in a discussion of the contours and effects of globalization in the region.

What does globalization mean in the Southern African context? The quote above from Patrick Bond's book *Unsustainable South Africa* highlights that negative views of globalization have been absorbed into government policy-speak in Southern Africa, as the quote from the original New Partnership for Africa's Development (NEPAD) proposal quoted by Bond emphasizes. However, Bond goes on to put the perspective of many left-wing critics by stating that 'Africa's continued poverty and degradation ("marginalization") *are a direct outcome of globalization*, not of a lack of globalization' (Bond, 2002a: 369 emphasis added). Marginalization and chronic poverty, which manifests itself not only as lack of income but also in terms of access to basic services such as water and sanitation, is the lot of many if not most Southern Africans and Africans. Globalization has often been blamed for these problems, both in terms of its marginalization effects and as the way in which it widens the gap between rich and poor, both within states (especially in Africa) and globally.

But is this because of globalization? Or is this explanation for poverty and lack of development not just a coincidental meeting of the minds between inefficient and/or corrupt government elites and disgruntled left-wing academics? And are they speaking about the same thing when they refer to globalization? Melber (2004: 5) indicates that 'globalization' is often taken to mean the current period of capitalist economic expansion that takes a particular form under the so-called neoliberal 'Washington Consensus'. Within this understanding (which forms perhaps the underlying impetus as well as the source of tension within NEPAD) there is an elitist pragmatism which Melber (ibid.) refers to as 'better this capitalism than no capitalism at all'.

Scholte (2005a; 2005b) points out that much of what is referred to as globalization in popular academic and media discourse is in fact old wine in new bottles, and clearly this is the case in South and Southern Africa. As Scholte (2005a: 54–9) puts it:

> In sum much talk of globalization has been analytically redundant . . . Four main definitions have led into this cul-de-sac: globalization as internationalization; globalization as liberalisation; globalization as universalization; and globalization as westernization . . . Deployed on any of these four lines, 'globalization' provides no distinct value added . . . Critics of 'globaloney' are right to assail the historical illiteracy that marks most claims of novelty associated with these conceptions of globalization . . . Of course, this is not to suggest that debates about international interdependence, neoliberalism, universalism-versus-cultural diversity, modernity, and imperialism are unimportant. Indeed,

> a well fashioned concept of globalization could shed significant light on these issues. However it is not helpful to . . . treat (globalization) as equivalent to – internationalization, liberalization, universalization or westernization. Not only do we thereby merely rehash old knowledge, but we also lose a major opportunity to grasp – and act upon – certain key circumstances of our times.

It is worth quoting Scholte at some length because it helps to clarify in which ways globalization does – and does not – shed light on current historical processes globally, and how such processes shape political and socio-economic dynamics in different parts of the world. If globalization is not equivalent to international interdependence, for example, as is currently described in the popular media, then what does it mean? And what does it mean to us in Southern Africa, where the region's economies have long been structurally dependent on international markets? Do colonialism and neocolonial patterns of trade have any bearing on what we understand as a dynamic, an effect or an outcome of globalization? The pronouncements of the South African government and, from another angle, critics like Bond (2002a; 2002b) and the South African anti-globalization movement would both say yes.

Yet the critical aspect of economic globalization is what Scholte has initially termed deterritorialization and later changed to supraterritoriality (Scholte, 2005a: 85; 2005b: 77). Supraterritorial refers to the degree to which economic and other activities take place on a global scale that *transcend the territoriality* of the international state system. Examples of this would be e-communications and cyberspace in general; global travel; global factories and global commodity chains; the spread of global products and product names like Nike, Coca-Cola and Toyota.[1] Other 'transworld' activities and/or evidence of supraterritorialism or globality, as Scholte (2005a: 67) calls them, include global finance, global businesses, global civil society organizations, global military activities, global ecological and health concerns, global laws and globalized social relations.

Important to the understanding of supraterritoriality and transworld practices is their *decentredness*. Indeed Scholte argues that understanding globalization requires a shift in methodology away from our tendency to treat the global arena as composed of distinct territorial spaces of activity (what he calls methodological territorialism). Globalization, then, refers to activities which call upon us to think about the global arena differently, and to understand globalization in terms of a new language which reflects the simultaneous contraction of time and space with regard to 'transworld' and 'transborder' connections (Scholte, 2005a: 86–7).

Scholte (2005b: 77) also urges us to remember that our current social space 'is both territorial and supraterritorial'. In other words, he is not arguing that state activity or their geographical significance has no relevance, but he focuses attention on the need to examine what is truly global about how we understand globalization in general and in terms of how it affects lives at different levels in different corners of the globe. As our discussion here emphasizes, while the dynamics of what is new about globalization might refer to supranationality, the fundamental *developmental* impact of globalization is very definitely territorial, if Southern Africa is anything to go by. As figures on development (or the lack of it) clearly underline, globalization has had an impact on different geographical areas in different ways and global structural inequalities have been aggravated by globalization (Leysens and Thompson, 2006). Recent statistics show that even states in the region with 'medium human development' ranking in terms of UNDP indicators have high levels of poverty. South Africa, the wealthiest state in SADC, has a Human Poverty Index (HPI) of 30.9 per cent, and Madagascar (a Low Human Development state and one of the poorest in SADC) has an HPI of 35.3 per cent. Mauritius is in fact the only state in the SADC grouping with an HPI below the percentage value of 30. Life expectancy is another indicator that shows the region's poverty dilemma. The probability of not surviving to age 40 is between 43.3 per cent (South Africa) and a staggering 74.3 per cent (Swaziland). Only Mauritius (5 per cent) and Lesotho (27.8 per cent) have slightly better statistics (UNDP, 2005). While HIV/AIDs plays a role in the latter statistics, poverty exacerbates the situation.

Sklair (2002: 8) identifies the 'unique' aspect of globalization (i.e. that which is different from the internationalization of global capital) as what he terms transnational practices (TNPs). The transnational corporation (TNC) 'is the major locus of transnational practices . . . transnational corporations are the most important and most powerful globalising institutions in the world today and by virtue of this they make the capitalist global system the dominant global system'. Thus TNCs, through transnational practices, make the role of the state less important and bring to the fore issues about global labour organizations and social movements as well as impacts of global economic institutions like the WTO on global economic and social relations, as well as their civil-society critics such as the anti-globalization movement. To Sklair (2002: 9) consumerism is very definitely part of globalization as it forms a fundamental part of TNPs. Transnational practices and consumerism – as dynamics of globalization – affect the Southern African region very differently. Those countries which are the most marginalized – states like Malawi and Tanzania for example – display very few signs of either: both with a GDP of $580 and Human Development Index Scores of 0.388 and 0.407 respectively, they fall off the map in terms of marginalization (UNDP, 2004, quoted in McGowan, 2006: 310). Is this a cause or an effect of globalization?

The caveat that globalization is both supraterritorial as well as territorial is critical, in my view, to retaining a sense of the way in which globalization processes do not necessarily have a homogeneous 'globalized impact'. If we examine globalization in the context of the development debate trajectory, it is clear that globalization has different impacts on societies and communities. Some may be affected by the sphere of 'time-space' shrinkage only partially or in nominal ways in terms of direct impact. After all, in Southern Africa there are many people who have never seen a computer, much less sent an email or used the Web. In 2005, Lesotho had only 147 host computers (linked to the Internet or Web), Malawi had 288 and Tanzania 9,444. This compared with South Africa which had 451,500 (CIA, 2005 and Internet Consortium online, quoted in McGowan, 2006: 314).

Cox (1987; 1997) has discussed at some length how certain economic groups are peripheralized through the globalization of production, trade and financial networks and processes. These marginalized groups occur all over the world but are more prevalent in the South. As the discussion below indicates, Southern Africa shows marked characteristics of bifurcated societal relations where organized business and labour form part of globalization dynamics, and marginalized semi-formal labour and semi-subsistence agriculturalists, who do not. Leysens (2005) applies Cox's framework to Southern Africa, using Afrobarometer data, demonstrating the ways in which poor communities in the region are marginalized from mainstream political and economic practices.

The variable impact of globalization in Southern Africa

A good illustration of the varied impact of globalization on the region is the changing nature of norms, values and decision-making procedures – what Keohane and Nye (1987) would call the 'regime' nature – within the regional organization, SADC. SADC can be examined both in terms of its regional institutional dynamics and in terms of the changing nature of the norms, values and decision-making procedures which characterize the nature of the organization. These norms and values form part of the knowledge frame which holds the organization together. This, according to Keohane and Nye (1987) and others, is the 'glue' that holds international and regional regimes together.

How have the norms and values entrenched in the organization changed since 1992 to reflect the economic, political, cultural and social aspects of globalization? SADCC/SADC has gone from being a loose arrangement of states seeking economic independence from South Africa, though still committed in many cases to various forms of rather dubious 'socialist' economic practices when it was called the Southern African Development Coordination Conference (SADCC) (1980–92), to its current configuration (as the Southern Africa Development Community SADC) as a grouping of rather avid proponents of capitalism seeking foreign assistance to achieve as rapid an absorption into the global capitalist system as possible (Tapscott and Thompson, 2000).

The current revamping of the economic aspect of SADC is called the Regional Indicative Strategic Development Plan (RISDP) which draws attention to the need for regional integration European Union (EU) style, including goals to have a common currency in the next ten years as well as general macroeconomic convergence (Le Pere and Tjonneland, 2005: 27). These policies are being pursued with a simultaneous opening up to international (especially EU) markets as the recent SA–EU trade deal illustrates; discussions with the US on the possibility of a free trade area have also taken place (Schoeman, 2005). The RISDP is ostensibly also aligned with other continental and international initiatives such as the NEPAD and the Millennium Development Goals (MDGs). Given the level of economic development in the region, the advisability of these regional and global economic strategies remains a moot point, and one that is strongly criticized by the anti-globalization movement in Southern Africa (Bond, 2002a; 2002b). It is clear though that the governments of the region, and South Africa in particular, have shifted their policies in response to what they understand as economic globalization, even if they are critical in their pronouncements about its effects. Bond refers to this phenomenon of government behaviour as that of 'talk left, act right' and points out that anti-globalization pronouncements by the South African government usually follow from social movement activism which shows the government's inability to address the plight of the poor (Bond, 2002a: 361–2).

While regional integration in itself does not necessarily indicate globalization, as it prioritizes regional rather than global interconnections (Scholte, 2005a; Keohane and Nye, 2005), SADC nevertheless shows the impact of globalization in four rather different and multidimensional ways. These connect issues of growing regional and international interdependence to the spread of globalization. They are manifestations within the organization of four facets of globalism, as outlined by Keohane and

Nye (2005: 76–7). They are: 'long distance flows of goods, services and capital, as well as the information and perceptions that accompany market exchange'. SADC's real (as opposed to policy speak) form of integration into the global political economy occurs increasingly in terms of regional market dependencies on the world trade system – not just individual states, but the global networks of production, finance and trade. The changing knowledge frame of the organization itself, and its commitment to globalized production and marketing strategies, illustrate the reach of globalized knowledge structures. Keohane and Nye's four facets of globalism are as follows.

Military globalism, according to Keohane and Nye (2005: 76), refers to 'long distance networks of interdependence in which force, and the threat or promise of force' are employed. SADC's 'two headed' institutional nature in the 1990s, is, as Schoeman (2005: 13) perceptively puts it, a result of the fact that SADC has moved from a 'historical-symbolic shared history and a shared security configuration' which is now being replaced by 'economic considerations'. While Ngoma (2005) has deliberated at length about the potential of the region to become a regional security community, it is more likely that SADC's security concerns reflect globalized security concerns, such as retaining regional peace and stability to ensure the flourishing of a combination of regional and transnational economic practices. Strong evidence of this are the regional moves afoot to establish free trade areas with other stronger economic blocs such as the EU and the United States (Schoeman, 2005: 20). The US has also for many years placed pressure on South Africa to play a more prominent peacekeeping role in the region with a clear agenda of keeping the region stable to ensure 'economic stability' (read integration into global markets).

Environmental globalism, according to Keohane and Nye (2005: 76), refers to 'the long distance transport of materials in the atmosphere or oceans, or of biological substances such as pathogens or genetic materials that affect human health and well-being'. There is another aspect to this which Keohane and Nye do not mention, namely global protocols on the environment such as the Kyoto protocol, which attempt to regulate developmental practices in the South, as well as to curb ongoing global environmental degradation (such as the hole in the ozone layer). SADC has a number of environmental treaties regarding various aspects of environmental protection, but is also on the receiving end of toxic-waste dumping (Bond, 2002a).

The third and fourth facets, *social and cultural globalism*, involve according to Keohane and Nye (2005: 77), 'the movement of ideas, information, images and people (who of course carry knowledge and information with them)'. It is in terms of these two facets of globalization that SADC illustrates the ways in which the region has become more fully a part of globalization practices, at least at the state level. While Scholte (2005a; 2005b) cautions us about equating economic neoliberalism with global-ization, we cannot ignore the very obvious fact that currently Foreign Direct Investment (FDI) and transnational practices are integrally part of the spread of international capitalism and the ideology and culture of economic neoliberalism. This of course does not mean that all societies and communities in the region are affected by the social and cultural aspects of globalization in the same way. In this sense the region is char-acterized by what Held (2004), Keohane and Nye (2005) and others call 'thin' globalization.

Thin or thick globalization refers to the relative density of the economic, political, social and cultural networks, processes and dynamics that characterize globalized patterns of behaviour. Because the spread of these networks and dynamics are very uneven in Southern Africa, the form of globalization we have here is a thin one (although this does vary from state to state in the region, with South Africa having notably thicker globalization networks at all levels). State-level interactions, as well as the networks and dynamics that characterize formal economic practices in the region, display many of the characteristics of globalization discussed above. The more social and cultural aspects of community integration are harder to estimate, but are discussed in more detail in the following section of this chapter.

In short, there is no doubt that the underlying ethos of SADC as an organization has changed radically in response to the economic impera-tive of economic globalization. SADC illustrates the power of globally located businesses by drawing attention to the ways in which emergent industries and businesses in the South find it harder and harder to compete with the 'lean and mean' economic imperatives of transnational eco-nomic practices. Another salient feature of SADC is that its current eco-nomic *modus vivendi* is funded by the EU to the tune of supplying 86 per cent of all SADC funding (Schoeman, 2005: 17). This funding does not come without strings attached. The spread of international capital and transnational practices occurs in a number of different ways, and 'spheres of economic influence' are still seen as important by the big (state and regional) actors in the global political system. It is clear at this level, that as Held (2004) and others warn, we should not be tempted to equate eco-nomic globalization with a decline in importance of states or state alliances in the global system – not least the ways in which powerful states and blocs push their economic agendas through by supplying economic assistance.

Yet many people in the region have never heard of SADC, and many communities remain peripherally involved in the type of 'supranational' activities that Scholte describes. To make sense of what globalization means to societies in the Southern African context requires thinking about state and societal layers of regional realities simultaneously. If we focus at the state level on recent changes to national and regional development strategies and relate that to the literature on globalization, there are a number of significant policy changes which have occurred in the last two decades which would seem to give us sufficient proof that economic globalization is having an impact regionally through shifting strategies of regional integration, particularly in terms of the spread of ideas and ideology as well as in terms of communication and 'development expertise' (as illustrated through EU support of SADC at this level). This is embodied in the shift in SADC from an economically non-committal sector integration strategy to embracing the principles of economic neoliberalism through its aspiration to become a regional economic bloc based on the EU model.

The entrenchment of neoliberalism regionally and continentally is taken one step further by the establishment of NEPAD and its commitment to the principles of international capitalism, in particular the replacement of former notions of continental economic interdependence with ideas of global integration. At this level we are taking into account state and inter-state policies which reflect not only the interests of international capital and the transnational capitalist class but also the interests of state leaders themselves whose future political careers are shaped by the ways in which the international economic system as a whole (particularly trade, finance and production) reacts to national and regional political and economic strategies. Taylor and Nel (2002: 166) state that the driving force behind NEPAD is 'the linkage between globalization, export driven trade policies and a nascent transnational elite', and that NEPAD only helps to legitimize the negative aspects of globalization by recognizing that Southern Africa and Africa must perforce be integrated rather than face the alternative of further marginalization (see also Melber, 2004: 6). As Sklair (2002: 6) puts it: 'governments will go along with globalization not because they cannot resist it but because they perceive it to be in their own interests'.

If we move on to other levels, particularly the societal and cultural, at which coming to terms with globalization in Southern Africa has different impacts and meanings, these are no less demonstrative of the effect that globalization can have, in as much as it has changed the way the world functions, as well as what has been 'left out' of the time-space shrinkage that is supposed to characterize true 'global dynamics'. This should perhaps caution us from too rigid definitions of what globalization means – or does not – in different geographical contexts: because we need to think about how Southern Africa is connected to the global system, both regionally and nationally *and societally*. There is an actual level of economic activity regionally which excludes the public sector.

Statistics released by SADC show that economic integration occurs primarily with richer states in the North. Le Pere and Tjonneland (2005: 29–30) show that approximately 22 per cent of SADC trade is intra-regional, and most of SADC trade is with the EU, the US, Japan and China. There is also major regional inconsistency with regard to the reduction of trade tariff barriers, which make the process of regional integration very uneven (ibid.: 30). This is old news, as this development trajectory dogged the old SADCC and is unlikely to go away easily given current levels of economic development as well as regional infrastructural limitations. Yet more importantly, the national economies of SADC remain unevenly integrated into the global system. Indeed there are states like Malawi, Lesotho and Swaziland, for example, who show little sign of being integrated into global transnational economic practices. In this sense thinking about territory is still important to the extent that some economic, political and social practices are still very much informed by geographical locality.

A related point is that Foreign Direct Investment has been largely unforthcoming in the region, showing that in spite of governmental policy commitment to providing a fertile national and regional landing ground for FDI, international capital and transnational corporations do not necessarily spread their activities and ventures evenly in the global system (ibid.). In this context a lot has been said about the marginalization of Africa in the global political economy. Held (2004: 45) points out that the gap between rich and poor globally is shrinking in some regions (Asia for example) and growing in others (sub-Saharan Africa). The gap between rich and poor globally, regionally and nationally is an often cited argument against economic globalization, claiming that the spread of TNPs amongst other aspects of globalization is inherently exploitative, as these practices tend to follow cheaper and less organized labour.

A more important inconsistency from the point of view of measuring the impact of globalization is the degree to which the broader majority of societies in the region are drawn into more formally recognized economic activities, and/or begin to show signs of being drawn in ideologically and culturally into different (consumerist) patterns of consumption and expenditure. These impacts are hard to generalize, but we can perhaps draw attention to the differential impact of globalization by looking systematically at some of the framing questions regarding the impact of globalization on the region as highlighted in this book as a whole. It is to these that we now turn.

To what extent is the current phase of globalization new?

Almost all critical analysts of globalization agree that much of what is commonly understood by the term globalization is not new. We have discussed above the ostensibly 'outstanding' features, which include the notion of the spread of networks and dynamics characterized by time-space shrinkage (cyberspace, global telecommunications, international travel) and transnational economic practices. How does this affect the region? If we look at SADC as an example of the regional impact of globalized production, trade and market strategies, there is evidence at the level of policy of the impact of economic globalization as discussed above.

There is another dimension to the organization, however, where what Schoeman (2005) refers to as the two-headed nature of SADC surfaces, through its twin commitments to deepening market penetration and integration in the region and regional political and military stability. Added to this is SADC's organizational schizophrenia which involves a strong commitment (in policy pronouncements at least) to regional integration with commitments to establishing a common currency and to free trade and the freer movement of people in the region; but at the same time, a distinct lack of regional economic integration and lack of coordinated economic policies aimed in this direction. As Schoeman (2005: 20) points out, while intra-regional trade in SADC has increased from 5 per cent in 1985 to 25 per cent, in 2005 this is because South African business has moved aggressively into the region and accounts for an increase of intra-regional bilateral trade of 248 per cent. The economic interdependencies of SADC states remain much the same as they always have, with the exception of the fact that South Africa provides even more of a hegemonic role as the long-standing bastion of Western economic and political ideals in the region. What is depressingly the same, despite the ideological inroads of globalization, is the grinding poverty in the region, particularly in rural areas, and as discussed earlier even states with better HDI rankings tended to have high HPI indicators. This is a very strong illustration of the degree to which globalization has made the world smaller for some, and larger, even more inexplicable and impenetrable for others, as poverty levels continue to escalate despite positive trends in economic growth and development indicators.

What are the main (political, economic and social) forces driving globalization? Who are the main actors?

It should be clear from the preceding discussion that the driving actors of globalization in the region are states and big business. Interestingly,

SADC as a regional economic integration organization has played a significant role in grounding the more intangible knowledge dimensions of globalization, such as commitments to transnational practices of multinational companies and foreign direct investment. In its previous incarnation, in the form of the SADCC (and even the early SADC) there was a distinct lack of enthusiasm for these forms of economic 'opening up' on the part of states in the region (Thompson, 1996). Even while these TNPs have not established themselves evenly in the region, the commitment encouraging FDI through TNPs, as well as a growing tendency to allow this with minimal state regulation, shows a commitment to the principles of economic globalization. Bond (2002a) also discusses the role of the World Bank and IMF in particular in entrenching some of the more negative aspects of globalization in the region. The emphasis on cost recovery for basic services is one very obvious example of how neoliberal thinking can erode principles of environmental and social justice for the poor.

Van der Westhuizen (2006: 197–8) also highlights how the effects of globalization on developing states leads to 'shadow' economies characterized by both licit and illicit forms of trade. The reason for this is as follows:

> as globalization reduces the autonomy of the state to determine national development policy, and expands the market, the regulative capacity of (an already weak) state declines as the size and scope of the shadow economy increases . . . In those cases where state weakness has already become highly pronounced – the Democratic Republic of the Congo, Sierra Leone, Somalia – rival social actors emerge, challenging not only the states' monopoly of violence but also even its exclusive licence to tax. In these social spaces unsavoury social forces position themselves: mafias, strongmen and viligante movements (like Mapogo a Mathamaga in South Africa's northern Province).

Thus while they might not be driving globalization, these social actors have a parasitic relationship with the set of global and governmental actors and dynamics described above which occur as a result of globalization's unequal structural impact on developing economies.

What are or should be the main responses to globalization?

The discussion to this point has tended to refer to civil society somewhat indirectly and has focused on states' responses to globalization in the region. At the societal level, in general, manifestations of local citizen action that have global reach have not been especially significant if we take the region as a whole. South Africa's civil society organizations have tended to have more success in establishing the kinds of local – global linkages and connections which are referred to in the literature on the social and cultural aspects of globalization, while the rest of the region has lagged behind.

The anti-globalization lobby in South Africa, the HIV/AIDS Treatment Action campaign, as well as the environmental movement are examples of this (see Bond, 2002a; Robins, 2005; Thompson, 2005). For the most part, societies in the region remain poorly integrated into participatory democratic practices as it is, let alone into global networks on governance issues (Van der Westhuizen, 2006). 'Uncivil' society refers to the bulk of the population in Southern Africa who remain unintegrated or marginally integrated into formal economic and political practices and networks. These groups remain largely untouched by the processes that are supposed to characterize globalization. There is another category of uncivil society becoming prevalent in South Africa, which consists of a large number of urban migrants with aspirations to the kind of consumerist lifestyles they observe around them, but without the income or chronic poverty relief they need to do anything about these aspirations, nor the political will to lobby sufficiently hard to get local government representatives to take up their cause for things like better basic services and housing. Many of these communities live in relative, rather than absolute, deprivation, and are affected by economic globalization in terms of the reality of its limited reach, rather than the (neoliberal) imagery of its all encompassing embrace. This is yet another aspect of economic as well as cultural globalization.

So is globalization a bad thing? Like any either/or question, it invites pronouncements on globalization and its alternatives. Held (2004: 48) asks the crucial question 'How might global market integration hinder or retard the development of the world's poorest countries?'. He goes on to discuss the merits of Garrett's view that 'global economic integration alone cannot be adequate medicine for low income countries to escape a development trap. While it would be wrong to argue in favour of widespread protectionism, sequencing openness in a set of reforms, and only advocating openness once substantial progress has been made in relation to the development of human capital, physical infrastructure and independent political institutions is a sensible way to proceed' (see also Castells, 2005). While, as we discussed earlier, the further internationalization of capitalism is not coterminous with globalization, Held (2004) refers to the dominant global *ideology* of globalization which has at its heart a specific set of ideas and practices most tellingly embodied in the neoliberal (Washington) consensus of how development should proceed. It is this ideology which has clearly taken root in SADC's approach to regional development, if not in all the states which belong to it, even while more insidious forms of globalization are manifesting themselves simultaneously, such as Van der Westhuizen's (2006) markets and mafias referred to earlier.

However, the troublesome aspects of globalization, as Held (2004: 90–1) states, indicates that it fundamentally represents the interests of 'leading states and vested interests'. He goes on to say that 'despite vociferous dissent of many protest groups in recent years, the promotion of the global market has taken clear priority over many pressing environmental and social issues', and he also mentions that developed states ensure which rules of the game are enforced and where. Agricultural protectionism continues at the same time as developing states are urged to operate on global free market principles. This accords with the analysis of Bond (2002a) on South Africa's unsustainable development, and how globalization has affected Southern Africa negatively, especially in terms of what have become known as 'brown' (as opposed to green) environmental issues – that is the appalling urban (and semi-urban) environments in which many poor South (and Southern) Africans find themselves in an effort to earn more income.

There is no doubt then that globalization has had a negative effect on Southern Africa insofar as it has widened the gaps between the 'haves' and the 'have-nots', and overall has aggravated rather than alleviated the poverty concerns of the region. Governments have learned to toe the line or face the consequences. Therein lies the root of 'talking left, acting right'. This phenomenon is the consequence of the reduced autonomy that globalization brings on governments – especially those with limited resources such as those in Southern Africa. The fact that globalization does not serve the interests of the poor is negated by the fact that it does serve the interests of the rich – and the powerful – in the region: business and governments. The prioritization of free markets and economic liberalism also have their negative spinoffs for service delivery and urban poverty relief in general as Bond (2002a) makes very clear through analysis of the poor housing, water and sanitation delivery and the influence of neoliberal economic thinking on water pricing and basic services for the poor.

Held (2004: 90–1) also discusses 'the troubling fact that while nearly 3,000 people died on 9/11, almost 30,000 children under the age of five die each day in the developing world of preventable diseases, diseases which have been practically eradicated in the west', and the 'moral gap' defined by

> a world in which, as indicated earlier, over 1.2 billion people live on less than a dollar a day, 46 per cent of the world's population live on less

than 2 dollars a day, and 20 per cent of the world's population earn eighty per cent of its income.

As already mentioned, these disparities manifest themselves in Southern Africa as well. Most sub Saharan Africa countries (with the exception of South Africa fall into the 'low income' category, and according to World Bank statistics the region receives considerably more aid flows than it does Foreign Direct Investment (World Bank, 2006).

Southern Africa and Africa have taken up some of these challenges through organizations such as the African Union at international fora including World Trade Organization meetings and in terms of lobbying the G8 for debt relief (the Gleneagles conference is a good example of this limited lobbying power). The extent to which government concerns reflect those of social movements is very limited, as the latter are usually very critical of many aspects of government policy as well as how issues of major concern are taken up and resolved at the global level. Regionally the extent to which civil society is able to make inroads at the level of global governance structures remains at present somewhat limited. As Bond (2002a: 362) puts it with reference to the environmental movement and activism on brown environmental issues in South Africa, 'only in exceptional cases do the social and environmental justice movements reach a sufficiently high level of irritation and relevance to worry the ANC'. While regional social movements remain relatively weaker than in South Africa, this does not mean that the status quo cannot change over time. South Africa is already showing signs of an increasing groundswell of social movement activity, even among those understood as being more marginalized, and it is only a matter of time before this begins to manifest more regionally. Ironically, it appears the more globalization processes and networks become thicker, the more sustained the level of civil society participation and resistance becomes. In the long run, this will definitely be a positive, if not *the* positive consequence of globalization in the South.

Note

1 All of these supraterritorial practices are facilitated by what Scholte (2005a: 69) terms global money: 'that is some units of account, some means of payment, stores of value and mediums of account that have transplanetary circulation. For example the US dollar, the "Japanese" yen, the "British" pound and other major denominations are much more than national currencies. As supraterritorial monies, they are used anywhere on earth at the same time and move (electronically and via air transport) anywhere on earth effectively in no time.'

References

Bond, P. (2002a) *Unsustainable South Africa*. London: Merlin Press.

Bond, P. (2002b) *Fanon's Warning: A Civil Society Reader on the New Partnership for Africa's Development*. Trenton, NJ: Africa World Press.

Castells, M. (2005) 'The Rise of the Fourth World', in D. Held and A. McGrew (eds), *The Global Transformations Reader* (2nd edn). Cambridge: Polity Press.

Cox, R. (1987) *Production, Power and World Order: Social Forces and the Making of History*. New York: Columbia University Press.

Cox, R. (ed.) (1997) *The New Realism: Perspectives on Multilateralism and World Order*. Tokyo: United Nations University Press.

Held, D. (2004) *Global Covenant: The Social Democratic Alternative to the Washington Consensus*. Cambridge: Polity Press.

Keohane, R.O. and J.S. Nye Jr (1987) 'Power and Interdependence Revisited', *International Organization*, 41, 4: 725–53.

Keohane, R. and J. Nye (2005) 'Globalization: What's New? What's Not? (And So What?)', in D. Held and A. McGrew (eds), *The Global Transformations Reader* (2nd edn). Cambridge: Polity Press.

Le Pere, G. and E. Tjonneland (2005) 'Which Way SADC? Advancing Co-operation and Integration in Southern Africa', Occasional Paper, 50. Midrand, South Africa: Institute for Global Dialogue.

Leysens, A. (2005) 'Social Forces in Southern Africa: Transformation from Below?', *Journal of Modern African Studies*, 44, 1: 31–58.

Leysens, A. and L. Thompson (2006) 'The Evolution of the Global Political Economy', in P. McGowan, S. Cornelissen and P. Nel (eds), *Power, Wealth and Global Equity: An International Relations Textbook for Africa*. Cape Town: UCT Press.

McGowan, P. (2006) 'The Southern African Regional Sub-system', in P. McGowan, S. Cornelissen and P. Nel (eds), *Power, Wealth and Global Equity: An International Relations Textbook for Africa*. Cape Town: UCT Press.

Melber, H. (2004) *South Africa and NePAD – Quo Vadis?* Hatfield, South Africa: Southern African Regional Poverty Network (SARPN), available at http://sarpn.org.za.

Ngoma, N. (2005) *Prospects for a Regional Security Community in Southern Africa: An Analysis of Regional Security in the Southern African Development Community (SADC)*. Pretoria, South Africa: Institute for Security Studies.

Robins, S. (2005) 'Aids, Science and Citizenship after Apartheid', in M. Leach, I. Scoones and B. Wynne (eds), *Science and Citizens: Globalisation and the Challenge of Engagement*. London: Zed Books.

Schoeman, M. (2005) 'SADC at 25: An Overview of Selected Issues', *Strategic Review for Southern Africa*, 27(2): 12–27.

Scholte, J. (2005a) *Globalization: A Critical Introduction* (2nd edn). Basingstoke, UK: Palgrave Macmillan.

Scholte, J. (2005b) 'What is Global about Globalization?', in D. Held and A. McGrew (eds), *The Global Transformations Reader* (2nd edn). Cambridge: Polity Press.

Sklair, L. (2002) *Globalization, Capitalism and its Alternatives*. New York: Oxford University Press.

Tapscott, C. and L. Thompson (2000) 'Thinking Beyond the Discourse: Towards Alternative Approaches to Development in Southern Africa', in *Development, Democracy and Aid*, CSAS Monograph Series, No. 1. Cape Town, South Africa: School of Government Publication.

Taylor, I. and P. Nel (2002) 'New Africa, Globalization and the Confines of Elite Reformism: Getting the Rhetoric Right, Getting the Strategy Wrong', *Third World Quarterly*, 23(1): 163–80.

Thompson, L. (1996) 'States and Security: Emancipatory versus Orthodox Approaches in Governance in Southern Africa', occasional paper series no 3 University of the Western Cape: School of Government.

Thompson, L. (2005) 'Managing Mobilisation? Participatory Processes and Dam Building in South Africa – the Berg River Project', working paper 254. IDS, University of Sussex.

United Nations Development Programme (UNDP) (2005) *Human Development Report*, accessed at www.sarpn.org.za.

Van der Westhuizen, J. (2006) 'Globalization and the South: Markets, Mafias and Movements', in P. McGowan, S. Cornelissen and P. Nel (eds), *Power, Wealth and Global Equity: An International Relations Textbook for Africa*. Cape Town: UCT Press.

World Bank (2006) *Development Indicators*, accessed at http://devdata.worldbank.org/wdi2006.

10
Super-Imperialism: A Perspective from East Africa

Mary Njeri Kinyanjui and Felix Kiruthu

The East African region is comprised of three countries, namely Kenya, Uganda and Tanzania. Geographically, the three countries share common borders and are also connected by Lake Victoria, the largest freshwater lake on the continent. The countries also share a common history as former colonies or protectorates of the British government, gaining independence at almost the same time in the 1960s. Today they constitute the East African Community (EAC, 2000). They are also united by the use of the English language and the spread of Christianity as well as Islam. Their experience of globalization has been somewhat similar. They shared the influence of Arabs and Asians prior to the colonial era (Patel, 1997), are former British colonies and have been subjected to the IMF and World Bank Structural Adjustment Programmes (SAPs) of the 1980s and 1990s. The SAPs involved the marketization and liberalization of their economies and democratization of their governments. The three East African countries have also had similar experiences of democratization through multipartyism.

Figure 10.1 provides a graphical presentation of the processes of globalization in the East African region. Three phases of globalization can be discerned. They are (i) the period of the Arab and Asian occupation when the region was linked to the rest of the world economically by the dhow traders; (ii) the colonization by the British government; and (iii) the period of Structural Adjustment Programmes controlled by the World Bank and the IMF, currently the prime movers of global capitalism in East Africa. The WTO and multinational corporations are also significant institutions that contribute to the configuration of globalization in this third phase. This phase is here referred to as the era of super-imperialism.

This chapter argues that 'globalization' has long historical roots in the East Africa region and that three successive periods of domination by

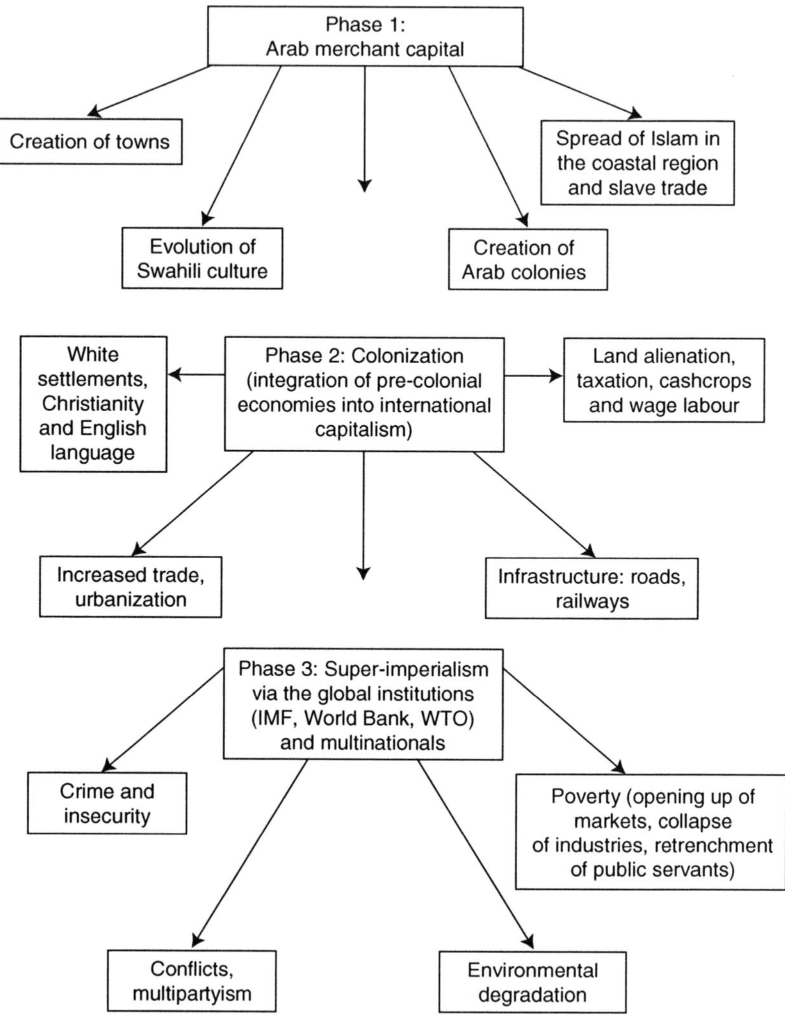

Figure 10.1 Phases of globalization in the East African region

outside powers can be discerned. The 1960s were a short interregnum in which political independence led to attempts to foster 'national development' in the region but this proved to be short lived following the intensification of the cold war between the Eastern and the Western bloc and the economic crises of the 1970s. What distinguishes the current phase of globalization, which we term super-imperialism, is that resources are drawn from the region by traders and multinational corporations (MNCs) without any social and moral responsibilities towards the welfare of workers in the factories, the small-scale agricultural producers or the community as a whole.

The Arab and Asian phase of globalization

The process of globalization began early in history. The first documented interactions between the East African region and the outside world were with Arabs, Asians and the Greeks. The region's interaction with these groups of people is reflected in the establishment of colonies on the East African coast and islands such as Zanzibar, Pemba and Lamu (Sheriff, 2002). Slaves and ivory were the main trade commodities between the interior of East Africa and the Arab world. The evolution of the Swahili culture and language, the spread of Islam, Arab architecture in the old towns of Mombasa and Dar-es-Salam are the remnants of the Arab experience with the East African region.

The colonization phase of globalization

The Arab experience was followed by the period of European explorations in the 15th century. During this period, European commercial expeditions moved into Africa, India and China in search of ivory, spices, silk and slaves. Slaves were taken to the Americas where they were involved in the production of cotton, minerals and sugar. The Industrial Revolution in Europe during the 19th century led to the reconfiguration of globalization based on the need for cheap labour and new markets for manufactured goods (Pillay, 1998). The European middle classes had developed the taste for beverages such as cocoa, tea and coffee that could be acquired in the tropics. They also required vegetable oils, such as palm oil, and industrial products, such as rubber from the tropics (Ake, 1981). These needs led to the scramble for Africa and the intensification of colonialism in the closing decades of the 19th century when East Africa was integrated into global capitalism. During colonialism countries in Africa in general and East Africa in particular became the sources of raw materials and markets for manufactured products. Since the colonial era, globalization has facilitated the accumulation of a disproportionate amount of wealth by the imperial powers at the expense of the East Africans (Stichter, 1982). European companies monopolized the extraction of mineral resources such as trona at Lake Magadi in Kenya, copper from the Kilembe mines in Uganda and diamonds from Shinyanga in Tanzania. Agricultural commodities such as tea, cotton, coffee, sisal and pyrethrum were introduced for sale in European markets to meet the industrial requirements of Europe (Leys, 2001).

The infrastructure, including roads and railways, was developed in a manner that served the flow of commodities from the interior to towns and to the ports, which served as the bulking centres for export. Ake (1981) observes that roads in Africa were constructed as adjuncts to the railway line and their main purpose was the flow of commodities to the metropole. Little has been done to reorganize the infrastructure to meet the changing needs of the East African communities to date. The Kenya–Uganda railway has remained as a major remnant of this process of infrastructure development.

Accompanying colonialism, Western education was introduced so that East African communities could adapt to the new social, cultural and economic processes. In particular, Western education, which was imparted alongside the English language in East Africa, was introduced to provide labour for the expanding capitalist economy. Christian missionaries imparted education whose main aim was to evangelize rather than to instil Western technology into the African communities (ibid.).

The main drivers of globalization during the colonial phase were the missionaries, trading companies and the colonial administrations aided by Asians. The colonized were mere recipients of this form of globalization. During this era, the African economy underwent a process of monetization: Asian traders traversed most of East Africa and introduced shops (*dukas*) where Western commodities such as clothes, blankets, utensils and glassware were sold. They also assisted the colonial powers in the extraction of resources by providing artisan skills in the construction of the railway (Patel, 1997).

Like the Asians, Christian missionaries assisted in the European colonization and control of Africa. They socialized Africans into accepting the values that were important for the exploitation of resources in East Africa. For instance, mission education emphasized total obedience to the colonial masters and manual skills such as masonry, carpentry and brick making for the success of the colonial economy (Ake, 1981). Ironically, it is evident that the global propagation of Western concepts and structures did not begin with human rights as the Western world has sought to portray. Rather, it took the violent and exploitative forms of colonial conquest and domination (Schuurman, 2001). The colonial experience in East Africa was, therefore, instrumental in universalizing Western features and patterns that were clearly at variance with human rights.

Africa is not poor: the colonial powers and multinationals that were introduced came to exploit the rich human and natural resources in the region. In the process, colonialism led to the death of thousands of people and shaped and entrenched the economic development frameworks designed to benefit the metropole. This necessitated the imposition of bureaucracies and repressive legislation designed to perpetuate this exploitation. These bureaucracies have continued into the present era of globalization (Nabudere, 1980).

The third phase of globalization: super-imperialism

The decolonization process that commenced in the post-World War II period accelerated the process of globalization when it gradually removed direct control of colonial rule over East Africa. However, the emergent states continued to be sources of raw materials and markets for manufactured goods from the developed world. Although political independence in East Africa took place in the 1960s, the East African states responded to this period differently. This could be explained in terms of the divergent conceptions of development each nation chose to peruse in the bipolar global environment of the cold war (Barkan, 1984). Kenya adopted capitalism, while the governments of Tanzania and Uganda under presidents Nyerere and Milton Obote, respectively, were more sympathetic to a socialist development path. Tanzania adopted the Arusha Declaration in 1967, which advocated the nationalization of the major means of production, while Uganda adopted the Common Man's Charter as the blue print of the economy (Aseka, 2005b).

These historical differences, however, did not last long and soon all three countries in the region were converging as a result of the policies introduced as a response to the global economic crisis of the 1970s. It was then that the world experienced a recession due to an increase in world oil prices. In response to the Yom Kippur war between the Arab states and Israel, which attracted Western political support, the Arab states initiated an oil boycott that led to a substantial increase in the world price of oil. This led to the deterioration of the terms of trade for many developing countries, resulted in a debt crisis and coincided with the neoliberal counter-revolution of the late 1970s (Lapeyre, 2004).

In the 1980s globalization therefore took the form of the Structural Adjustment Programmes (SAPs), which were imposed by the multilateral and bilateral donors. The policies of the IMF and the World Bank were influenced immensely by the neoliberal counter-revolution of the newly elected governments in the North. They advocated conditionalities such as the liberalization of the economy, retrenchment of public servants, the introduction of cost-sharing policies in hospitals and schools and the devaluation of local currencies (Gilpin, 2000).

Liberalization opened up and freed markets in each of the three East African countries. These weak economies were expected by the donor institutions to focus on tourism, agriculture and extraction of mineral resources, but not on manufacturing (Pillay, 1998). SAPs have been the basis of East Africa's new phase of integration with the global economy. This is a global economy in which Africa, as a continent, has been marginalized. Economically, Western Europe, the US, Japan and China account for two-thirds of the global production of goods. This amounts to US\$ 30,000 trillion compared to Africa's GDP of no more than US\$ 500 billion (Aseka, 2005a). Economic marginalization has been accompanied by political change: the despots in Africa who were previously protected by the superpowers during the cold war politics were now abandoned, as they had no more significance in global geopolitics (Leys, 2001).

This latest phase of globalization we call 'super-imperialism', at the heart of which lies the question of the human dignity of the people of East Africa. Like the hut and poll taxes that were introduced by colonial governments in Africa, whose ideology was to force Africans to work, the philosophy of SAPs is no different. SAPs were introduced to make African countries pay their debts, transform the orientation of their economies to market driven ones and to regulate business activities.

SAPs were intended to integrate African production into the latest phase of global capitalism. To meet this demand, African countries had to undertake reforms in all sectors of the economy and privatize state corporations. The Africans also needed 'capacity building' to realize their full potential because they were assumed to be uninterested in or incapable of changing their own situations. Implicit in the conditionalities of SAPs was the assumption that Africans had failed to establish institutions that would initiate development and accelerate economic growth. SAPs were to serve as the medium through which African economies could recover. Moreover, these conditionalities were non-negotiable: African countries had to adjust or receive no more aid.

As students of history, we have vehemently criticized and condemned the traditional African chiefs who signed treaties that transferred land to colonizing powers and contributed to the loss of control of mines and other resources. But in the current situation, East African governments are doing similar things by selling off parastatals and other public organizations to private local and foreign investors. This is done without regard to the fact that such parastatals represent local ownership of production and an economic independence that was at the heart of the struggle for independence from colonial masters.

During the current phase, global actors draw resources from the East African region without any social and moral responsibility for the welfare of the people involved. Unlike the preceding period whereby the colonial mother country – Britain – provided infrastructure and had some social responsibility towards her colonies, in this era of superimperialism the traders, MNCs and International Financial Institutions (IFIs) reap and recoup profits without having to pay for social and physical infrastructure costs. Global actors accumulate wealth and at the same time threaten to divest because of insecurity, poor infrastructure and high wage costs.

In addition to this general account of the three phases of globalization and its dynamics in the current phase there are specific experiences in each country in the region. Some of these specific effects are noted briefly below.

Kenya's experience in the era of super-imperialism

The explanation behind Kenya's sorry state of economic development has been blamed on over-reliance on the export of commodities. From 1964 to 1970 average per capita income grew by 2.8 per cent (World Bank, 2005) but in the 1970s the country experienced a serious economic downturn due to price fluctuations, which affected coffee and tea in the world market. The Kenyatta government responded to the situation by introducing price controls and marketing boards, which purchased agricultural products at government set prices. In the final analysis, this distorted prices. In some areas, farmers increased production of crops that were uncompetitive in the world market.

The Kenyan government also increased the number of state-owned bodies or parastatals, with the support of donor aid (Leys, 1975). As a result, the share of public sector output in GDP rose from 24 per cent in 1977 to 37 per cent in 1982. Unfortunately, these bodies provided the political class with an avenue for wealth accumulation and political patronage rather than improving the economy. Hand in glove with this development was the adoption of import-substitution policies with the support of the World Bank and the UNCTAD (Adams, 2005).

This economic structure had manifest problems and was reformed following the introduction of neoliberal policies in the 1980s. These policies, too, were to have clear problems. For example, with trade liberalization in the 1980s there was an influx of manufactured goods from Asia and Europe. As a result, deindustrialization took place. In Kenya leading garment and textile firms like Kicomi, KTM, Rivatex, Mountex, Raymonds and Yunken were all closed (Kinyanjui, 2003; McCormick and Rogerson, 2004). Closures were also experienced in leather industries such as Tiger Shoes and Bulleys Tanneries.

At the same time, recommendations were made by IFIs to reduce government intervention in national economies. It was argued that a significant proportion of the government's budget was directed to bailing out non-performing parastatals, institutions which were also seen as rewarding individuals who were loyal to the government. The private sector was earmarked as the alternative institution that would lead the process of economic recovery since the government had failed. Since there were no local firms with the resources to purchase these firms, foreign investors were invited to steer the process. The privatization of para-statals such as Kenya Airways, East African Bag and Cardage, Kenya Power and Lighting Company Ltd (KPLC), Kenya Commercial Bank (KCB) and Telkom therefore took place, while multinational corporations that had acquired local franchises during the Africanization process, such as Kenya Canners and East African Industries, reverted to their old names of Delmonte and Unilever respectively.

It is not only private capital that was unleashed. In the case of one multinational, it is alleged that dogs bit to death young boys who were suspected of stealing pineapples, while others drowned in River Chania while fleeing from security guards who wanted to arrest them for 'stealing' animal feeds. The long hours and tedious working conditions of women working in these firms are also documented.

The other critical unethical issue relating to private-sector-led development and to the dignity of citizens is that, for example, while Delmonte grows export pineapples for canning or for juice extraction, neighbouring small-scale farmers in Makuyu and Magogoni experience famine because they do not have facilities such as water to irrigate their farms. Essentially, it is a case whereby cargo planes taking fruit to international markets crisscross each other with those bringing food aid to famine stricken citizens.

Tanzania's experience in the era of super-imperialism

Following independence in 1961, Tanzania, under Nyerere, attempted to develop an African socialism. This was epitomized by the Arusha Declaration of 1967, underpinned by the *ujamaa* ideology. While this led to de-investment by some foreign investors, many donors still supported the country with vast amounts of donor aid as they believed in Nyerere's ideas of development.

This changed, however, with the shift to neoliberalism in the IFIs and when the country's integration into the global economy increased after the 1980s, especially after Nyerere retired as the president. Multilateral donors exerted pressure to undertake reforms including trade liberalization, the privatization of state-owned enterprises and public-sector reforms (Mkenda, 2005). These reforms impacted on virtually every sector of the economy. The textile sector was among the first ones to experience the adverse impact of globalization. Due to local protection and subsequent high operating costs, the local textile industry could not withstand competition from cheap imports. This translated into labour redundancies as factories were forced to close down (Mkenda, 2005). In the early 1980s there were 35 textile firms but this number dropped to only two in 1996. Tanzanian Breweries Ltd was also privatized in the 1980s leading to the laying off of many workers (Adams, 2005).

As in Kenya, market reforms in Tanzania involved the privatization of many public enterprises. Between 1993 and 2002, 265 government corporations were privatized (UNCTAD, 2002) leading to the retrenchment of thousands of workers. For instance, when the Tanzania Telecommunications Company Limited was privatized in 1998, over 1,000 workers lost their jobs. In the public service, the government retrenched a total of 63,000 workers between 1993 and 1998 (Mkenda, 2005). The country's state-owned and largest commercial bank, the Bank of Commerce, was privatized in the 1990s (World Bank, 2005).

Uganda's experience during the era of super-imperialism

Unlike in Kenya where the state procrastinated with globalization reforms, Uganda embraced the processes of globalization following a long period of instability in the 1970s and 1980s. The National Resistance Movement regime, that took power in the 1980s, not only accepted economic liberalization but also pursued it with vigour under the doctrine of a mixed economy (Mutibwa, 1992). To the chagrin of some of its most ardent supporters, the Museveni administration fully embraced the SAPs as dictated by the Bretton Woods institutions. This entailed massive devaluations, downsizing of the public service and the lifting of subsidies from agricultural commodities.

In addition, from 1993, and in accordance with World Bank policy advice, user charge fees were introduced in the health and education sectors ostensibly to cover the costs of providing the services. The Ugandan government also embarked on civil-service reforms in 1990 to downsize the staff from 320,000 in 1990 to 80,000 in 1995 (World Bank, 2005).

Despite the efforts to attract multinationals such as Coca-Cola, Bidco, Shoprite Tri-Star as well as MTN, the country's external debt has continued to increase. Much of this was accumulated during the 1980s as the former dictators channelled finances into non-productive sectors. Foreign aid in Uganda, as elsewhere in the region, has been largely ineffective. It has been channelled through governments' respective budgets thereby reinforcing the donor's control of the economy. Moreover, aid has effectively empowered the political elite while disempowering the population (Adams, 2005). Aid therefore contributed to a widening of the gap between the elite and the majority who could not take advantage of the new opportunities arising from trade liberalization in the era of SAPs. The privatization process undermined the public purse. For example, all the hotels privatized were sold at a great loss to the government. The most notorious was the privatization of the Hilltop hotel valued at 120 million Uganda shillings but sold for only 35 million shillings (Kibikyo, 2005: 190).

Multinational corporations and super-imperialism

As the foregoing account indicates, it is the multinationals that have benefited from current policies and shaped the forms of the regions' integration into the global capitalist economy. Indeed, since the colonial era, many MNCs entered the East African region with the aim of making profits. They are still entrenched in many fields ranging from mining to commerce to agriculture. Their presence indicates that, contrary to the popular image of Africa in the global media as a basket case constantly needing the help of the rest of the world, business operators – especially western MNCs in the extractive industries, merchant houses of all kinds of consumables, Chinese and Indian traders, western banks and financial corporations – confirm that Africa has always been good for business.

Although the investments of these multinationals contribute to an increase in industrialization in the region, poor wages and cheap land resources accompany this. In addition, most of these multinationals create new needs in terms of consumption patterns among the people. It is a matter of class to take bottled beer as it is to stay *bamboocha* by drinking Fanta and food supplements. The power of advertising has especially captured the youth who construct their identities around certain brands such as Coca-Cola, Embassy and Sweet Menthol. As Schuurman (2001: 6) observes, the Western notion of progress will sever indigenous people from their cultural roots and expose them as helpless victims to a global, exploitative capitalism that through manipulation in the Western-dominated media urges them to consume the wrong things for the wrong reasons, with money they do not have. This is occurring in East Africa. Furthermore, these corporations have a significant influence on policy formulation in the region and, as a result, they have benefited immensely during the privatization of government corporations and services.

The uneven distribution of benefits between multinational profits and workers' wages has resulted in workers' strikes in banks and Export Processing Zones as trade unions have sought to bargain for better working conditions and remuneration. MNCs have responded with a series of corporate codes of social responsibility but these do not get at the root causes of poverty. For example, in Kenya, the programmes to support the needy, such as Barclays Bank's girl-child initiative and Standard Chartered Bank's Nairobi Marathon, involve giving handouts and not structural support. Why not support poverty alleviation by paying workers well or forming linkages with local financial institutions that are banking with the poor? The current practices of corporate social responsibility fail to give back to the community what it takes from them.

Super-imperialism and human dignity: some outcomes

The latest phase of globalization has impinged on the dignity of East Africans, and all Africans, in many ways. For example, the global movement of Africans to the developed countries is controlled and is seen negatively in both the home and host countries. Migrant African professionals' movement is restricted on the basis of the fact that they constitute the so-called brain drain. They are accused of being unpatriotic to their home countries while in the recipient countries they are seen as economic refugees. The converse is true for human movement from developed countries to developing countries. Migrants from these countries are treated as expatriates who bring in skills and knowledge to recipient African countries. They come to work in top management jobs in corporate sectors, international NGOs and churches.

Globalization is also characterized by the preponderance of the 'knowledge economy' but this in turn accelerates the gap between the rich and poor nations given that Western nations finance most of the research in Africa and also claim the intellectual rights emanating from such research ventures. This explains the row that followed a joint research project between the University of Nairobi and Oxford University on an HIV/Aids vaccine in 2002.

The outcomes of present policies can also been seen in the basic socio-economic indicators for the region as shown in Table 10.1.

Table 10.1 Socio-economic indicators, selected years, East Africa

Indicator	Kenya	Tanzania	Uganda
Human Development Index (HDI)	0.509 (1980)	0.435 (1990)	0.412 (1985)
HDI 2003	0.474	0.418	0.508
HDI Rank (2003) (out of 177)	154	164	144
Population living below the national poverty line (latest year) (per cent)	42	55	n/a
Population without access to improved water (2003) (per cent)	44	38	27
Adult literacy rate (aged over 15) (per cent) 1990	70.8	62.9	56.1
Adult literacy rate (aged over 15) (per cent) 2003	73.6	69.4	68.9
Youth literacy rate (aged 15–24) (per cent) 1990	89.3	83.1	70.1
Youth literacy rate (aged 15–24) (per cent) 2003	80.3	78.4	80.2
Life expectancy at birth (1970–75)	53.6	49.5	51.1
Life expectancy at birth (2000–05)	47.0	46.0	46.8
Average annual population growth rate (1975–2003) (per cent)	3.2	3.0	3.3
Average annual GNI per capita growth (1990–2003) (per cent)	−0.6	1.0	2.6
Net foreign direct investment as a percentage of GDP (1990)	0.7	0	0
Net foreign direct investment as a percentage of GDP (2003)	0.6	2.4	3.1

Source: UNDP, *Human Development Report* (2005) New York: United Nations Development Programme.

As Table 10.1 shows, the countries in the East African region are ranked among the lowest in the world in the UNDP's Human Development Index. In both Kenya and Tanzania, the HDI score has actually fallen over the past decades. Substantial proportions of the population continue to live below the national poverty lines and do not have access to safe water. Population growth rates are among the highest in the world.

Per capita income growth has been negative over the past decade in Kenya and only 1.0 per cent per annum in Tanzania. Uganda has fared better but the figures are skewed by the impacts of civil strife in the 1990s. The opening of the economies to foreign direct investment has meant that FDI as a share of GDP has increased significantly in Tanzania and Uganda. But this shows no sign of benefiting the majority of the population. In fact, the most disturbing statistic of all is that average life expectancy in each of three countries is lower now than it was thirty years ago; East Africans can only expect to live until 47 years of age.

Even so, there have been some positive changes in some areas. For example, the adult literacy rate has risen in each of the three countries. In Kenya, however, the most recent improvement was due to the introduction of the free education system by the National Rainbow Coalition (NARC), notwithstanding the holding and withdrawal of foreign aid by the World Bank and IMF due to government's failure to speed reforms as well as curb high-level corruption. It is to an analysis of changes in the political system that we now briefly turn.

Competitive politics, multipartyism and super-imperialism

The period from the 1980s to the 2000s represents a unique phase of globalization in the East African region. In this period, we see the growth of non-governmental organizations and civil societies and the transition to multipartyism. Changes in the presidencies of all three countries have taken place.

The transition to multipartyism has been subject to different timing in each of the three countries of the region. In Uganda, for example, only one political organization, the National Resistance Movement, was recognized, while other political parties were prohibited from sponsoring candidates until 2006. These included the Uganda Peoples Congress (UPC), the Democratic Party (DP), the Conservative Party (CP), the Justice Forum and the National Democrats Forum. In Kenya, multiparty democracy was ushered in much earlier, in 1991, after the repeal of section 2a of the constitution of Kenya. It was not until 2002, however, when KANU, the dominant party, lost power to the National Rainbow Coalition (a coalition of many political parties including the Liberal Democratic Party, Democratic Party and National Alliance Party of Kenya). Chama Cha Mapinduzi (CCM) dominates Tanzania's brand of multipartyism. The other parties include the National Convention for Construction and Reform (NCCR-Mageuzi), Chama Cha Demokrasia na Maendeleo (CHADEMA), the Union of Multiparty Democracy and the Civil United Front.

Some of the impetus for the change to multipartyism came at the instigation of the IFIs and Western governments. For example, in the 1990s Kenya was denied aid by the bilateral and multilateral donors on the grounds that she needed to demonstrate transparency, accountability and good governance.[1] The destabilization of the economy, following the suspension of an IMF loan facility, held out the prospect of further inflationary pressures (which were realized in triple-digit inflation rates) since the effects of the immediate depreciation in the value of the Kenya shilling and rising import prices were amplified by tax increases (Cowen and Kanyinga, 2002: 129). This in turn provoked political violence in 1997 that led to the lynching of a plain clothes policeman at a political rally in Nairobi, and the slaughter of at least eight police officers and 110 civilians at Likoni Coast province (ibid.). This combined economic and political pressure forced Kenya – and other East African countries – to embrace multipartyism (Leys, 2001). These new East African governments are increasingly being forced to manage national politics and to adapt to the pressures of global market forces. As a result they have had to address the issues of adoption of PRSPs, domestic borrowing, public procurement and corruption. The new governments are more responsive to the global institutions and have no agenda for changing the internal status quo. A large proportion of their budget comes from external funding; the new multipartyism in reality is beholden to external actors.

Conclusion

Globalization consists of a web of relationships between countries at different levels of economic development or material well being. As a worldwide historical process of capital expansion, globalization in the East African region can be traced to the pre-colonial period. The Arab and Asian traders were the main agents of the process while ivory and slaves were the main exports from the region. During the colonial period, the Christian missionaries, white settlers and the Asians were the key agents. East Africa produced cash crops and mineral resources while Western Europe brought in manufactured goods to the region. The current phase of globalization is characterized by the activities of MNCs, the IMF and the World Bank.

Structural changes such as the initiation of trade justice, reducing inequalities between countries and addressing the unequal power relations between the developed and developing countries are needed if all are to benefit from an integrating world. The current measures of peer review mechanisms and Afro-barometer assessments will not provide the structural mechanisms for transforming Africa: they are all based on the Western model of the world political economy. For a country to be a member of the global economy it must adopt the American and Eurocentric ways of defining norms, values and institutions. Viewed in this way globalization is a new form of capitalism characterized by superimperialism. It is a process that involves the concentration of capital in very few corporations and individuals in the fragmented spaces of the global economy.

Note

1   Kenya has still not yet satisfied the World Bank and IMF conditionalities for fighting corruption.

References

Adams, J. (2005) 'The Right Approach to the Right Policies: Reflections on Tanzania in The Frontlines of Development', in G. Intermits and P. Todd (eds), *Reflections from the World Bank*. Washington, DC: World Bank.

Ake, C. (1981) *A Political Economy of Africa*. New York: Longman.

Aseka, E. (2005a) *Pitfalls of Ideology, Social Policy and Leadership in East Africa*. Nairobi: EME Research Initiatives and Publishers.

Aseka, E. (2005b) *Transformational Leadership in East Africa*. Kampala: Fountain Publishers.

Barkan, J. (1984) *Politics and Public Policy in Kenya and Tanzania*. Nairobi, Heinemann.

Cowen, M. and K. Kanyinga (2002) 'The 1997 Elections in Kenya: The Politics of Communality and Locality', in M. Cowen and L. Liisa (eds), *Multi-Party Elections in Africa*. Oxford: James Currey.

East African Community (2000) *Annual Report, 1998–2000*. Arusha, available at http://www.eastafricanlaw.com.

Gilpin, R. (2000) *The Challenge of Global Capitalism*. Princeton, NJ: Princeton University Press.

Kibikyo, D. (2005) 'Privatisation: Deindustrialisation and Politics in Uganda', in R. Mukama and R. Murindwa (eds), *Confronting 21st Century Challenges*, vol. 2. Kampala: Makerere University.

Kinyanjui, M. (2003) 'A Gender Analysis of Small Scale Garment Producers' Response to Market Liberalisation in Kenya', *African Geographical Review*, 22: 49–59.

Lapeyre, F. (2004) 'Globalization and Structural Adjustment as a Development Tool', *working paper* 31, Policy Integration Department: World Commission on the Social Dimension of Globalization. Geneva: International Labour Office.

Leys, C. (1975) *Underdevelopment in Kenya: The Political Economy of Neo-Colonialism*. Nairobi: East African Educational Publishers.

Leys, C. (2001) *Market-Driven Politics. Neo-Liberal Democracy and the Public Interest*. London: Verso Books.

McCormick, D. and C. Rogerson (2004) *Clothing and Footwear in African Industrialisation*. Pretoria: African Institute of South Africa.

Mkenda, B. (2005) 'The Impact of Globalization on Tanzania's Labour Market Evidence From the manufacturing Sector', paper prepared for a Policy Dialogue for Accelerating Growth and Poverty Reduction in Tanzania, held at the Conference Hall of Economic and Social Research Foundation (ESRF), 28 July.

Mutibwa, P. (1992) *Uganda Since Independence*. Kampala: Fountain Publishers.

Nabudere, D. (1980) *Imperialism and Nationalism in Uganda*. London: Onyx Press.

Patel, Z. (1997) *Challenge to Colonialism*. Nairobi: The Standard.

Pillay, D. (1998) 'Globalisation, Marginalisation and the Retreat of the State of Africa: The Role of Civil Society in the Pursuit of Democratic Governance, Social Economic Development and Regional Integration', International Society for Third World Research (ISTR), available at http://www.jhu.edu/istr/pubs/report/jul98.html.

Schuurman, F. (2001) *Globalization and Development Studies: Challenges for the 21st Century*. New Delhi: Vistan Publications.

Sheriff, A. (2002) 'The Spatial Dichotomy of Swahili Towns: The Case of Zanzibar in the Nineteenth Century', in R. Burton (ed.), *The Urban Experience in Eastern Africa Century 1750–2000*. Nairobi, Kenya: The British Institute of East Africa.

Stichter, S. (1982) *Migrant Labour in Kenya*. Harlow, UK: Longman.

UNCTAD (2002) *Investment Policy Review: The United Republic of Tanzania*. Geneva: United Nations.

UNDP (2005) *Linking Industrialisation with Human Development*. Nairobi: UNDP.

World Bank (2005) *Sustaining Growth and Achieving Deep Reduction in Poverty*. Washington, DC: World Bank.

11

Enforced Globalization and the Neoliberal Path to Development: A Perspective from South Asia

Nasreen Khundker

It is challenging to answer the question 'what is globalization?' in the South Asian context. It is nevertheless possible to summarize the experience of the diverse countries of the region, to come to a common perception of the process and what it implies. It is also felt that given the imperatives of the region, globalization has to be seen in the light of development objectives and ensuring a minimum standard of living for the population. South Asia therefore presents an interesting case study and a basis for comparison for other developing regions.

The main argument of this chapter is that in the South Asian context 'globalization' is the realization of the neoliberal agenda of free trade, and pro-market economic policies, with uncertain outcomes for development. The main agents of globalization are the global institutions, such as the World Bank and the IMF, and more recently, the WTO. The primary role of these agencies in shaping economic policies has been made possible by the considerable dependence on foreign aid and external finance by countries in the region, and thus their susceptibility to 'conditionalities' imposed by global financial institutions, determining important policy outcomes.

From the perspective of global institutions, the policy changes are part of a neoliberal economic agenda, justifiable on the grounds of achieving greater economic efficiency and higher rates of economic growth. A subsidiary theme is poverty alleviation, given the pervasive poverty in the region. Macroeconomic stabilization is a further desired goal.

As is well known, however, the neoliberal policy framework adopted by countries has not been separate from policy changes and ideological, as well as paradigmatic, shifts in the countries of the Centre, mainly the US and the UK. This worldwide dissemination in policies and ideology has again only been made possible through the agencies of the global financial institutions, which have themselves undergone considerable changes in philosophy and policy outlook.[1]

Globalization, moreover, has its historic roots in the colonial period, recognition of which is important in understanding the subsequent policies and strategies of the newly independent post-colonial states in the region, as well as the experience of globalization in its current context.

This chapter therefore discusses the meaning and content of globalization, its historical roots, the agents of globalization and the outcomes for the South Asia region, as well as the implications for development, with some concluding remarks.

The historical roots of globalization

Colonialism and globalization

South Asia comprises the countries of Afghanistan, Bangladesh, Bhutan, India, the Maldives, Nepal, Pakistan and Sri Lanka. These countries are also members of the South Asian Association for Regional Cooperation (SAARC), established in 1985. The countries geographically form a sub-continent and have a shared history and culture, which gives the region its unique character. They were part of the British Indian Empire. India, however, was partitioned on independence into two separate countries, India and Pakistan, in 1947, on the basis of religion, which proved to be untenable. Thus, Pakistan was further subdivided into Bangladesh and Pakistan in December 1971, after a war of liberation lasting for nine months. As Table 11.1 shows, the region comprises over a fifth of the total

Table 11.1　South Asia: basic statistics

	Population millions (2004)	*Gross national income per capita (US $) (2003)*	*HDI rank (2002)*
South Asia	1438.4		
Afghanistan	23.2	200	
Bangladesh	135.2	400	138
Bhutan	0.8	630	134
India	1066.0	540	127
Maldives	0.3	2,350	84
Nepal	24.7	240	140
Pakistan	148.7	520	142
Sri Lanka	19.5	930	96
World	6389.3		
S. Asia as % of world	22.5		

Source: Asian Development Bank, *Key Indicators*, 2005.

world population, and is characterized by low per capita incomes. Countries vary by population, size and incomes, with India dominating by both size and population. The region is also marked by considerable diversity in terms of religion, language and ethnicity. The main religions are Hinduism, Islam, Buddhism, Jainism and Christianity. Several languages are spoken including Hindi, Urdu, Bengali, Nepali, Tamil, Sinhalese, Bhutanese and a host of regional dialects.

The historical roots of the globalization process are to be found in the colonial past of South Asian countries. Patterns of trade from the region and a globally integrated production structure were already established during colonial rule. Major commercial and export crops were introduced, such as jute,[2] tea and indigo, which were processed in the mills and factories of Britain, and re-exported back to the region and elsewhere, as finished products.

Under patterns of imperial trade, cotton, imported from the United States, was processed in the Lancashire cotton mills then exported to India. According to many economic historians, this also served as a major setback, if not total demise, for the local manufacture of cotton fabrics in India, including the famous muslin of Dhaka. Similarly, the main incentive for indigo cultivation in Bengal was provided by increased foreign demand, as a result of the decline in its supply from traditional sources such as western India, parts of North America and the West Indies. Indigo, interestingly, was grown through coercion, the *raiyats* or peasant cultivators not finding it a profitable crop; and this led to a revolt in 1859–60 (Asiatic Society, 2003). The coercion was moreover necessary for the colonial government, mainly as a source of revenue, due to the decline in the export of cotton textiles from the region.

Interestingly enough, the colonial enterprise was marked not only by commodity flows, but also by considerable labour migration both within and outside the region. Thus new crops such as tea were grown in plantations in Sri Lanka with migrant labour of Tamil origin from India, while tea plantations in Bangladesh were developed with labour displaced from Orissa in India. Similar labour migration took place from India to East Africa, South Africa and the West Indies.

The patterns of production set during the colonial era established the countries of South Asia as producers and exporters of primary products and importers of manufactured goods. This also explains the persistent balance of payments deficits of countries associated with the long run tendency for the terms of trade to decline.[3] These deficits are one of the main reasons for external borrowing by countries, both from institutions such as the IMF, and, for Latin American countries, from private commercial banks. It also provides the rationale for the stabilization and Structural Adjustment Policies of the World Bank and the IMF. Interestingly, however, Great Britain could sustain deficits in its own balance of payments in the colonial period through the imposition of various taxes in the colonies (Patnaik, 2003).

Post-colonial aspirations

The patterns of production and trade established during colonial rule are also crucial in understanding the subsequent thrust towards import-substituting industrialization in the post-colonial era. If the terms of trade were by and large not favourable to less developed countries, local manufacture of the imported products had to be encouraged. In this regard, the path followed by countries of South Asia was no different from other developing countries with a colonial past.

It also explains the search for archetypes in terms of development models, and a focus on planning to achieve development objectives, with a concomitant role for the state. A widespread substitution of imports, as well as development planning, were thus considered as important strategies in newly independent countries to reduce their dependence on colonial centres and to achieve a better allocation of resources. Moreover, these new goals could not be left to the vagaries of market forces and required state intervention in the economy, in terms of regulation, imposition of taxes and subsidies, special incentives and protective tariffs.

In the Indian case, this led to the adoption in the mid 1950s of the Soviet type Mahalanobis model, by Nehru, in the Second Plan, with its emphasis on heavy industry. This planned strategy similarly served as a blueprint for development in varying degrees for other countries of the region. Politically, it led to the non-aligned movement, which also found leadership from the region. However, geopolitical and cultural differences, as well as differences in aspirations for development, surfaced leading to new boundaries for many of the nation states in the region being established.[4] These differences have continued to the present day, influencing the form and extent of integration with the world economy, as well as links within the region.

Thus, while the focus of the political leadership in the post-colonial period was on the building of nation states, these efforts failed to take into account the separate identities and aspirations of minority ethnic and national identities. For many countries of the region, therefore, particularly India, Bangladesh, Pakistan and Sri Lanka, violent conflicts between the governments representing the majority population and religion and ethnic minorities that were both politically and economically deprived, proved to be unavoidable. One could mention in this context the Tamil separatist movement in Sri Lanka, the Sikh rebellion in the Punjab and various other rebellions in the north-eastern states of India, the Baluch separatist movement in Pakistan and the conflict in the Chittagong Hill Tracts of Bangladesh[5]. This is not to say that the majority population itself does not feel deprived, as epitomized by the Maoist rebellion in Nepal.

The post-colonial period also saw the emergence of aid relationships, as well as the birth of 'development economics' on the intellectual front, both to justify foreign aid and external finance, and to take into account the differences in economic and social structures of developing countries in articulating a set of policies appropriate to their diverse structures and levels of development. No less important was the realization that the international economic order was not conducive to the aspirations of developing countries, and it was necessary to establish a new international economic order that would fundamentally restructure the world economy.

Globalization as neoliberalism – the current context

Agents of globalization

The main thrust of this section is to explain the globalization process in South Asia in its present context. It is argued that the defining feature of contemporary globalization is neoliberalism and the main agents of change have been the international institutions such as the World Bank, the IMF and more recently the WTO. It also includes regional institutions such as the Asian Development Bank. All these institutions have shown a remarkable convergence in terms of ideas and have effected major policy changes in the region through their lending policies.

All countries in the region have adopted neoliberal economic policies with their thrust on the private sector, privatization of state-owned enterprises, trade and financial liberalization, and deregulation of markets. The timing of these changes has however been different, while the context has been the same. The latter mostly originated in the external situation and the balance of payments deficits of countries, although the internal situation was responsible to the extent that the pattern of growth followed in earlier decades was not sustainable, leading to both fiscal deficits and heavy external debts, partly attributable to inward-looking policies.

Sri Lanka was one of the first to adopt structural adjustment policies, with a World Bank–IMF loan as early as 1977, in response to a balance of payments and foreign exchange crisis originating in the fall of international prices for its major export crops such as tea, rubber and coconut, and rising import prices (Sinnathamby, 2000). External factors were similarly important in the case of Bangladesh, particularly a crisis in terms of foreign exchange reserves and declining terms of trade since the mid-1970s, following the oil price shocks of 1973 and 1980 (Syeduzzaman, 1991). The first IMF loans for the country were negotiated in 1974 and 1975, under standby arrangements, and a major adjustment programme was launched in December 1980, when it took a loan from the IMF under its Extended Fund Facility. Bangladesh was also one of the first of 35 countries to be contracted into the Structural Adjustment Facility of the IMF, set up in 1986.

Nepal adopted a stabilization programme in 1985 supported by an IMF standby arrangement and, subsequently, Structural Adjustment Programmes of the World Bank, in the face of a balance of payments crisis and fiscal deficits. Pakistan and India were relatively latecomers to the scene. The former took Structural Adjustment Facility and Extended Structural Adjustment Facility loans under an IMF standby arrangement in December 1988. In India's case, the process was initiated as late as 1991 with a Structural Adjustment Loan under an IMF standby arrangement. Several factors contributed to the balance of payments crisis in India, such as a fall in worker remittances due to the first Gulf war, an outflow of deposits of non-resident Indians, and the collapse of the Soviet Union, India's largest trading partner (Ratnam, 2000).

The policy changes were also affected by ideological shifts of newly elected governments, or at the very least required a change in the 'mindset' of countries. In the case of Sri Lanka, for instance, the party that came to power in 1977 was openly committed to pro-market reforms and a redirection of national economic policies towards greater openness. This was very different from the pre-1977 situation, when Sri Lanka followed a primarily socialist agenda and a standoff attitude towards the international financial institutions (Sinnathamby, 2000). In the Indian case, on the other hand, the first IMF loans were contracted by the Indian National Congress, despite its commitment towards a planned economy and a socialist agenda, largely due to the pressures on the balance of payments. For Bangladesh, the socialist agenda was very briefly pursued and abandoned in the mid 1970s, after a change of power and assassination of the first president and founding father of the nation. Subsequent governments that initiated the reform process were military dictatorships, but the policies have continued to this day with democratically elected governments.

The usual sequence of policy changes for all countries in the region have been macroeconomic stabilization packages of the IMF, followed by structural adjustment loans of the World Bank. The purpose of the former is to reduce the fiscal deficit of countries by curtailing current expenditures, including social sector expenditures, food and other subsidies, and improving tax collections; while the money supply is restricted to control inflation. The structural adjustment measures are meant to support stabilization policies. Thus, income and value-added taxes are increasingly emphasized in lieu of tariffs. Trade liberalization involves the reduction in tariffs and the establishment of a uniform tariff structure, removal of quotas and licences, along with exchange rate adjustments, devaluation and a move towards the convertability of currencies.

The privatization agenda was actively followed along with other public sector reforms, such as the subcontracting of services, and the involvement of private firms in areas previously dominated by the public sector. Financial sector reforms including banking reforms and the creation and strengthening of capital and securities markets are also an integral part of the policy package. The IMF loans, originally short term and on commercial terms, have also been replaced by longer-term concessionary financing under Structural Adjustment Facilities (SAF) and Extended Structural Adjustment Facilities (ESAF). The latest initiatives in this regard are the Poverty Reduction Growth Facilities (PRGF). The World Bank loans are Structural Adjustment Loans (SAL) and Sectoral Adjustment Loans (SECALS).

Privatization was thought to be necessary to reduce losses of state-owned enterprises and improve efficiency. In Bangladesh, 1,089 enterprises were privatized from 1972 to 1996, leading to a widespread retrenchment of workers (Khundker, 2000). In India privatization took the form of selling shares in public enterprises, with the government retaining the controlling share and the proceeds being used to reduce fiscal deficits (Ratnam, 2000). Forty out of 240 public enterprises of the central government were (partially) privatized in this manner from 1991 to 1997, with a reduction in employment of 200,000 (ibid.). This was also the case in Sri Lanka, though workers were gifted with 10 per cent of shares. Privatization was concentrated on small-to medium-sized enterprises (Sinnathamby, 2000). In Pakistan, the privatization plan was announced in 1991, selecting 108 public sector enterprises for privatization, and offering 10 per cent of shares to employees (Fasihuddin, 2000). A similar privatization act was announced in Nepal in 1991 along with other changes in the industrial sector such as greater emphasis on export industries (Pyakuryaly, 2000).

While public expenditure cuts, through withdrawal of food and input subsidies, particularly in agriculture, have affected various groups throughout the region, they have also, interestingly, affected the competitiveness of multinational corporations and emphasized their 'footloose' character. Thus, in Bangladesh a recent withdrawal of food rations to tea estate workers has initiated the sale of a major multinational to local companies.

Trade liberalization is another cornerstone of the new policy framework. Countries have been encouraged to reduce tariffs and rationalize their tariff structures, putting in place a set of uniform tariffs. The timing of these changes has again been different for countries closely following the sequence of stabilization and adjustment measures. There were moreover policy reversals, with periods of accelerated liberalization and other reforms towards the free market, followed by brakes on this process (World Bank, 2004). These reversals are in most part dictated by domestic exigencies, including the need to generate tariff revenues, while the external pressures remained to continue with the reforms.

In the Indian case, for instance, the liberalization process lost momentum between 1997 and 2001, but resumed in the 2002/03 and 2003/04 budgets, though agriculture continued to be protected. In Pakistan, on the other hand, trade liberalization has been a continuous process since the 1980s, with a new impetus since 1996/97. The same is true of Nepal, which generally has low tariffs, including in agriculture. Further tariff reductions however are not envisaged, given the Maoist guerilla conflict and the government's need to finance security measures. About 80 per cent of Bhutan's trade in merchandise is with India, and tariffs are exempt from each other's imports under a free trade agreement. Tariffs are also generally low in Sri Lanka, and all textile tariffs were abolished in 1997. Trade liberalization slowed down in Bangladesh from about 1995, but there were further reductions in tariffs and 'para tariffs' in the 2002/03 budget (World Bank, 2004).

There has also been a remarkable continuity in the broad parameters of change, as advocated by the international financial institutions. While stabilization and structural adjustment policies have dominated much of the 1980s and the 1990s, the latest initiatives are the Poverty Reduction Strategy Papers (PRSPs), to be implemented through government budgets and prepared by countries in order to access the Poverty Reduction Growth Facility (PRGF) of the IMF.[6] It is interesting that the nature of conditionalities has not changed, despite the new focus on reduction of poverty by half by 2015 and targets set for countries accessing loans in terms of the Millennium Development Goals. Thus in Bangladesh, the PRGF loan of the IMF is also tied to increases in the domestic price of oil in line with international prices, thus reducing oil subsidies. The effect on the poor is to be cushioned through expansion of the social safety nets such as old-age pensions and 'Vulnerable Group Development'.

PRSPs are supposed to be country 'owned' and to incorporate the voices of civil society, in both the process of formulation and of monitoring, though this is often cosmetic. While the explicit set of conditionalities, as mentioned, are a reduction in rates of poverty by 2015 and achievement of targets in terms of the UN Millennium Development Goals, the policy framework for achieving these goals is private-sector development, trade liberalization, privatization, financial sector reforms and market efficiency. A further emphasis is on good governance, elimination of corruption and gender equality (World Bank, 2005), as well as investment in social and physical infrastructure and social safety nets, without recognizing that corruption, bad governance and marginalization of the poor may be integral to the policy framework itself. The changed focus on 'soft' sectors such as social infrastructure, gender and governance, it may be mentioned, has also been a priority focus of the World Bank in recent years.

The policy changes have been further strengthened by aid coordination of major bilateral donors and imposition of a common set of condition-alities, strongly emphasizing the free market rationality. This is mani-fested through formation of donor consortiums and regular meetings of aid groups to assess country performance and to suggest common policy reforms. It is also reflected in the analysis of country strategy papers of the key donors.

Globalization is thus not simply greater integration of the world econ-omy but the emergence of a New World Order, with its supporting institu-tions and ideas. This has in effect shaped the economies of the region and has given meaning and content to the globalization process in South Asia.

Features of globalization

International institutions have been instrumental in restructuring the domestic economies of South Asian countries in a different sense. For example, the Multi-Fibre Arrangement (MFA) provided countries, particu-larly Bangladesh, with the opportunity to take advantage of quotas imposed on exports of ready-made garments to the United States from a number of neighbouring countries. This resulted in a shift to an export-based industrialization strategy, almost totally dependent on this single item (Sobhan and Khundker, 2001). The ending of the MFA imposes add-itional competitive pressures on Bangladesh, and considerable stress in continuing with its industrialization strategy, while it has given a boost to Indian production of textiles and ready-made garments. In a broad sense, negotiations under the WTO have become increasingly important for countries in the region for their long term agricultural and industrial development. The question of market concessions and duty-free access for their products, as well as the continuation of farm export subsidies in the West, affects the ability of countries in the region to withstand global competitive pressures and also to sell in the global market place.

Globalization is similarly apparent in international migratory flows. A large part of the labour force in the South Asia region are temporary migrants to countries in the Middle East, newly industrialized countries such as Malaysia, as well as other countries of the world. The remittances of these workers are an important source of foreign exchange earnings. There are, however, important differences between countries. While remittances are the most important source of foreign exchange earnings in the case of Bangladesh, most of the out-migration from Nepal is to India, mostly for seasonal work (Nepal South Asia Centre, 1998). Nepal also experiences considerable in-migration from India of relatively skilled labour for work in the manufacturing sector. These migratory flows are also significant within the region and have an important social dimension. For example, one of the issues is the inter-regional trafficking of women. Most of these women are trafficked into brothels in Bombay from Bangladesh and Nepal, and thence forth to other countries. Child trafficking to the Middle East from countries in the region, such as Bangladesh, has been a similar outrage. The children are employed as camel jockeys.

Flows of foreign direct investment to the region have not been substantial, though it did increase by almost five-fold between 1993 and 2003 as shown in Table 11.2. The countries that have recorded substantial increases in FDI in recent times are Bangladesh and India. What is important, however, in terms of development outcomes, is the structure of FDI. For the case of India, for instance, most of the foreign investment has been in junk foods and telecommunications. A similar pattern is observable in other countries.

As shown in Table 11.3, both the trade: GDP ratio and exports, as a percentage of GDP, have increased in the countries of the region, indicating a greater level of integration with the world economy, as well as greater regional integration. For Sri Lanka, Bhutan and the Maldives, trade flows have always been significantly high, though for the latter two countries this is mostly intra-regional trade. The direction of trade also shows interesting changes in the last decade and a half (Asian Development, 2005). For Afghanistan and Nepal for instance, merchandise exports have drastically declined to Europe and increased to Asia. The same is somewhat true for India. For the Maldives and Pakistan, exports to both

Table 11.2   FDI flows to South Asia (US $million)

	1993	1996	2000	2003
South Asia	1114.5	3611.4	3270.3	5162.7
Afghanistan	–	–	–	–
Bangladesh	14.1	13.5	280.4	102.5
Bhutan	–	0.1	−0.1	0.2
India	550.4	2426.1	2496.0	4269.0
Maldives	6.9	9.3	13.0	13.5
Nepal	–	19.2	–	14.8
Pakistan	348.6	922.0	308.0	534.0
Sri Lanka	194.5	119.9	173.0	228.7

Source: Asian Development Bank, *Key Indicators 2005*, table 23.

Table 11.3   South Asia: extent of integration with the world economy (total trade and exports as % of GDP)

	1990		2003		2004	
	Trade	*Exports*	*Trade*	*Exports*	*Trade*	*Exports*
Afghanistan	–	–	46.8	–	–	–
Bangladesh	17.2	5.1	29.7	12.6	31.5	13.4
Bhutan	51.4	–	56.3	18.4	–	22.9
India	3.3	5.7	23.6	10.0	–	11.3
Maldives	–	84.5	–	–	85.6	–
Nepal	22.7	6.2	38.2	10.7	–	11.1
Pakistan	30.0	12.5	28.4	13.1	29.9	13.3
Sri Lanka	57.3	25.0	64.7	28.1	68.7	28.7

Source: Asian Development Bank, *Foreign Trade Indicators* (various years).

Asia and Europe have declined, while they have increased to North and Central America. For merchandise imports, on the other hand, trade within the region has increased, with the notable exception of Afghanistan, where imports have increased from Europe.

The volume of intra-regional trade has increased from about 2.4 per cent of total trade of the region in 1990 to 4.9 per cent in 1998 (World Bank, 2004). Most of this intra-regional trade is again through bilateral agreements between countries.

The scope and importance of intra-regional trade is also recognized through the formation of SAARC, the signing of the South Asia Preferential Trade Arrangement (SAPTA) in 1993, and the formation of the South

Asia Free Trade Area (SAFTA) in 2005. It can be argued that both a desire for greater regional cooperation and the increasing number of such regional arrangements among developing countries in other parts of the world has led to the establishment of SAARC. In the present context, such regional cooperation also provides a forum for developing a common stance in the WTO negotiations, although this is not always achieved.

Countries in the region differ in the basis of their integration with the world economy. For example, 76 per cent of Bangladesh's foreign exchange earnings come from the export of ready-made garments, primarily to the US and countries in the European Union. This industry, as well as textiles, is similarly important in the case of Sri Lanka and for Pakistan, accounting for 52 per cent and 60 per cent of total exports respectively (Joshi, 2002). In the Indian case, on the other hand, the IT industry has successfully developed since the mid 1990s as a globally integrated sector, accounting for 19 per cent of total exports in 2003–4, and 24 per cent of global off-shored IT/ITES services in 2002 (Upadhya, 2004). Non-resident Indians who had earlier migrated to the Silicon Valley in the US played a key role in the evolution of this industry. It has also led to the formation of a new transnational capitalist class who are the most vocal advocates of globalization.

Outcomes

Table 11.4 shows the growth rates of GDP in countries of the region in recent years. By 2004, annual growth rates of GDP had surpassed 6 per cent for Afghanistan, Bangladesh, Bhutan, India and the Maldives. It was over 5 per cent for Sri Lanka and 6 per cent for Pakistan. The notable exception is Nepal, with declining rates of GDP growth.

Table 11.4   Growth rates of GDP in South Asia, 1999–2004

	1999	2000	2001	2002	2003	2004
Afghanistan	–	–	–	–	5.4	8.3
Bangladesh	4.9	5.9	5.3	4.4	5.3	6.3
Bhutan	7.8	9.5	8.6	7.1	6.8	6.7
India	6.1	4.4	5.8	4.0	8.5	6.9
Maldives	7.2	4.8	3.5	6.5	8.4	8.8
Nepal	4.5	6.1	4.9	−0.4	2.9	3.4
Pakistan	3.7	4.3	1.9	3.2	5.1	6.0
Sri Lanka	4.3	6.0	−1.5	4.0	6.0	5.4

Source: Asian Development Bank, *Asian Development* (2005).

Underlying these aggregate growth rates are changes in the structure of production. In most countries it is the service sector which has grown fastest, particularly since 2000. What is also striking is the deceleration in growth rates in agriculture over the period, particularly for India and Sri Lanka. The growth rate is actually negative in some years for these two countries. This has accompanied other structural changes such as changes in the input structure and nature of crops, requiring increased use of credit, leading to greater indebtedness of farmers. Market liberalization has exposed them to greater fluctuation in terms of both the domestic and international markets. All this has caused acute distress amongst farmers and an increased number of suicides in several states of India (Vyas, 2004). In the case of industry on the other hand, Bhutan seems to be the only country in the region where industrial growth has been increasing at a fast rate.

Of special interest are the poverty levels in the countries of the region. From all accounts, globalization has not been able to make any significant dent in poverty. Poverty levels continue to be very high, especially in rural areas, as indicated in Table 11.5. In the countries for which data since 1990 are available, two of the three have seen increases in the poverty rate. Poverty levels in the region vary from country to country and reflect past policies, levels of aid, and so on. Thus poverty levels are the lowest for Sri Lanka and also lower for Pakistan and Bhutan, compared to Bangladesh, Nepal and India. Sri Lanka followed a successful basic needs strategy in the 1970s with a positive impact on poverty, education and other basic needs indicators. Pakistan has received high levels of aid throughout the 1980s for geopolitical reasons.

Table 11.5   Population in poverty (%) and inequality in South Asia (national poverty lines)

	1990	*Latest year*	*Total*	*Urban*	*Rural*	*Gini coefficient*
Afghanistan	–	–	–	–	–	–
Bangladesh	–	2000	49.8	36.6	53.0	0.3
Bhutan	–	2000	–	25.3	–	0.341
India	36.0	2000	28.6	24.7	30.2	0.33
Maldives	–	1998	43.0	20.0	50.0	–
Nepal	–	2004	30.9	9.6	34.6	0.40
Pakistan	28.6	1999	32.6	25.9	34.8	0.3
Sri Lanka	20.0	1996	25.0	15.0	27.0	0.3

Source: Asian Development Bank, *Key Indicators* (2005).

Neoliberal policies, while achieving higher rates of economic growth, have not been similarly successful in poverty reduction. Given these outcomes in terms of development indicators, the continued adherence to neoliberal policies appears to be dogmatic rather than judicious. It also calls into question the possibility of reducing poverty by half by 2015, one of the core elements of the UN's Millennium Development Goals. While poverty reduction is an avowed goal of global institutions, the perception of the organizational and productive capacities of the poor is limited, leading to policy prescriptions which stress the acquisition of more skills and better use of market opportunities.

The social transformations induced by globalization have been marked. In the Bangladesh case, it has led to the participation in the labour force, in unprecedented numbers, of young females, mostly migrants from rural areas, in the ready-made garments industry.[7] This has increased the visibility of women in the public space and paved the way for their greater participation in other spheres. Similarly significant has been the effect of global market fluctuations. Thus, the phasing out of the MFA and adjustments by domestic manufacturers of ready-made garments, from woven to higher-valued knitwear items, have currently reduced the need for female labour. In the same manner, immediately after 9/11, reduced demand for ready-made garments in the United States led to factory closures in Bangladesh. Many women workers lost their jobs as a result.

The dualistic structures of development, characteristic of Third World countries, have been entrenched and intensified by globalization and neoliberal economic policies. This is marked not only by the rural–urban divide, but also by the internal structures of cities, by services, and so on. Thus there has been a marked increase in investments in the services sector, ranging from fancy shopping malls[8] to expensive private universities and similarly expensive private medical services, at the same time as access to basic services by the poor has declined and there has been a deterioration in the services of the public sector, which is struggling to survive under expenditure cuts and an outflow of resources to the private sector. Many of the public-sector services have been taken over by NGOs, although they have, in many cases, successfully reached the poor.[9]

Globalization and neoliberalism have also restricted the ability of countries to pursue more egalitarian paths to development through distributive measures or in terms of diverse structures of ownership of productive resources. This, despite the inequalities inherent in market structures, various forms of rent-seeking through the market mechanism and inequalities in control and ownership of resources in private property relations.

And this despite the existing biases in the international trading and financial system.

Conclusion

The most articulate group initially opposing globalization and the neoliberal policies has been the trade-union lobby, given the widespread job losses in the formal sector of the economy. There has been a marked loss in trade-union strength, as well as an erosion of workers' rights, including that of lower wages and safety standards. Casualization of much of the workforce by multinational companies and the private sector has similarly eroded much of the social security benefits. In the case of India, unemployment rose in the 1990s due to deflationary policies in agriculture and public expenditure cuts following its initial IMF loan (Patnaik, 2000), while the plight of farmers has been similarly acute.

Trade unions, as well as other marginal groups, have however slowly lost their voice. This also applies to intellectual opposition, since economists in particular, perhaps lacking a sense of the history of economic philosophy, have been overawed by both the rhetoric and rationale of the World Bank and the IMF to either critique or seriously search for viable alternatives.

Ironically, the opposition to state policies, if not directly to the forces of globalization, may manifest itself in more violent forms, such as the insurgency in Nepal or in the north-eastern states of India, or in terms of attempts at domination by radical Islamic groups in Bangladesh, Afghanistan and Pakistan. This opposition is itself a result of global influences and a response to US domination of countries in the Middle East, particularly Iraq. The most recent events in Nepal and worker unrest in Bangladesh also suggest that this opposition can become more widespread.

The discussion and analysis of this chapter raises the question as to why this neoliberal agenda is being so actively pursued. The obvious answer is that this convergence to a new world order is based on political imperatives. These imperatives are an attempt to restructure and reshape the world in which US hegemony is maintained and also reflects the search for new alignments by the US and its allies in the post-cold war era. To a large extent, it also reflects the triumph of neoliberal ideas, institutions and power configurations within the US and other countries of the Centre. Interestingly, attempts to challenge this hegemony, for example by China, has also led to the embrace of the economic philosophy of neoliberalism by that country and the need to unleash market forces.

The proponents of 'globalization' as synonymous with trade liberalization and free markets are therefore at pains to chalk out the advantages and opportunities the process offers, primarily for growth and poverty reduction, ignoring the manifold social and political tensions and the limitations of the approach. The limitations too are seen in terms of *challenges* or *risks*. Current development strategy therefore boils down to maximizing the opportunities and minimizing the risks from globalization.

The diversity in patterns of development and ideologies is likely to threaten this endeavour of world dominance. For countries in the South Asia region, therefore, as elsewhere, the present reality is one that makes it necessary to strategize in relation to global politics for survival and to meet the challenges of globalization. The choice is not between autarky and openness, but in how far to accept the externally defined parameters of development.

Notes

1   For the World Bank, for instance, the 1970s was a time when Third World countries were encouraged to give priority to meeting basic needs. Thus countries were encouraged to prepare Social Accounting Matrices or SAMs, which would indicate the benefits accruing to different income and social classes from the process of economic growth. Redistribution with growth was a similar strategy to be followed by countries. This is very far from the present policy focus of the World Bank.
2   Jute mills were set up in Calcutta, but also in Dundee, Scotland.
3   This is the famous Prebisch doctrine in development economics (Thirlwall, 1994).
4   The partition of India and Pakistan into two nation states in 1947, purely on the basis of religion, and the subsequent birth of Bangladesh in 1971, asserting ethnic and political, rather than religious, identity, are examples.
5   For a description and analysis of these various conflicts see Ali (1993). The conflict in the Chittagong Hill Tracts and the north-eastern states of India are mainly between the mountain population and settlers from the plains, who were politically induced to settle in these regions.
6   Not all countries, notably India and Nepal, have availed themselves of the PRGF. Although India did not adopt the PRSP it did adopt the same policy framework for reforms.
7   There are at present 1.5 million workers in the ready-made garments industry of Bangladesh, over 70 per cent of whom are women. 87 per cent of the workers in the garment industry in Sri Lanka are also women. For India the figure is 34 per cent. The rates of participation of women workers in this industry, however, are much lower in Pakistan and Nepal, at 10 per cent and 15 per cent respectively. Thus various social factors and attitudes are important in explaining the employment of women in the export sector besides the lower opportunity costs of female labour.
8   Many of the malls have been erected in lands owned by state mills after a transfer of ownership to private hands.
9   This is particularly true for Bangladesh.

References

Ali, S. (1993) *The Fearful State*. London: Zed Books.

Asian Development Bank (2005) *Key Indicators*. Manila, Philippines: ADB.

Asiatic Society of Bangladesh (2003) *Banglapedia*. Dhaka: Asiatic Society of Bangladesh.

Fasihuddin (2000) 'International Financial Institutions' Policies and Initiatives in Social Development: A Case Study of Pakistan', in *IFI's Policies and Initiatives in Social Development in Asia and the Pacific*. Singapore: International Confederation of Free Trade Unions Asian and Pacific Regional Organisation (ICFTU-APRO).

Joshi, G. (2002) 'Overview of Competitiveness, Productivity, and Job Quality in South Asian Garment Industry', in G. Joshi (ed.), *Garment Industry in South Asia, Rags or Riches*. New Delhi: SAAT/ILO.

Khundker, N. (2000) 'International Financial Institutions' Policies and Initiatives in Social Development: A Case Study of Bangladesh', in *IFI's Policies and Initiatives in Social Development in Asia and the Pacific*. Singapore: International Confederation of Free Trade Unions Asian and Pacific Regional Organisation (ICFTU-APRO).

Nepal South Asia Centre (1998) *Nepal Human Development Report*. Kathmandu, Nepal: Nepal South Asia Centre.

Patnaik, U. (2003) 'Global Capitalism, Deflation and Agrarian Crisis in Developing Countries', Social Policy and Development Programme Paper, 15. Geneva: United Nations Research Institute for Social Development.

Pyakuryaly, B. (2000) 'International Financial Institutions' Policies and Initiatives in Social Development: A Case Study of Nepal', in *IFI's Policies and Initiatives in Social Development in Asia and the Pacific*. Singapore: International Confederation of Free Trade Unions Asian and Pacific Regional Organisation (ICFTU-APRO).

Ratnam, V. (2000) 'International Financial Institutions' Policies and Initiatives in Social Development: A Case Study of India', in *IFI's Policies and Initiatives in Social Development in Asia and the Pacific*. Singapore: International Confederation of Free Trade Unions Asian and Pacific Regional Organisation (ICFTU-APRO).

Secretary of State for International Development, UK (2000) 'Eliminating World Poverty: Making Globalization Work for the Poor', White Paper on International Development, October.

Sinnathamby, M. (2000) 'International Financial Institutions' Policies and Initiatives in Social Development: A Case Study of Sri Lanka', in *IFI's Policies and Initiatives in Social Development in Asia and the Pacific*. Singapore: International Confederation of Free Trade Unions Asian and Pacific Regional Organisation (ICFTU-APRO).

Sobhan, R. (ed.) (1991) *Structural Adjustment Policies in the Third World: Design and Experience*. Dhaka: University Press.

Sobhan, R. and N. Khundker (2001) *Globalization and Gender, Changing Patterns of Women's Employment in Bangladesh*. Dhaka: The United Press Limited.

Syeduzzaman, M. (1991) 'Bangladesh's Experience with Adjustment Policies', in R. Sobhan (ed.), *Structural Adjustment Policies in the Third World*. Dhaka: University Press Limited.

Thirlwall, A. (1994) *Growth and Development* (5th edn). London: Macmillan. Chapter 15.

Upadhya, C. (2004) 'A New Transnational Capitalist Class? Capital Flows, Business Networks and Entrepreneurs in the Indian Software Industry', *Economic and Political Weekly*, 39(48): 5141–51.

Vyas, V. (2004) 'Agrarian Distress: Strategies to Protect Vulnerable Sections', *Economic and Political Weekly*, 39(52): 5576–82.

World Bank (2004) *Trade Policies in South Asia: An Overview,* vol. II, September, Washington DC: World Bank.

World Bank (2005) 'Bangladesh PRSP Forum Economic Update, Recent Developments and Future Perspectives', Bangladesh Development Series, paper 1, November, Dhaka: World Bank.

12
A Roller Coaster Ride: A Perspective from South East Asia

Walden Bello

On the roller coaster

Perhaps an apt image for South East Asia's experience over the last 20 years is that it has been on the roller coaster of globalization interpreted here as meaning the accelerated integration of the national economy into the global economy. When massive quantities of Japanese investment streamed into the region beginning in 1985 they triggered a period of growth and prosperity, which, it seemed, would go on and on.

It didn't.

The so-called 'South East Asian Miracle' came to a screeching halt with the Asian financial crisis of 1997–8, a cataclysm brought about by the policies of capital account liberalization, followed by the more advanced economies of the region, at the strong urging of the International Monetary Fund (IMF) and the US Treasury Department. Weakened by the crisis, these economies faced attempts by the Northern powers to liberalize their trading structures and policies via the World Trade Organization and free trade agreements in the succeeding years.

These struggles over trade and trade-related policies such as intellectual property rights unfolded even as the cutting edge of global capitalism shifted from the Western Pacific rim to China. China's sizzling economy became one of the forces that brought South East Asia from relative stagnation a few years after the financial crisis. This development was, however, viewed with ambivalence by many, for it carried the risk of South East Asia becoming an appendage of the Chinese economy. Confronted by a China that was super-competitive in nearly all economic sectors, South East Asia's economies were woefully unprepared for the demands of a world dominated by big national or regional players.

It was a condition that had not been inevitable. The outcome might have been different had the governments of the region taken seriously the opportunity for regional integration and cooperation provided by the establishment of the Association of Southeast Asian Nations (ASEAN) nearly 40 years earlier. They failed to do so. In 2006, ASEAN, the grandfather of regional associations in Asia, remained a very weak entity, a hollow framework that could not hide the disarray with which its member governments confronted the multiple economic challenges faced by the region.

The developmental state in South East Asia

South East Asia's integration into today's globalized economy occurred in earnest in the decade 1985–1995. The process was export orientated and foreign investment led. But it was not integration propelled by the adoption of neoliberal policies. While the leading role of the state in development was not as prominent as in Korea and Taiwan, it was nevertheless salient.

Thailand began to register the 8 per cent to 10 per cent growth rates that dazzled the world when it was moving to a 'second stage of import substitution' – the use of trade policy to create the space for the emergence of an intermediate goods sector – during the second half of the 1980s (Sakasakul, 1992). There, the effective rate of protection for manufacturing stood at 52 per cent (Christensen, 1995: 354).

In the case of Malaysia, while it is true that some privatization and deregulation favouring private interests took place in the late 1980s, it would be a mistake to overestimate the impact of these policies. Two examples suffice to underline the central – and positive – role of state intervention. Petronas, the state oil company, was consistently rated as one of East Asia's best-run firms. And certainly, one of the most innovative – and successful – enterprises in the whole region was a state-directed joint venture between a state-owned firm and a foreign automobile transnational corporation, Mitsubishi, which produced the so-called Malaysian car, the Proton Saga. The Proton Saga now controls two-thirds of the domestic market and turns a profit for its producers. Yet its development exemplified all the so-called sins of industrial policy that neoclassical economists have warned against: discriminatory tax treatment of competitors, strategic industrial targeting or a systematic plan to manipulate market incentives to create a local car industry, and forced local sourcing of components to encourage the growth of local supplier industries (see Doner, 1987: 511–96).

As for Indonesia, some change along market-orientated lines did take place in the 1980s and 1990s, but up to the end of the Suharto period in May 1998, the state continued to be the most important actor in the economy. Hardly any of the big state enterprises passed to the private sector. State enterprises contributed about 30 per cent of total GDP and close to 40 per cent of non-agricultural GDP. Government production accounted for 50 per cent of the mining sector, 24 per cent of manufacturing, 65 per cent of banking and finance, and 50 per cent of transport and communications (see Hill, 1990: 54–5) Indeed, in the last years of the Suharto regime, there was a resurgence of statist policy in the form of trade policy, subsidies and other mechanisms directed at the creation of a heavy-industry nucleus around which to centre the economy, including the development of an automobile industry, an integrated steel complex, a shipbuilding complex and an aircraft industry.

Externally induced growth

South East Asia's remarkable high-speed growth in the period 1985–1995 did not, however, stem principally from a determined effort by state elites using trade and other policies to lift their countries by the bootstraps to industrial status, as was the case in South Korea. Nor was it due to asset and income redistribution, another key element in the economic take-off of Korea and Taiwan. The critical factor was foreign investment, specifically Japanese investment. In the period 1985–93, an estimated $51 billion worth of Japanese capital swirled through the Asian Pacific in one of the most rapid and massive outflows of foreign capital towards the developing world in recent history. The cause of the outflow was the Plaza Accord of 1985. By sharply raising the value of the yen relative to the dollar and other major hard currencies, this agreement made production in Japan prohibitive in terms of labour costs, forcing the Japanese to move the more labour-intensive processes of their manufacturing operations to low-wage areas, in particular China and Southeast Asia.

Some $15 billion worth of Japanese direct investment flowed into South East Asia between 1985 and 1990.[1] The inflow of Japanese capital allowed these countries to have access to foreign capital at a time when US and international banks were tightening up on lending owing to the Third World debt crisis. Even more important, Japanese investment allowed the core South East Asian countries to surmount recession and move on to a path of high-speed growth as they not only received Japanese capital but were transformed into essential parts of a regional economy that was being forged around a Japanese centre. As one Japanese diplomat candidly put it, 'Japan is creating an exclusive Japanese market in which Asia Pacific nations are incorporated in the so-called *keiretsu* [financial/ industrial bloc] system' (Okasaki, 1992).

Thai technocrats, for instance, had no doubts about the source of their country's dynamism. As one of them wrote, 'The current explanation of Thailand's accelerated growth was the 1985 appreciation of the value of the yen, rendering Japanese production more costly. Japanese multi-nationals were forced to look for new lower-cost production locations. In 1987, Japanese investment approvals by Thailand's Board of Investments exceeded the cumulative Japanese investment for the preceding 20 years' (TDRI, 1992: 2). The truth is that whatever might have been the Thai government's policy preference – protectionist, mercantilist or market-orientated – the vast amounts of Japanese capital coming into Thailand could not but trigger rapid growth. The same was true in two other favoured recipients of Japanese investment, Malaysia and Indonesia.

Why Japanese capital bypassed the Philippines

It was not true for the Philippines. The Japanese tsunami bypassed the Philippines, and that made all the difference. Relying on various sources, Japanese expert Kunio Yoshihara (1994: 49) estimates that between 1987 and 1991, a paltry $797 million worth of Japanese investment entered the Philippines while Thailand received $12 billion. Including invest-ment from Taiwan and Hong Kong that followed in the Japanese wake, the difference was even more marked: Thailand received $24 billion in investment during the same period, or 15 times the amount invested in the Philippines, which came to $1.6 billion. 'This difference in the flow of foreign investment from the three countries,' Yoshihara (1994: 52) rightly noted, 'produced a significant disparity in growth performance of the two countries [Philippines and Thailand] during that period.' Moreover, in contrast to Thailand, the Philippines was barely integrated into the dynamic regional economy being constructed around the Japanese centre.

Why was the Philippines bypassed? Probably on account of simple profit calculations on the part of the Japanese. The Japanese are strategic investors – that is, they invest if there is the prospect of a growing market. They are not just interested in cheap labour or using a country as an export-production platform; they are keen to exploit local markets. And in the late 1980s the Philippines was anything but an attractive market.

Owing to pressure from international creditors, the International Monetary Fund and the World Bank, repayment of the Philippines'

$26 billion external debt was the priority agenda item of the administration of President Corazon Aquino that took over power after the ousting of the Marcos dictatorship in 1986. With the country subjected to a recessionary Structural Adjustment Programme and with from a third to a half of the government budget devoted to debt repayment every year, the outcome was predictable: an average growth rate of 1.5 per cent between 1983 and 1993. The Japanese were not about to make major commitments to a strategically depressed market. And so the Japanese tsunami skirted the Philippines and deprived it of the externally induced boom experienced by its neighbours.

Financial liberalization torpedoes the South East Asian miracle

Contrary to neoliberal prescriptions, the key South East Asian economies maintained high tariffs and quantitative restrictions on imports. When it came to financial flows, however, they acquiesced to IMF and US Treasury Department pressure to liberalize their capital accounts and financial systems.

The reason for this policy inconsistency was not simply because of the pressure coming from Northern banks, fund managers and portfolio investors who wanted a piece of the 'Asian miracle'. With the externally induced boom triggered by Japanese investment, the region had become addicted to foreign capital. Thus, when Japanese direct investment inflows began to taper down in the early 1990s, South East Asian technocrats wondered about how to continue to feed their foreign capital-dependent economies. The billions of dollars in speculative capital knocking to enter appeared to offer a solution.

To attract speculative capital, Thailand's technocrats, advised by fund managers and the IMF, formulated a three-pronged strategy pioneered by Mexico in the early 1990s. They liberalized the capital account and the financial sector as a whole; maintained high domestic interest rates relative to those in the Northern money centres to lure portfolio investment and bank capital; and fixed local currency at a stable rate relative to the dollar, to ensure foreign investors against currency risk.

Portfolio investment in both equities and bonds rose, and so did credit from international banks to Thai financial institutions and enterprises, which sought to take advantage of the large differential between the relatively low rates at which they borrowed from Northern money-centred banks and the high rates at which they could relend the funds to local borrowers.

In the short term, the formula was wildly successful in attracting foreign capital. Net portfolio investment came to around $24 billion in the three years before the crisis erupted in 1997, while at least another $50 billion entered in the form of loans to Thai banks and enterprises. These results encouraged finance ministries and central banks in Kuala Lumpur, Jakarta and Manila to copy the Thai formula, with equally spectacular results. According to Washington's Institute of International Finance (1998: 3), net private flows to Malaysia, Indonesia, the Philippines, Thailand and Korea shot up from $37.9 billion in 1994 to $79.2 billion in 1995 to $97.1 billion in 1996.

In retrospect, Thailand illustrated the fatal flaws of a development model based on huge, rapid infusions of foreign capital. First, just as in Mexico a few years earlier, there was a basic contradiction between encouraging foreign capital inflows and keeping an exchange rate that would make the country's exports competitive in world markets. The former demanded a currency pegged to the dollar at a stable rate in order to draw in foreign investors. With the dollar appreciating in 1995 and 1996, so did the pegged South East Asian currencies. Consequently, the international prices of South East Asian exports rose.

The second problem was that the bulk of the funds coming in consisted of speculative capital seeking high, quick returns. With little regulation of its movements, foreign capital did not gravitate to the domestic manufacturing sector or to agriculture, which were considered low-yield sectors that would provide a decent rate of return only after a long gestation period. The high-yield sectors with a quick turnaround time to which foreign investment and foreign credit inevitably gravitated were the stock market, consumer finance and, in particular, real estate development. In Bangkok, at the height of the boom of the early 1990s, land values were higher than in urban California.

Not surprisingly, a glut in real estate developed rapidly. Bangkok led the way with $20 billion worth of new commercial and residential space unsold by 1996. Foreign banks had competed to push loans on to Thai banks, finance corporations and enterprises in the boom years of the early 1990s. By the middle of the decade, lenders woke up to the realization that their borrowers were loaded with non-performing loans.

Alarm bells began to sound. The flat export growth rates for 1996 (an astonishing zero growth in both Malaysia and Thailand) and burgeoning current account deficits were worrisome. Since a foreign exchange surplus earned through the consistently rising exports of goods and services was the ultimate guarantee that the foreign debt contracted by the private sector would be repaid, the slowing of exports was a blow to investor confidence. What the investors failed to realize was that the very policy of maintaining a strong currency, calculated to draw them in, was also the cause of the export collapse.

By 1997 it was time to get out of the region, many investors concluded. Because of the liberalization of the capital account, there were no mechanisms to slow down the exit of funds. With hundreds of billions of Thai baht chasing a limited number of dollars, the outflow of capital could be highly destabilizing. Many big institutional players and banks began to leave, but what converted a nervous departure into a catastrophic stampede was the speculative activity of the hedge funds and other arbitrageurs. Gambling on the authorities' eventual devaluation of the overvalued baht, they accelerated the process by unloading huge quantities of the Thai currency in search of dollars.

In the Thai debacle, hedge funds played a key role. Specializing in combining short and long positions in different currencies, bonds and stocks in order to net a profit from the combined transactions, these funds had been attacking the Thai baht occasionally since 1995. But the most spectacular assault occurred on 10 May 1997, when in just one day, hedge funds are said to have bet US$10 billion against the baht in a global attack (Khantong, 1998). Under such massive attacks, the Bank of Thailand lost practically all its $38.7 billion of foreign exchange reserves between the end of 1996 and mid 1997. On 2 July, the decade-long peg of 25 baht to the dollar was abandoned, and the Thai currency lost over 50 per cent of its value over the next few months.

Jakarta, Kuala Lumpur and Manila experienced the same conjunction of massive capital inflow, property glut and rise in the current account deficit. The nervousness had existed there, too, but the baht collapse was what triggered mass panic and exit from these three markets. As Jeffrey Winters (1998) describes it:

Suddenly, you receive disturbing news that Thailand is in serious trouble, and you must decide immediately what to do with your Malaysian investments. It is in this moment that the escape psychology and syndrome begins. First, you immediately wonder if the disturbing new information leaking out about Thailand applies to Malaysia as well. You think it does not, but you are not sure. Second, you must instantly think about how other EMFMs [emerging market financial managers] and independent investors are going to react, and of course they are thinking simultaneously about how you are going to react. And third, you are fully aware, as are other managers, that the first ones who sell as a market turns negative will be hurt the least, and the ones in the middle and end will lose most value from their portfolio – and [are] likely to be fired from their position as an EMFM as well. In a situation of low systemic transparency, the sensible reaction will be to sell and escape. Notice that even if you use good connections in the Malaysian government and business community to receive highly reliable information that the country is healthy and is not suffering from the same problems as Thailand, you will still sell and escape. Why? Because you cannot ignore the likely behavior of all the other investors. And since they do not have access to the reliable information you have, there is a high probability that their uncertainty will lead them to choose to escape. If you hesitate while they rush to sell their shares, the market will drop rapidly, and the value of your portfolio will start to evaporate before your eyes.

As the region's economies unravelled, the US and the IMF derailed a Japan-led proposal to create an Asian Monetary Fund (AMF), which could have allowed countries whose currencies were being targeted to access the reserves of the cash-rich Asian countries with minimum conditionalities. With the AMF threat defused, the IMF assembled multibillion 'rescue packages', but these were meant to enable countries to meet their financial commitments to the creditors pounding on their gates, not stabilize the economies in crisis. Moreover, to access these loans, governments were forced to adopt expenditure-slashing economic programmes that mistakenly identified inflation as the threat to be thwarted and thus simply accelerated the economic free-fall.

Aftermath of the crisis

One of the key consequences of the financial debacle is that it led to South East Asia's distancing itself from the IMF and to a crisis of the IMF itself. Prime Minister Mohamad Mahathir of Malaysia broke with the IMF when he imposed capital controls at the height of the crisis. Vehemently opposed to it at the time, the Fund eventually conceded that this move stabilized the economy at a critical period (Soros, 2002: 119). Indeed, of all the key South East Asian economies, Malaysia recovered the fastest, from a − 7.4 per cent GDP growth rate in 1998 to 6.1 per cent in 1999.

The IMF (1999: 62) eventually acknowledged – though in euphemistic terms – that its reliance on fiscal belt-tightening to stabilize the currency and restore investor confidence in Thailand and Indonesia was mistaken: 'The thrust of fiscal policy . . . turned out to be substantially different . . .

because . . . the original assumptions for economic growth, capital flows, and exchange rates . . . were proved drastically wrong.' This was, of course, a ghastly mistake – one that drove Indonesia's GDP down by 13 per cent in 1998, Malaysia's by 7.4 per cent, Thailand's by 10.5 per cent and the Philippines' by 0.6 per cent. In the space of a few weeks, 22 million Indonesians and one million Thais found themselves to have fallen under the poverty line (Chomtongdi, 2000: 18, 22).

Not surprisingly, in Thailand, Thaksin Shinawatra ran on an anti-IMF platform in 2001 and won, and he proceeded to adopt fiscally expansionary, Keynesian policies that helped restore economic growth, though not at the pre-crisis rates. In 2003, Thaksin declared that Thailand had paid off all its debt to the IMF and declared 'financial independence'. The Philippines refrained from incurring new loans from the Fund, and in May 2006, Indonesia said it would be able to pay off all its debts to the IMF in two years' time. India and China, which had a ringside view of the destructive impact of the IMF's policies, also skirted the Fund.

This 'boycott' turned out to be Asia's 'revenge' on the Fund. Indeed, the Asian financial crisis and its aftermath turned out to be the 'Stalingrad' of the IMF, a debacle from which it never recovered. It translated not only into a crisis of legitimacy but also a budget crisis, since over the last two decades the IMF's operations have been increasingly funded from loan repayments by its developing country clients rather than from the contributions of wealthy Northern governments, which deliberately shifted the burden of sustaining the institution to the borrowers. The situation worsened when Argentina and Brazil paid off all their debts to the IMF in 2006 and also declared financial sovereignty. The upshot of these developments is that payments of charges and interests, according to Fund projections, will be cut by more than half, from \$3.19 billion in 2005 to \$1.39 billion in 2006, and again by half to \$635 million in 2009 (Woods, 2006: 2).

For both the Fund and the more developed South East Asian countries, then, the Asian financial crisis was a watershed. For the latter, it ended the long period of high-speed growth of the South East Asian 'tiger' economies. Recession, then unimpressive and erratic growth in what were once the region's more advanced big economies – Indonesia, Thailand, Malaysia and the Philippines – marked the succeeding decade. Domestic demand became the main stimulus of economic growth in these countries for a few years after the crisis, though the opportunities here were limited by the absence of significant measures of income and asset redistribution. Large-scale poverty made a comeback in most countries, and income inequality increased in all.

In the aftermath of the financial crisis, the weakened states of the region faced increased pressures to deregulate, privatize and dismantle trade barriers, with neoliberal commitments being key components of the IMF stabilization packages for Indonesia and Thailand, as the US, in particular, took advantage of the crisis to advance its 15-year-old effort to pry open South East Asian markets and liberalize investment laws for its corporations.

Adjusting South East Asia

In Thailand, local authorities agreed to remove all limitations on foreign ownership of Thai financial firms, accelerate the privatization of state enterprises and revise bankruptcy laws along lines demanded by foreign creditors. As the US Trade Representative noted, the Thai government's 'commitments to restructure public enterprises and accelerate privatisation of certain key sectors – including energy, transportation, utilities, and communications – which will enhance market-driven competition and deregulation – [are expected] to create new business opportunities for US firms' (Barshefsky, 1998). In Indonesia, said the same official:

> the IMF's conditions for granting a massive stabilisation package addressed practices that have long been the subject of this [Clinton] Administration's bilateral trade policy . . . Most notable in this respect is the commitment by Indonesia to eliminate the tax, tariff, and credit privileges provided to the national car project. Additionally, the IMF program seeks broad reform of Indonesian trade and investment policy, like the aircraft project, monopolies and domestic trade restrictive practices, that stifle competition by limiting access for foreign goods and services.
>
> (Barshefsky, 1998)

The national car project and the plan to set up a passenger aircraft industry had elicited the strong disapproval of Detroit and Boeing, respectively.

Skirmishes with the WTO

The late 1990s and the first five years of the millennium saw the spectre of the WTO cast its shadow over the region. Only Thailand, an agro-export power whose commercial interests would benefit from freer trade in agriculture, was enthusiastic about participation in the new global trade body, which replaced the General Agreement on Tariffs and Trade (GATT) in

1995. Export-orientated Malaysia was more circumspect, supporting trade liberalization but opposing Northern efforts to extend liberalization to 'trade-related' issues such as investment, competition policy, government procurement and trade facilitation. Indonesia was identified by a World Bank study as one of the expected losers in global trade liberalization.

The case of the Philippines was paradigmatic not only for the region but for the developing world. There, liberalization of agricultural trade via the WTO's Agreement on Agriculture meant opening up the country's market to cheap subsidized grain, produce and foods from, among others, the United States and the European Union. The results were predictable. During the national debate on whether or not to ratify the WTO, the government admitted that 350,000 farmers would be displaced annually, with 45,000 of them being corn farmers.[2] Over the next few years, domestic corn growing, in particular, suffered as the country eliminated quotas on the entry of foreign corn. While production remained stagnant, land devoted to corn across the country contracted sharply from 3,149,300 hectares in 1993 to 2,510,300 hectares in 2000.[3]

On the other hand, the shift of farmers to higher value added crops, that neoliberal economists promised, did not occur; nor did an expansion of Philippine agricultural exports, which was supposed to be one of the benefits of the adherence to the WTO Agreement on Agriculture. The value of exports registered no significant movement, rising from $1.9 billion in 1993 to $2.3 billion in 1997, then declining to $1.9 billion in 2000. In contrast, massive importation, the big fear of WTO critics, became a reality, with the value of imports almost doubling from $1.6 billion in 1993 to $3.1 billion in 1997 and registering $2.7 billion in 2000. The passage of the Philippines from a net food exporting country to a net food importing country was underlined by the movement from an agricultural trade surplus of $292 million in 1993 to a deficit of $764 million in 1997 and $794 million in 2002.[4]

Faced with massive displacements in agriculture, Indonesia and the Philippines took the lead in forming the 'Group of 33' (G 33) in the lead-up to the WTO Ministerial in Cancun in September 2003. Though they were not big agricultural exporters, agriculture was the lifeblood of these economies, which faced massive displacements of agricultural labour from WTO liberalization. The most cogent statement of the concerns of this group was put forward by a Philippine delegate at one of the sessions of the WTO Agricultural Committee in the lead up to the Cancun Ministerial:

> Our agricultural sectors that are strategic to our food and livelihood security and rural employment have already been destabilized as our

small producers are being slaughtered by the gross unfairness of the international trading environment. Even as I speak, our small producers are being slaughtered in our own markets [and] even the more resilient and efficient are in distress.[5]

The key demands that came to be advanced by the G 33 was the exemption from liberalization of what they termed 'special agricultural products' (SPs) that were essential to food security and the establishment of 'special safeguard mechanisms' (SSMs) such as tariff increases that would match the levels of subsidization of agricultural products in developed countries.

Courted with FTAs

As resistance from developing countries challenged and slowed down the WTO, South East Asian countries became the objects of pressures to sign on to bilateral free trade agreements (FTAs), which many powerful states saw as an alternative route to free trade compared to the lumbering multilateral trade body. The preference for FTAs was, in fact, explicitly stated by then US Trade Representative Robert Zoellick (2003) shortly after the collapse of the WTO's fifth ministerial in Cancun: 'As the WTO ponders the future, the US will not wait; we will move towards free trade with can-do countries.'

An FTA between the US and Vietnam was signed in 2000, followed by one between the US and Singapore in 2003. A move to conclude an FTA with Thailand, however, was delayed by strong mass resistance. The US–Singapore FTA put Thai activists on alert that the likely provisions of the FTA being negotiated in secret with Thailand were likely to be 'TRIPs-plus', that is, more restrictive than the WTO Trade Related Intellectual Property Rights Agreement. Restrictions contained in the US–Singapore trade included limitations on a country's ability to do compulsory licensing or the government's allowing firms to break a patent monopoly in the public interest; extension of a drug company patent term beyond 20 years; and a five-year term of data exclusivity.

Of special concern to the Thais was the threat this posed to the country's HIV-AIDS treatment programme. By allowing Thai firms to do compulsory licensing in the interests of public health, the government facilitated access to relatively affordable medicines to over 80,000 people living with HIV/AIDS. According to an authoritative source:

[I]f the US provisions are accepted, thereby ruling out the generic competition that could drive down prices for newer patented drugs, the Thai government will not be able to continue to expand access to treatment and provide effective second-line drug combinations which are needed when the initial drug combinations no longer work. The current cost of one second-line drug is over $3,500 per patient per year – nearly ten times the cost of the most commonly-used first-line triple combination.

(Médecins sans Frontières, 2006)

Pressure from civil society groups, which took the form of a demonstration of some 10,000 people near the negotiations venue in Chiang Mai on 9 January 2006 forced Thailand's chief negotiator to resign and contributed to an impasse in the negotiations.

China: threat or opportunity?

Thailand's sensitivity to FTAs was sharpened by an 'early harvest' FTA negotiated between China and Thailand in 2003. In the experimental arrangement the two countries agreed that tariffs on more than 200 items of vegetables, and fruits would be immediately eliminated. Under the agreement, Thailand would export tropical fruits to China while winter fruits from China would be eligible for the zero-tariff deal. The expectations of mutual benefit evaporated after a few months, however, with most Thai commentators admitting that Thailand had got the short end of the stick. As one assessment put it, 'despite the limited scope of the Thailand–China early harvest agreement, it has had an appreciable impact in the sectors covered. The *appreciable impact* has been to wipe out northern Thai producers of garlic and red onions and to cripple the sale of temperate fruit and vegetables from the Royal projects' (Chanyapate, 2005).

The Thai 'early harvest' experience created consternation throughout South East Asia, since China was seeking FTAs with a number of ASEAN countries, looking for the best terms from each of the targeted governments. It stoked fears of ASEAN becoming a dumping ground for China's extremely competitive industrial and agricultural sectors, which could drive down prices owing to cheap urban labour that was continually replenished by dirt cheap labour streaming from the countryside. People wondered if FTAs with China would not simply legalise the dumping of Chinese goods, a great deal of which were already being smuggled across their borders.

Fears of being swamped by Chinese goods were coupled with worries that China was causing local and foreign manufacturers to phase out their operations in relatively high wage South East Asia and moving them to

China. There seemed to be some support for this. When China devalued the yuan in 1994, it was able to divert some foreign direct investment away from South East Asia (Ariff, 2001: 65). The trend of ASEAN losing ground to China accelerated after the financial crisis. In 2000, foreign direct investment in ASEAN shrank to 10 per cent of all foreign direct investment in developing Asia, down from 30 per cent in the mid 1990s. The decline continued in 2001 and 2002, with the United Nations *World Investment Report* (UN, 2003: 41) attributing the trend partly to 'increased competition from China'. Japanese investors were the most dynamic foreign investors in South East Asia, so there was great apprehension in the key Asian countries when an official survey (UN, 2002: 44) revealed that 57 per cent of Japanese manufacturing TNCs found China to be more attractive than the ASEAN-4 (Thailand, Malaysia, Indonesia and the Philippines).

Yet the relationship with China was not one way. Demand from China's red hot economy was a key factor in South East Asian growth beginning around 2003, after a period of low growth dependent on domestic demand. Indeed, this was also the case for Korea and Japan. For Asia as a whole, in 2003 and the beginning of 2004, noted an UNCTAD (2004: 20) report, 'China was a major engine of growth for most of the economies in the region. The country's imports accelerated even more than its exports, with a large proportion of them coming from the rest of Asia.' By the first decade of the millennium, the cutting edge of global capitalism had definitively moved from the Pacific Rim to China . . . and the Chinese locomotive was pulling almost all countries in the South East Asian region with it.

In any event, China moved aggressively to clinch free trade agreements with ASEAN countries. At the 10th ASEAN Summit held in Vientiane, Laos, in November 2004, the ASEAN countries issued a joint statement expressing agreement of the goal of removing all tariffs between ASEAN and China by the year 2010. A positive spin on the China–ASEAN Free Trade Agreement was provided by Philippine President Gloria Macapagal-Arroyo, who hailed the emergence of a 'formidable regional grouping' that would rival the United States and the European Union.

The benefits to China of an FTA with ASEAN were clear. The aim of the strategy, according to Chinese economist Angang Hu (2004: 59), was to more fully integrate China into the global economy as the 'centre of the world's manufacturing industry'. A central part of the plan was to open up ASEAN markets to Chinese manufactured products. In light of growing protectionist sentiment in the US and the European Union, South East Asia, which absorbed only 8.2 per cent of China's exports, was seen as an important market with tremendous potential to absorb more Chinese goods. Also key, noted Hu (2004: 53), was the Chinese government's plan for attracting investment 'into the western region of China from ASEAN nations, weaving the western region more thoroughly into the fabric of regional and international trade'.

Despite President Arroyo's brave words, how ASEAN would benefit from the ASEAN–China FTA was much less clear. It was highly doubtful that China would depart from what Hu (2004: 52) has characterized as China's 'half open model', which is marked by 'open or free trade on the export side and protectionism on the import side'.

Certainly, the benefits would not come in labour-intensive manufacturing, where China enjoyed an unbeatable edge by the constant downward pressure on wages exerted by migrants from a seemingly inexhaustible rural workforce that makes an average of $285 a year. Certainly not in high tech, since even the US and Japan were scared of China's remarkable ability to move very quickly into high tech industries even as it consolidates its edge in labour-intensive production. Certainly not in labour services, since China could produce engineers, nurses and domestic workers that would perform the same work but at lower wages than their ASEAN counterparts. For instance, China's deployment of seafarers threatened the Philippines premier position as a source of seamen globally.

Agriculture? But, as the 'early harvest' experience with Thailand showed, China was clearly super-competitive in a vast array of agricultural products from temperate crops to semi-tropical produce, and in agricultural processing. Vietnam and Thailand might be able to hold their own in rice production, Indonesia and Vietnam in coffee, and the Philippines in coconut and coconut products, but there might not be many more products to add to the list. Raw materials? Yes, of course, Indonesia and Malaysia had oil that was in scarce supply in China, and Malaysia did have rubber and tin and the Philippines had palm oil and metals. But a second look made one wonder if the relationship with China was not reproducing the old colonial division of labour, whereby low-value-added natural resources and agricultural products were shipped to the centre while the South East Asian economies absorbed high-value-added manufactures from Europe and the United States.

Thus, drastic imbalance was likely to be the result of the China–ASEAN FTAs. But, from the point of view of many analysts, the blame for this was not largely China's. China was simply trying to exploit its advantages. The responsibility was largely ASEAN's. China's rise merely exacerbated ASEAN's fundamental problems, which its member governments had long placed on the backburner. The South East Asian nations had over 30 years to build an 'ASEAN house', and they had squandered the opportunity. Had

ASEAN evolved along the lines envisioned by its founders, it would not have displayed the disarray with which its members confronted the Asian financial crisis, the WTO, FTAs and the rise of China. To this dismal story we now turn.

ASEAN in the doldrums

Founded in 1967, ASEAN's initial economic aspirations were expressed in the Kansu-Robinson Report produced under the auspices of the then Economic Commission for Asia and the Far East (ECAFE), which envisioned an integrated trading zone that would serve as a platform for regional import substitution (Soesastro, 2001: 292–3). Cooperative industrialization via coordinated trade policy was the essence of the original ASEAN idea.

During its first two decades ASEAN was hijacked by politics. The main function ASEAN played in the 1970s and 1980s was to serve as the front-line formation against 'Vietnamese expansionism', in alliance with China and the United States. Later, 'ASEAN Brotherhood' was transformed by the South East Asian governments into solidarity against external criticism of human rights abuses. Dominated by strongmen like Suharto in Indonesia, Lee Kwan Yew in Singapore, and Marcos in the Philippines, ASEAN acquired the reputation of being Dictators Inc. in the 1980s.

ASEAN as an economic framework contributed little to the dynamic growth of the South East Asian economies in the late 1980s. Regional economic integration was not, however, completely forgotten. The ASEAN Industrial Projects (AIP) Scheme aimed at building one capital-intensive industry per country that would service the regional market. The ASEAN Industrial Complementation (AICO) programme offered regional incentives for enterprises that built complementary transborder facilities, with each country assigned a particular phase of production. The AIP failed to take off because it involved market sharing, 'which ASEAN members were not ready to accept' (Soesastro, 2001: 293). As for AICO, it was mainly Japanese automobile and electronic transnationals that took advantage of the incentives the plan offered when they split up and relocated different parts of the labour-intensive phases of their operations from Japan to different South East Asian countries to offset the rising value of the yen in the late 1980s. Thus, some industrial integration took place across borders, but this was not the integration of ASEAN enterprises dreamt of by the founders of ASEAN but one driven by the logic of profitability of Japanese transnationals.

When the US-backed Asia Pacific Economic Cooperation (APEC) threatened to make the ASEAN economic project irrelevant by creating a trans-Pacific free trade area in the early 1990s, the ASEAN governments set up the ASEAN Free Trade Area (AFTA) to initiate a process of tariff reduction leading to a single market. Commitment slackened, however, in the mid 1990s, when the APEC project fizzled out and the threat from an alternative regional arrangement disappeared. Later in the decade, governments sought to give a new momentum to AFTA by bringing forward the completion of tariff reductions on products in its 'Inclusion List' from 2008 to 2003. There have been difficulties meeting this revised schedule, with Malaysia, for instance, seeking an extension of tariff liberalization for its auto industry. Moreover, some 26 per cent of ASEAN tariff lines – those of strategic value to the different countries – are either in the 'Temporary Exclusion List', 'General Exclusion List', or 'Sensitive List', meaning tariff reductions are either deferred indefinitely or permanently.

With compliance slackening, the ASEAN leaders meeting in Vientiane (Laos) in November 2004 drew up yet another declaration, this time to abolish tariffs in 11 'priority sectors' by 2007. The end-point of the liberalization process is supposed to be 2020, when ASEAN will be a single market and a single, integrated production base. Not surprisingly, the new benchmark has evoked scepticism. Why has ASEAN regional integration remained so distant after nearly 40 years? Aside from its having been overpoliticized, ASEAN as an economic project has had three fundamental flaws.

First, the ASEAN governments have had no common vision of the goal of a free trade area. While some governments are guided perhaps unconsciously by the vision of the original Kansu-Robinson report, which saw the creation of a platform for accelerating and deepening the industrialization of the region by maintaining barriers to the entry of strategic goods and services from third countries, others saw regional free trade in neoliberal terms, along the lines articulated by neoclassical economist Mohamed Ariff (2001: 59): 'The long-run goal should be to liberalise trade globally without discrimination. It is important to view AFTA as a transition or stepping stone towards that objective. AFTA can be used as a *training ground* where the ASEAN countries can learn to compete with one another before they compete in the international market place.' Needless to say, these are two different visions of the objective of a trading arrangement that are incompatible.

Second, ASEAN has remained principally a project of government leaders and technocrats, with national industrial elites evincing little interest in industrial integration and jealously guarding their markets. Indeed, as late as 2001, intra-ASEAN exports accounted for only 20 per cent of ASEAN's total exports – the same proportion as in 1970! Japan and the US remain overwhelmingly the main trading partners of ASEAN's member countries.

Third, ASEAN has remained a technocratic project, with little effort to make it a popular democratic enterprise. Not surprisingly, 'ASEAN brotherhood' (for ASEAN elites do not speak of 'ASEAN sisterhood') has very little resonance at the grassroots. To build an economic project on a fragile political entity that most South East Asians have probably not heard of, much less affectively identify with, is courting failure.

In short, ASEAN remains a very weak economic entity, despite the flurry of economic diplomacy seemingly centred on ASEAN, such as the ASEAN-Plus-Three formation for financial cooperation and the Asian Economic Summit. Moving quickly to a free trade agreement with China would be to court disaster. Even if many exemptions from steep tariff reductions are agreed upon by China, ASEAN would be locked into a process where the only direction that barriers to super-competitive Chinese industrial and agricultural goods would go is downwards. An ASEAN–China FTA at this juncture can only lead to de-industrialization and an agricultural crisis in ASEAN.

The challenge to the ASEAN governments in 2006 was to either take the 40-year-old project of regional integration seriously or face the strong possibility of being reduced to appendages of the burgeoning Chinese economy. In short, ASEAN as an economic framework may have contributed little to South East Asia's dynamic growth in the 1980s and 1990s, but in the current period, where the dynamo of global capitalism has moved from the Pacific Rim to China, ASEAN as a project of regional integration has become necessary to avoid the steady marginalization of its member economies.

Conclusion

As in the early 1980s, before the massive inflow of Japanese capital, South East Asia today is at a crossroads. From the red hot wonders of the world economy, the more advanced economies of the region have exhibited unimpressive performances over the last six years, with all of them still burdened with the consequences of the Asian financial crisis.

Large-scale poverty has made a comeback and inequality is at its highest in years. The engine of growth in most of the economies of the region after the crisis was domestic demand, but with few reforms in income and asset redistribution, the possibilities of squeezing growth from this area were limited. In the last three years, the enormous demand of the Chinese economy has become the main source of growth of the South East Asian economies.

The rise of China and the relative stagnation of South East Asia pose a grand challenge to the region. Can it avoid becoming an appendage of the Chinese economy? The answer probably lies in what use its member countries make of ASEAN. Will they let ASEAN remain what it has been so far, a fragile economic scaffolding with little substance? Or will they finally turn to the hard task of making it a regional economic bloc, where, in accordance with the vision that originally inspired it, trade policy – along with technology policy, foreign investment policy and incomes policy – are coordinated to consciously bring about the larger objective of cooperative regional development?

Notes

1   Figures from the Japanese Ministry of Finance.
2   This was admitted by proponents of ratification of the WTO Accord in television debates in 1994.
3   *Selected Agricultural Statistics, 1998, 2002* (Quezon City: Department of Agriculture, 1998, 2002).
4   Ibid.
5   Submission of the Republic of the Philippines, WTO Committee on Agriculture, Geneva, 1 July 2003.

References

Ariff, M. (2001) 'Trade, Investment and Interdependence', in Simon Tay *et al.* (eds), *Reinventing ASEAN*. Singapore: Institute of Southeast Asian Studies.
Barshefsky, C. (1998) Testimony before the House of Representatives Ways and Means Subcommittee, 24 February.
Chanyapate, C. (2005) 'Dangerous Advice on Free Trade Pacts', available at http://www.bangkokpost.com/News/20Sep2005_opin24.php.
Chomtongdi, J.-C. (2000) 'The IMF's Asian Legacy', in *Prague 2000: Why We Need to Decommission the IMF and World Bank*. Bangkok: Focus on the Global South.
Christensen, S. (1995) 'Thailand: The Institutional and Political Underpinnings of Growth', in D. Leipziger (ed.), *Lessons from East Asia*. Ann Arbor, MI: University of Michigan.
Doner, R. (1987) 'Domestic Coalitions and Japanese Auto Firms in Southeast Asia', Dissertation, University of California at Berkeley, Berkeley, California.
Hill, H. (1990) 'Ownership in Indonesia: Who Owns What and Does It Matter?', in H. Hill and T. Hull (eds), *Indonesia Assessment 1990*. Canberra: Research School of Pacific Studies, Australian National University.
Hu, A. (2004) 'A Free Trade Agreement Policy for the Northeast Asian Countries and ASEAN: A View from the People's Republic of China', in H. Hira Kawa and Y. Kim (eds), *Co-Design for a New East Asia After the Crisis*, Nagoya, Japan: Economic Research Center, Nagoya University.
Institute of International Finance (1998) *Capital Flows and Emerging Market Economies*. Washington, DC: Institute of International Finance.
International Monetary Fund (1999) 'IMF-Supported Programs in Indonesia, Korea, and Thailand', IMF occasional paper, 178, Washington, DC, 30 June.

Khantong, T. (1998) 'The Currency War is the Information War', talk at the seminar Workshop on 'Improving the Flow of Information in a Time of Crisis: The Challenge to the Southeast Asian Media', Subic, Philippines, 29–31 October.

Médecins sans Frontières (2006) 'US-Thailand Free Trade Agreement: MSF Calls on Thailand to Protect Access to Medicines in the Face of US Pressure', MSF Press Release, 11 January.

Okasaki, H. (1992) 'New Strategies toward Super-Asian Bloc', *This Is* (Tokyo), August, pp. 42–90, reproduced in *Foreign Broadcast Information Service Daily Report: East Asia Supplement*, 7 October, p. 18.

Sakasakul, C. (1992) *Lessons from the World Bank's Experience of Structural Adjustment Loans (SALs): A Case Study of Thailand*. Bangkok: Thailand Development Research Institute.

Soesastro, H. (2001) 'ASEAN in 2030: The Long View' in S. Tay *et al.* (eds), *Reinventing ASEAN*, Singapore: Institute of Southeast Asian Studies.

Soros, G. (2002) *On Globalization*. New York: Public Affairs.

Thailand Development Research Institute – (TDRI) (1992) *Thailand's Economic Structure: Summary Report*. Bangkok: TDRI.

United Nations (2002) *World Investment Report 2002: Transnational Corporations and Export Competitiveness*. Geneva: United Nations

United Nations (2003) *World Investment Report 2003*. New York: United Nations.

United Nations Conference on Trade and Development (UNCTAD) (2004) *Trade and Development Report 2004*. Geneva: UNCTAD

Winters, J. (1998) 'The Financial Crisis in Southeast Asia', paper delivered at the Conference on the Asian Crisis, Murdoch University, Fremantle, Western Australia, August.

Woods, N. (2006) 'The Globalizers in Search of a Future: Four Reasons why the IMF and World Bank Must Change, and Four Ways They Can', Brief, CDG (Center for Global Development) April.

Yoshihara, K. (1994) *The Nation and Economic* Growth. Kuala Lumpur: Oxford University Press.

Zoellick, R. (2003) US Trade Representative Press Conference, Cancun, Mexico, 14 September.

13

From Benign Force to Contested Terrain: A Perspective from East Asia

Kwong-leung Tang

Globalization has generated much interest in East Asia in the last decade. Its impacts and processes have been extensively debated among scholars, states and international organizations since the Asian financial crisis. Few would disagree that it is a multidimensional concept, lacking a unanimously agreed meaning. For East Asia, globalization is mainly seen in economic and political terms: in particular, economic globalization is perceived to be a hotly contested terrain in which the idea of market supremacy clashes with that of the state rather than as a neutral process. On this battleground, neoliberal economists seek to establish the claim that economic liberalization promotes growth and reduces poverty, due to a) the intensifying competition between domestic and external economic actors and b) increased exposure of management and workers to improved practices. They point out that liberalization of trade and investment regimes by developing countries has attracted more direct foreign and portfolio investment, which in turn accelerates the rate of economic growth and, the assumption is, lifts the poor out of poverty. Contrary to this claim, critics contend that a neoliberal regime of liberalization only fosters conditions that ensures the continued production of poverty in the developing countries by shrinking their prospects of economic growth (Nuruzzaman, 2005).

Without question, Asia has been the scene of rapid economic development. Neoliberal thinkers see East Asia's economic prosperity (and the alleged arrival of 'the Asian century') as heralding the beneficial impacts of trade liberalization. However, one must not envisage economic globalization simply as the rapid acceleration of the flow(s) of goods, services and capital across national borders over the last 50 years. It also involves the expansion of capitalist economies that, ultimately, supplant local control. Such processes are directed by the ideology of neoliberalism: countries are encouraged to exploit all their resources, and public goods are to be opened up to complete privatization (Foster, 2003).

While globalization is widely acknowledged, neoliberal arguments and their critiques were not seriously debated prior to 1997 in most parts of East Asia. One reason was that many East Asian nations had been prey to colonial powers since the 15th century. Even after World War II, when most of these nations gained independence, these issues did not surface immediately. Following the post-war reconstruction of Japan, East Asian countries such as Hong Kong, Korea, Singapore and Taiwan were transformed. The adoption of export-led, industrialization-based approaches to economic development produced rapid rates of economic growth in the region, which resulted in significant increases in per-capita incomes. Therefore, longtime economic realities were not critically examined. The onset of the 1997 Asian financial crisis changed this, however, as it more fully showed the destructive force of economic globalization. To some extent, it even revealed the fallacies of the neoliberal argument. After the Asian crisis, the problems of poverty and income inequality were either severe or worsening in countries like Hong Kong, Taiwan, Singapore and South Korea. Rural poverty plagued countries like China, Japan, Taiwan and South Korea. The crisis aftermath also showed that trade liberalization, far from alleviating poverty, only facilitated capital accumulation by the transnational capitalist class at the global level. In the end, we see that globalization can never be a benign force.

This chapter, then, looks at how globalization has challenged and impacted East Asia (in particular Japan, China, Hong Kong, Korea, Taiwan, Singapore) over time and at how states responded to neoliberal globalization after the Asian financial crisis. East Asia had experienced globalization in the form of imperialism in the past, with negative results. This was imperialism by outside powers as well as Japan from within the region. However, in the post-1945 period, countries gradually adopted the policy of integrating into the international economy (first Japan, then South Korea, Taiwan, Hong Kong and then China). However, they did this on the basis of the developmental state and export-led growth (rather than following a neoliberal path). This led to some spectacular economic results and international integration was seen as a benign force. However, the Asian financial crisis changed all that and globalization is now seen as much more contested. This contestation comes in two forms: from civil society and from states adopting different responses. With respect to the latter, Japan, Hong Kong and Singapore are taking a neoliberal response whereas South Korea, China and Taiwan are being much more cautious in the embrace of neoliberalism.

East Asia and imperialism

East Asia is large and geographically diverse, and there is no consensus on which states fall under the rubric of 'East Asia'. Many scholars include these key states: China, Korea (North and South), Japan, Hong Kong, Taiwan, Macau and Mongolia. Others would add Malaysia, Philippines, Vietnam, Laos, Cambodia, Thailand, Indonesia and Burma. On the other hand, a cultural definition of East Asia would certainly incorporate the nation state of Singapore, which has a strong affinity with the Chinese societies of China, Hong Kong and Taiwan. In this chapter, we will focus on China, Japan and the four Asian tigers (Hong Kong, South Korea, Taiwan and Singapore) and consider some of the others only briefly.

First and foremost, East Asia has a number of distinctive features. It has the world's most populous state (China), the world's second-largest economy (Japan), and the world's economically freest states (Hong Kong and Singapore). In their own ways, small and peripheral states like North Korea, Mongolia and Macau are distinctive as well. Since 1945, North Korea has distanced itself from the world, while Mongolia and Macau are much less secluded but, due to their location or physical size, are often not treated in many discussions of East Asia. One trait is common to most, if not all Asian nations: they suffered in the age of colonialism and imperialism.

If we assume that globalization means a breakdown of international borders (Ericson and Doyle, 1999) yielding enhanced human interaction within a one-world system (Giddens, 1999), then East Asia has always been 'globalized'. Historically, scholars acknowledge both the existence of an early-modern global economy and China's role as a crucial component of it, corresponding roughly to the Ming/Qing dynasties in China (from the 15th to the early 20th centuries). This did *not* mean that there was a single world system grounded on an integrated division of labour centred on China (Hung, 2001). In the beginning, there was intensive trade between Europe and China, institutionalized under a system of ports of trade that kept the political economy of China intact.

That stability would not remain forever. In the 19th century, there was a marked transformation as East Asia became the target of Western powers (and later Japan). According to some theorists, imperialism and its corollary colonialism, were a kind of distorted capitalism which, through the export of capital, enabled imperial powers to benefit from colonial regions to offset a lack of domestic investment opportunities. Many East Asian nations had been under the aegis of colonial powers. For instance, Imperial China (the Qing dynasty under Manchu rule) was strong until the middle of the 19th century, when it was defeated in a series of wars with various

Western powers. Consequently, while Hong Kong had featured in the first contacts between China and organized Western merchants, it was ceded to Britain in 1842 after China was defeated in the opium wars. Around the same time, Japan and Korea opened their doors to Western powers. On the other hand, Macau, the neighbouring city of Hong Kong, was first captured by the Portuguese in 1553, but it was not until many years later that it was ceded to Portugal. The Treaty of Tianjin formally recognized Macau as a Portuguese colony in 1862.

Elsewhere, European powers found Asian lands conducive for growing cash crops. For instance, the Dutch ran Indonesia while the British took the port of Singapore, Malaysia and Burma. Three colonial powers that looked for trading posts in Asia (Portugal, Holland and Spain) took control of Taiwan in various periods starting from the 16th century. But soon Taiwan was ceded to Japan in 1895 after the Sino–Japanese War. Similarly, during the 19th century, Korea tried to handle unlimited foreign trade and influence by closing its borders to all Western nations. This was not successful, as evidenced by the signing of the Kangwha Treaty in 1876 with Japan, whereby Korea was forced to open to foreign trade. In 1881, Korea signed a similar treaty with the United States that carried somewhat similar but unequal clauses. In the early-20th century, Korea eventually fell into the hands of imperial Japan.

Post-war modernization of East Asia

With only a few exceptions (Hong Kong and Macau), most of the Asian states were granted independence from their colonial masters after World War II. Fifty years later, it is clear that the economic development record of these nations is spectacular. Overall, sustained growth rates of such magnitude were linked to the creation of wage employment opportunities on a large scale; this trend undoubtedly contributed to the pervasive increase in the region's standards of living. The demand for low-cost wage labour drew substantial numbers of workers out of subsistence agriculture and the informal sector and, as income increased, social indicators improved.

Even in poorer countries there have been successes. After years of economic stagnation, China has seen very impressive growth rates since the 1980s. It has emulated the East Asian economic development experience, and there have been significant although varied improvements in social conditions in these nations. As a result, East Asian nations have become modern and economically prosperous. Despite this, there are some pockets of extreme underdevelopment, with North Korea and Mongolia remaining at the bottom of the world economic hierarchy.

The development path taken by many East Asian nations shows its early integration into the world capitalist system. Contrary to the prevailing economic wisdom of the time, which recommended the nurturing of domestic industry through import-substitution policies, these countries adopted an export-led industrialization approach designed to provide the markets of the industrial nations of Europe and, particularly, North America with low-cost but high-quality manufactured goods. This approach emerged because the United States, for reasons of political advantage, provided substantial economic aid to Japan, Taiwan and South Korea for industrial investment and access to US markets to promote post-war reconstruction. Soon afterwards, Hong Kong and Singapore were emulating the export-led approach.

In the development literature, the East Asian economic model is 'preached' as a miracle of efficiency. Orthodox thinking in development economics explains economic growth by private enterprise, the economic benefits of trade liberalization, and a restricted role for the state. Despite the widespread use of free-market rhetoric to characterize the East Asian approach, the region's governments actively engaged in promoting economic development. Many scholars believe that their efforts comprised a new *dirigisme* in which development became an overriding purpose of statecraft. Indeed, these nations were often described by some scholars as 'developmental states' (Johnson, 1982) and by the late 1980s, their successes seemed to offer a viable alternative to the growing influence of the neoliberal ideology, which strongly opposed government intervention in economic and social affairs. As White (1998) points out, the experience of the 'rational authoritarianism' of the Asian tigers is cited as evidence of a developmentally viable and politically appropriate alternative to democratic govern-ance. The case of colonial Hong Kong is illustrative. Though the colonial state did not actively guide economic development, it played a critical role in providing massive physical and social infrastructural development to facilitate capitalist development. There was a strong state-capitalist alliance, and towards this end, education, health and housing were developed and social security and social-work services were introduced in the early 1970s. In this climate, the East Asian nations seemed to offer the only viable alternative to the growing hegemony of neoliberal ideology.

This is not to say that neoliberal ideas have not gained any foothold in East Asia. It is worth pointing out that Japan had embraced economic globalization much earlier than other Asian countries. Economic globalization took the form of a shift from a manufacturing to a service economy in the 1980s (Hasegawa, 2005). At this time, the trade surplus, financial deregulation and the stronger yen drove large Japanese firms to direct overseas investment (FDI) and securities investment. Such rapid increase in FDI in manufacturing undermined the domestic manufacturing sector since Japanese firms increasingly relocated production sites to the United States and low-wage Asian countries. The decline in the domestic manufacturing sector along with the expansion of the service sector resulted in casualization of labour and proliferation of low-wage jobs. Simultaneously, due to a large debt and trade frictions, the Japanese government pursued a neoliberal austerity policy, suppressing spending in social security, education and aid to smaller firms, launching a large-scale administrative reform and privatized government-run firms (such as Japan National Railways and the Nippon Telegraph), and cutting social assistance payments (Hasegawa, 2005). Such cutbacks came at the worst time. The 'bubble economy' that emerged in the 1980s burst in 1989. A recession ensued in 1992 that has haunted Japan ever since. With the cutback in the social assistance system, unemployment and homelessness became serious problems. When the Asian crisis struck, these problems became cause for common concern.

The Asian financial crisis

Faith in the East Asian model of development gradually dissipated after the crisis set in. In 1997, the region experienced a major fiscal crisis that resulted in capital flight, currency devaluations, the bankruptcy of many firms, a sharp rise in unemployment and an increase in poverty, homelessness and other social problems. The crisis showed that the East Asian economic model was vulnerable to international economic influences. Economically, it was in this context that the major normative approach for addressing the political, economic and social problems arising from the crisis was advocated. This approach was the neoliberal one put forward by the IMF, the World Bank and the Asian Development Bank (ADB). Politically, the poor economic environment, the dominance of neoliberal ideas and the emphasis on managerialism put a limit to the expansion of the government's efforts. Socially, this normative approach proposed a limited role for government in social welfare, greater individual and family responsibility and more extensive use of the market.

The origins of the Asian financial crisis are complex and are not the main focus of this chapter. Some analysts attribute it to factors such as 'crony capitalism' and rigidities in the banking sector. Similarly, the IMF argues that close business–government linkages, non-transparent financial markets, and a myriad of market rigidities undermined many Asian economies (Singh and Weisse, 1999). Notably, Higgott and Phillips (2000) argue that the economic crises in 1997–9 in Asia, Brazil and elsewhere represented collectively the first post-cold war 'crisis of globalization' and were a signifi-cant setback for the process of international economic liberalization. Prior to the crisis, the ADB and Asia Pacific Economic Cooperation Forum were, in the main, based on attempts to advance neoliberal ideas about economic governance in Asia (Taylor, 2004). This was not too successful. Seen in this light, the Asian financial crisis provided yet another oppor-tunity for the neoliberal thinkers to promote their cause through large inter-national organizations such as the World Bank and the IMF. Needless to say, the Asian crisis was also illustrative of the deleterious impact of neolib-eral globalism.

The crisis was precipitated by the withdrawal of deposits by international investors concerned that banks in Thailand and other countries in the region had engaged in excessively risky loans. To a certain extent, these events were linked to globalization and the free transfer of capital, which is often cited as the prime cause of the crisis (Singh and Weisse, 1999). While greater liberalization from the mid 1980s stimulated the explosive growth of portfolio equity capital flows, it also exposed developing economies to serious systemic risks (Rasiah, 2000). Wade (1998) further argues that the single most irresponsible action in the whole crisis was capital account liberalization without a framework of regulation (also known as the 'panic-triggering debt deflation in a basically sound but under-regulated system' theory). Financial firms from Britain and the United States, allied with their treasuries and with the IMF, the WTO and the OECD, saw themselves at a chronic disadvantage in the Asian system of long-term relationships. This (mostly) Western alliance, supported by segments of the Asian political and financial elite, achieved dramatic domestic financial-sector liberaliza-tion and capital-account opening in Asia over the 1990s, setting up the conditions for the crisis.

Still, the roots of the crisis go deeper and farther back in time. By the mid 1990s, the region was already experiencing economic difficulties. By this time, the growth rate of the mighty Japanese economy had slowed, and unemployment had begun to increase. Some economists were concerned that currencies in the region, in particular the Japanese yen, were over-valued. Investor confidence in the banking systems of several East Asian countries had fallen and, faced with evidence that the Thai banks would default, institutional investors in the United States and Europe began to withdraw their deposits.

These developments were followed in 1997 by sudden currency-value declines, stock market crashes and capital flight. Many Asian countries were seriously affected, including some of the most successful East Asian economies (South Korea), as well as newer industrializing economies

(Indonesia and Thailand). It seemed that the East Asian development model had failed and that it could no longer offer a credible formula for economic and social prosperity. Indeed, faced with the crisis, several governments in the region turned to the IMF for assistance. They were encouraged by that organization, as well as by the American government, to abandon their statist predilections and embrace neoliberal reforms.

The economic crisis had serious social ramifications, and the social benefits resulting from rapid economic growth in recent decades were eroded. It is estimated that some 24 million people in East Asia lost their jobs as a result of the crisis, and that the poverty rate increased (ILO, 1999). Hong Kong, with a per capita GNP close to that of Japan prior to the crisis, recorded a GNP decline in 1998 and 1999. Hong Kong's fiscal deficit reached record levels in 2002, and the unemployment rate reached a record high of 8.6 per cent in 2003. Many more people applied for public assistance and income disparities worsened, as the Gini coefficient for the city-state reached a record high of 0.525 in 2001. Although Singapore has fared better than Hong Kong, its economy has also suffered. The economy contracted by 2 per cent in 2001 and unemployment reached 4.7 per cent by the end of 2001, the highest level since the last recession in 1986 (*The Straits Times*, 28 February 2002). It is estimated that some 20,000 workers were retrenched in 2002. Since then, Singapore's government has introduced a series of social and economic measures in an attempt to meet this challenge and assist the unemployed.

Taiwan emerged relatively unscathed from the Asian financial crisis of 1997. However, its economic environment has deteriorated since the election of President Chen Shui-bian in 2000. Many banks in Taiwan also faced problems, and defaults have increased. The country's unemployment rate reached a record 4.5 per cent in mid 2001 (*Lateline News*, 23 July 2001). Notably, the Asian crisis did not have much effect on Japan and China, economically or politically, though Japan's economic problems stemmed back to the bursting of the bubble economy in the early 1990s. Its woes have continued since then, with the unemployment rate reaching a record high of 5.5 per cent in 2002. Although communist China was not much affected by the Asian crisis, it is not free from economic difficulties and particularly from the problem of unemployment. While the country's economy grew by 8 per cent in 2001, the reform of debt-ridden state-owned enterprises has taken a toll on the labour force. Massive lay-offs of urban industrial workers in the past ten years have cast a shadow over its economy. Chinese leaders acknowledge that unemployment, and the resulting sense of insecurity among retrenched workers, is a major challenge to Communist Party rule. Accordingly, the government has taken steps to address the rise of poverty among retrenched workers. Not surprisingly, workers and jobless people in Korea, Indonesia and Hong Kong affected by the economic downturn took to the streets, demanding that their governments create jobs and provide welfare protection. In this regard, Korean workers were the most active. Facing increasing unemployment, the trade unions in Korea organized protests against lay-offs and against the Structural Adjustments Programmes proposed by the IMF.

These post-crisis social protests revealed the extent to which the economic downturn had not only created serious social problems but also intensified political pressures that could not be ignored. In the initial stage of the economic crisis, many Asian states were at a loss, showing arbitrariness and a lack of coherence in policy responses. In addition to this lack of response to the *economic* and *fiscal* impacts of the crisis, neither did governments respond effectively to the *social* consequences. In part, this reflected a historical lack of commitment to formulating comprehensive social-welfare policies. But it also reflected a mistrust of increased social spending on vulnerable groups in times of economic adversity. Many governments believed that increasing social spending in bad economic times would only undermine the prospect of economic recovery. They retained a strong faith in economic recovery and believed that, with patience and appropriate stimulus policies, rapid growth would again characterize their economies. These stimulus policies often favoured the business community. Policies designed to address the needs of the unemployed were mostly haphazard and increasingly meagre.

Neoliberalism: the IMF and the World Bank

Many Asian governments also sought a quick economic solution to the social problems arising from the crisis. They believed that renewed economic growth alone would eliminate most if not all of these social problems. This belief was bolstered by international organizations, primarily the IMF, but also the World Bank, and the ADB, all of which supported the adoption of neoliberal economic policies (IMF, 1999). Even after the crisis, East Asia has been cited as a success story on the grounds that economic growth over the last two decades has greatly reduced the number of the poorest people. On an even more optimistic note, Collier and Dollar of the World Bank (2001) predict that, if the trends of the 1990s persist, poverty in the developing world will be almost halved by 2015.

Faced with serious problems, several Asian nations applied for such aid from the IMF and the World Bank. South Korea received some US$58 billion from the IMF. By providing this support, the IMF exerted considerable influence and was able to pressure these countries to adopt its normative approach (Taylor, 1997). Representing this view, Alan Greenspan (cited in Wade, 1998: 1536) contended that the crisis in Asia showed the excessive government intervention in markets, marking the beginning of the end of the outmoded state-directed Asian system. He observed:

> The current crisis is likely to accelerate the dismantling in many Asian countries of the remnants of a system with large elements of government-directed investment, in which finance played a key role in carrying out the state's objectives. Such a system inevitably has led to the investment excesses and errors to which all similar endeavors seem prone.

However, the IMF did acknowledge the 'human dimension' of the crisis and the need for limited, short-term social programmes to assist the unemployed and others affected by the events of 1997 (IMF, 1999). Because of the serious political and social ramifications of the crisis, these organizations endorsed the introduction of programmes that would alleviate the worst excesses of the crisis. Yet, the social policies proposed by the IMF were neither comprehensive nor permanent. Any relaxation of fiscal controls was meant to be short lived. Above all, the IMF strongly emphasized 'cost-effective' social programmes that, in its view, would not create market disincentives. It also encouraged private insurance and other commercial social-service provisions that would replace government programmes.

Their views do not go unchallenged. For instance, scholars see the IMF's post-crisis remedies as merely 'tools of neoliberal immiseration' (Heuer and Shirmer, 1998). In fact, other influential international organizations took a different approach to that of the IMF and the World Bank when it came to remedying the social ills of the crisis. The International Labour Organization (ILO) and the OECD were very concerned with the social impact of the crisis and called for the adoption of social policies that could address these problems. For example, the collapse of the South Korean economy in 1998 caused worldwide jitters. The IMF intervened, imposing standard structural adjustments on the economy in exchange for a large financial bailout. This line of approach was seriously questioned. Critics argued that economic restructuring and massive lay-offs, along with a reduced government budget, would destabilize a country whose unemployment rate had already shot up. The IMF and the Korean state then revised the bailout packages, making allowance for an expanded unemployment-insurance programme.

Global social protests

After the crisis, many analysts predicted that the days of rapid economic growth and full employment in East Asia were over. Some, including Marxists, were pessimistic about deteriorating social conditions and rising levels of unemployment and poverty (McNally, 1998), and this thinking reflected the Marxist view of the new era of globalization as a consolidation of rabid capitalism. The Marxist critique of globalization has not been widely known in Asia, particularly when compared with the worldwide social protests against globalization.

Global activism against the ills of globalization captured much world attention as the 20th century ended. Of special importance was 'the Battle in Seattle' in 1999 – demonstrators against the WTO caused a four-day closure of the retail core of Seattle, as thousands of protesters clashed violently with the police.

Global protests do not spring from nowhere. As some observers (Smith, 2001) note, the protests against the WTO in Seattle were preceded by various social protests that erupted and gained in strength as a result of the fight against and victory over the Multilateral Agreement on Investment (MAI) talks at the OECD in 1998. The stalling of the MAI boosted activists' confidence and gave new meaning to global grassroots activism. Years of protest against the North American Free Trade Agreement had also strengthened linkages between protesters in that region. In short, global (and regional) economic negotiations and corporation-dominated trading arrangements shaped transnational dissent. Neoliberal ideas and accords, as they fuelled economic globalization, also served as lightning rods for these protests.

Street protests against globalization and neoliberal ideas in Asia are relatively few. But this area is not completely immune to protest movements. Anti-globalization protests have taken place in India, Indonesia, Thailand, Japan, South Korea and the Philippines. Spurred by the neoliberal agenda, globalization has deeply impoverished marginalized groups in the developing world, inciting some resistance to globalized capitalism. East Asia is now one of these sites of resistance, and analysts have assessed responses by these groups. Mittelman's (2000) discussion of the impact of globalization on Asian countries (including Malaysia, the Philippines and Vietnam) shows a 'growing pattern of resistance' in civil society, such as farmers' associations, environmental groups and other political movements.

The latest such episode occurred in December 2005 when these groups protested in Hong Kong against the Sixth Ministerial Meeting of the WTO. Global protests are renowned for the diffuse character of their concerns.

A wide variety of issues have indeed been raised: labour rights, the growth of poverty and inequity, loss of democratic sovereignty, and environmental degradation. The goals are diverse – eradication of poverty and promotion of equity between groups, advancing humanitarian principles, and championing human and labour rights and social standards – but all are directed against the adverse impacts of crude market liberalism.

The protest was orchestrated by the Hong Kong People's Alliance Against the WTO (HKPAA-WTO) which is a network of grass-root organizations covering trade unions, community labour groups and organizations that represent migrant workers, students, women, the church, human rights, research organizations and regional organizations that are based locally in Hong Kong. Without doubt, the most prominent organization was the Korean Farmers' Association. The farmers are fighting against WTO rules that force their government to cut tariffs on agricultural products, causing bankruptcy for tens of thousands, which paves the way for food occupation by transnational grain corporations and dispossession of food sovereignty. Likewise, thousands of Indonesian and Filipino women workers in Hong Kong used the occasion to press their demands for higher pay and better job security for migrant workers. Radical groups were present in the protest: the Marxist contingent of the demonstration, represented by such groups as Pioneer (Hong Kong) and Workers' Democracy Association (Taiwan), stood for resistance to capitalism and genuine socialism based on workers' democratic control of the economy and state. The socialist Committee for a Workers International called for a strong, young working class that could overcome the betrayals and setbacks of workers' organizations.

Prior to the Sixth Ministerial Meeting, the pro-WTO Hong Kong government (somewhat naïvely) launched a series of propaganda-like advertisements regarding the worldwide benefits of economic globalization. Simultaneously, the government undermined the credibility of these protest groups by labelling them 'violent troublemakers' and using other scare tactics. However, once the meeting – and the protests – began, there were some notable effects. Common people in prosperous Hong Kong did not simply listen with amusement to the slogans 'Junk the WTO!', 'Derail the WTO!' and 'Stop the Doha Round!'. The protests became an educational process for them, since they had not been aware of the plight of marginalized farmers, workers and migrants in China, Taiwan, Indonesia and Korea. The HKPAA-WTO shared true stories of suffering and impoverishment, such as Indonesian farmers, fishermen and workers being forced to work overseas because, due in part to globalization, they cannot find jobs in their home country. 'No to commodification of migrants – stop GATS!' was another eye-catching slogan, aimed at the WTO's infamous General Agreement on Trade in Services which, if approved, would intensify the exploitation of workers. In addition, the protest tactics and styles impressed both the common people and the media. Hong Kong people were deeply moved by the Korean farmer protesters' 'three steps, one kneeling', a peaceful and painful way of protest.

Conclusion

East Asia is facing the stark reality of globalization. In the eyes of those Asian states that rely heavily on external trade, the current stage of neoliberal globalization has the following features: the demise of the socialist challenge and the growing importance of WTO; advances in the communications revolution that greatly undermine the barriers of time and space between national markets; increasing globalization of trade; and deeper integration of Asian states with other global partners (Kim, 2000). Experiencing an ever-changing global environment, the East Asian states' primary goal is that of economic development. As noted, the neoliberal argument provides a vision and a strategy to these countries – owing to the rising density of international economic integration, world poverty and income inequality fell over the past two decades for the first time in more than a century and a half. As the argument goes, the evidence therefore confirms that globalization generates benefits. Outwardly, many states accept this version of the development strategy, and they duly receive support and accolades from neoliberal proponents. Thus the Asian tigers of Hong Kong and Singapore in January 2006 were rated the world's freest economies by the right-wing American think tank, The Heritage Foundation.

At the same time, the Asian crisis is a reality check and a spur to rethinking significant aspects of the neoliberal project (Higgott and Phillips, 2000). What has been the response thus far from Asian states? There is no uniform answer. But collectively, Asian economies have learnt some good lessons from the crisis. For instance, contrary to neoliberal claims, some Asian states realized that it is important to utilize foreign direct investment effectively and to prevent systemic volatility generated by portfolio capital movements (Rasiah, 2000). All these mean that Asian states must have generally effective governments.

Interestingly, some post-crisis Asian states like Japan, Hong Kong and Singapore have strongly embraced neoliberal globalization while maintaining a strong state, using the ideas of the New Management School to carry political and social reforms. To a certain extent, they welcome somewhat the imposition of American-style capitalism as the US is seen as the sole hegemonic power. In post-crisis Hong Kong, for instance, neoliberal ideas gave rise to 'managerialism' in political and economic governance. In the context of economic austerity, the Hong Kong government has increasingly subscribed to the philosophy of 'New Public Management' which stresses the contracting out of social services; developing partnerships; delimiting government responsibility, consumerism and user involvement; and streamlining and re-engineering service structures through downsizing and merging. The government now touts itself as a 'big market, small government' system (Lee 2005; Tang and Midgley, 2002).

Likewise, some details about Japan's pro-neoliberal stance can be ascertained from the recent privatization of Japan Post, the multifunction postal service which employs close to half a million workers. The planned privatization of Japan Post had always been a pet project of the Koizumi administration (*The Economist*, 23–29 June 2001), despite extreme legislative reluctance. In 2005, Koizumi put forth such a bill, but it was voted down in Parliament and, in response, Koizumi called a new election in which his candidates did quite well. With this strong mandate from the public, Koizumi moved quickly on his privatization plan, designed to curb government spending and the growth of the national debt.

A similar pattern of response can be seen in Singapore. Since the Asian economic crisis, the Singapore government has embraced neoliberal globalization to a degree not matched elsewhere in East or South East Asia. However, it must be pointed out that the consolidation and expansion of Singapore's state companies is integral to this strategy (Rodan, 2004). Seeking to make inroads into various sectors of the Singapore economy, international capital companies are highly critical of such an approach. Likewise, the Hong Kong Government's role in the economy is no smaller than before, even though it outwardly champions the cause of neoliberalism.

The responses of these countries do have two major implications: first, this neoliberal approach is hardly compatible with the region's historic statist traditions; and, second, the adoption of neoliberalism has exacerbated the existing neglect of social welfare by East Asian governments and failed to address adequately the region's growing social problems. According to a recent study in Taiwan, for instance, an overwhelming majority of people (83 per cent) was concerned about rising income inequities (*Apple Daily* (Taiwan), 3 January 2006). Four years ago, the figure stood at 61 per cent. As Hewison (2001) points out, opposition to neoliberal globalization has been especially intense since the Asian crisis. Many expect that such social protests will intensify as neoliberal globalization deepens in this part of the world.

Three other states in East Asia have taken a different stance. As noted, South Korea has taken a more opposing and uncompromising stance, refusing to embark on a neoliberal political and economic-governance model. Taiwan is more ambivalent, and the current government under President Chen has exhausted its energy on internal strife with opposition parties; he has just survived an opposition-led bid to recall him over allegations that some of his relatives engaged in insider trading (*Washington Post*, 28 June 2006). There is certainly some pro-globalization sentiment on the part of the Taiwanese government, as evidenced by its wish to join the WTO following China. At the same time, particularly after witnessing the anti-WTO movement in Hong Kong, it is wary of the fact that globalization has not brought benefits to all people (Wang, 2006). Not surprisingly, given its tense relationship with China, discussions about globalization often focus solely on the issue of 'Sinicization'. In other words, such debates are structured around its economic relationships with China. Without bilateral trade with China, Taiwan would show a trade deficit; without investment cooperation with China, Taiwanese businesses would lose market opportunities and fail to keep ahead of business rivals from other nations. Therefore, actively opening cross-strait economic links is the only way to achieve a win-win situation, and failing to establish the three direct cross-strait links runs counter to the spirit of globalization.

Clearly, one of the biggest winners of economic globalization is China. This comes with a price. The rise of China poses a huge challenge to the region and the question 'Can it avoid becoming an appendage of the Chinese economy?' is frequently asked. Locally, China's former President Jiang Zemin who is known for his zeal for the market economy warned of the adverse impacts of globalization when he stated trade liberalization might 'aggravate the uneven distribution of world resources and an unbalanced economic development, widen the gap between the North and the South, sharpen the polarization between the rich and the poor and cause further environmental degradation' (APEC CEO Summit, 18 October 2001) Critics of neoliberal free trade in China warn the government that the WTO is a double-edged sword. Though China is richer after joining the WTO, workers' rights have been undermined.

Even though China has been the beneficiary of open and free trade, and even though its accession to the WTO in 2001 was widely publicized, China's official stance towards neoliberal globalization is not without hesitation and betrays a high degree of pragmatism. This cautious attitude does not come from the government's communist roots. Rather, facing rising income inequity and peasant unrest, China is increasingly aware of the harmful effects of free trade, competition and deregulation on its people (Oi, 1999). The Asian crisis shows the threat of international economic forces to the survival of nations. This makes the country more cautious and proactive on the development front. As a Beijing University professor who also serves as policy advisor to the central government puts it, the China confronted with globalization is a 'learning society' (Yuan, 2006), but the current leadership, under President Hu Jin-tao and Premier Wen Jia-bao, is becoming more sympathetic to the 'losers' of economic reforms (unemployed workers and landless farmers, for example).

However, rather than arguing for one best way to counter neoliberal globalization, the conclusions drawn from this review are that a multi-faceted approach is the norm among East Asian states. This is very much mediated by one factor: the growing consciousness of the ills of globalization among professionals, the middle class and common people. Importantly, anti-globalization forces are gaining strength in East Asia, especially after the recent series of worldwide social protests against globalization. Obviously, proponents of neoliberalism have found it increasingly difficult to push their agenda in East Asia without facing both subtle and manifest resistance from civil society. One can safely predict that the link between international political processes and the rise of transnational social organizations and coalitions could mean significant transnational mobilizations in the future. Even at the level of state control, trade liberalization and privatization are viewed with caution by countries' leaders. In this way, the crisis in 1997 has become a double-edged sword: as it opened up East Asia for the encroachment of neoliberal globalization, it created massive hardships for the common people, inciting resistance. There is thus an inherent contradiction between the spread of neoliberal globalization and the uplifting of the social and economic well being of the country. Without a doubt, the potency of the contemporary counter movement in civil society against free trade, regional poverty and inequities, as well as the pragmatic attitudes taken by some Asian states, should not be taken lightly.

References

Collier, P. and D. Dollar (2001) 'Can the World Cut Poverty in Half? How Policy Reform and Effective Aid Can Meet International Development Goals', *World Development*, 29(11): 1787–802.

Ericson, R. and A. Doyle (1999) 'Globalization and the Policing of Protest: The Case of APEC', *British Journal of Sociology*, 50(4): 589–609.

Foster, J. (2003) 'A Planetary Defeat: The Failure of Global Environmental Reform', *Monthly Review,* January, 54, 8: 1–9.

Giddens, A. (1999) *Runaway World: How Globalization is Reshaping Our lives.* London: Profile Books.

Hasegawa, M. (2005) 'Economic Globalization and Homelessness in Japan', *American Behavioral Scientist*, 48(8): 989–1013.

Heuer, U. and G. Shirmer (1998) 'Human Rights Imperialism', *Monthly Review*, 49(10): 5–16.

Hewison, K. (2001) 'Nationalism, Populism, Dependency: Southeast Asia and Responses to the Asian Crisis', *Singapore Journal of Tropical Geography*, 22(3): 219–36.

Higgott, R. and N. Phillips (2000) 'Challenging Triumphalism and Convergence: The Limits of Global Liberalization in Asia and Latin America', *Review of International Studies*, 26(3): 359–79.

Hung, H. (2001) 'Imperial China and Capitalist Europe in the Eighteenth-Century Global Economy', *Review: A Journal of the Fernand Braudel Center*, 24(4): 473–513.

International Labour Organization (ILO) (1999) The ILO Governing Board to Examine Response to Asian Crisis, Press statement, 16 March, Available at http://www. ilo.org/public/english/bureau/inf/pr/1999.

International Monetary Fund (1999) *Economic and Financial Situation in Asia: Latest Developments*, Background paper prepared for presentation by Michel Camdessus, Managing Director of the International Monetary Fund, Asia Europe Finance Ministers Meeting, Frankfort, Germany, 16 January, available at: http://imf.org/External/np/speeches/1999/011699.HTM.

Johnson, C. (1982) *MTTI and the Japanese Miracle: The Growth of Industrial Policy 1925–1975*. Stanford, CA: Stanford University Press.

Kim, S. (ed.) (2000) *East Asia and Globalization*. Lanham' MD: Rowman and Littlefield.

Lee, E. (2005) 'The Renegotiation of the Social Pact in Hong Kong: Economic Globalisation, Socio-economic Change, and Local Politics', *Journal of Social Policy*, 34, 2: 293–310.

McNally, D. (1998) 'Globalization on Trial: Crisis and Class Struggle in East Asia', *Monthly Review*, 50(4): 1–14, available at http://www.monthlyreview.org/volume50.htm.

Mittelman, J. (2000) *The Globalization Syndrome: Transformation and Resistance*. Princeton, NJ: Princeton University Press.

Nuruzzaman, M. (2005) 'Economic Liberalization and Poverty in the Developing World', *Journal of Contemporary Asia*, 35(1): 109–27.

Oi, J. (1999) 'Two Decades of Rural Reform in China: An Overview and Assessment', *The China Quarterly*, 159: 616–28.

Rasiah, R. (2000) 'Globalization and Private Capital Movements', *Third World Quarterly*, 21(6): 943–61.

Rodan, G. (2004) 'International Capital, Singapore's State Companies, and Security', *Critical Asian Studies*, 36(3): 479–99.

Singh, A. and B. Weisse, (1999) 'The Asian Model: A Crisis Foretold', *International Social Science Journal*, 160: 203–15.

Smith, J. (2001) 'Globalizing Resistance: The Battle of Seattle and the Future of Social Movements', *Mobilization*, 6(1): 1–19.

Tang, K. (2000) *Social Welfare Development in East Asia*. New York: Palgrave.

Tang, K. and J. Midgley (2002) 'Social Policy after the East Asian Crisis: Forging a Normative Basis for Welfare', *Journal of Asian Comparative Development*, 1(2): 301–18.

Taylor, I. (2004) 'APEC, Globalization, and 9/11 – The Debate on What Constitutes Asian Regionalism', *Critical Asian Studies*, 36(6): 463–78.

Taylor, L. (1997) 'The Revival of the Liberal Creed: The IMF and the World Bank in a Globalized Economy', *World Development*, 25(2): 145–52.

Wade, R. (1998) 'The Asian Debt-and-Development Crisis of 1997: Causes and Consequences', *World Development*, 26(8): 1535–53.
Wang, H. (2006) 'Globalization is not Sinicization'. *Taipei Times*, 16, January (in Chinese).
White, G. (1998) 'Constructing a Democratic Developmental State', in M. Robinson and G. White (eds), *The Democratic Developmental State*. New York: Oxford University Press: 17–51.
Yuan, M. (2006) 'The Cultural Consciousness in the Context of Globalization', public lecture delivered on 16 January 2006 at the Chinese University of Hong Kong.

14
The Lexicon of Globalization: Comparative Regional Perspectives

Paul Bowles and Henry Veltmeyer

The regional perspectives presented in this book, together with the national perspectives contained in the companion volume, do not lead to a single reading of 'globalization'. Rather they provide a lexicon, an interpretive guide, to the understanding of the meaning, impacts and responses to globalization. In this chapter we draw out some of the most important entries in this lexicon. Specifically, we provide an analysis of seven major points. In discussing these we rely primarily on the regional perspectives presented in this volume although we also supplement this in places with some of the arguments contained in the national perspectives volume where this adds further insights to the discussion.

Inter-regional themes

There are some common themes that emerge across some of the regions that are linked to wider continental experiences and to their position within the international political economy. With respect to the continental themes, one striking theme that emerges from the East, West and Southern Africa chapters is the fear of marginalization as a result of the process of globalization. This is explicit in Sesay and Olayode's discussion of West Africa but is also evident in Thompson's analysis of Southern Africa and Kinyanjui and Kiruthu's chapter on East Africa. In all three cases, the predominant lens through which globalization is viewed is that of development. All three chapters distinguish sharply between these two concepts despite the prevalent discourse among neoliberal scholars to conflate the two into globalization as development. From the perspective of the African regions, globalization is assessed in terms of its prospects for development and, in each case, the regions are seen as being both integrated into global capitalism and yet at the same time increasingly marginalized from its centres of power and wealth. The regions of Africa are far from being ignored by globalization – they are integrally involved in its processes, but these are themselves seen as leading to the marginalization of the continent's regions in terms of their global significance and share of global wealth. Marginalization is seen as an outcome of globalization's processes rather than as an indicator of its absence.

In Africa, globalization is seen as being a neoliberal project with the international financial institutions, the IMF and the World Bank, as the major agents of this project. In the Arab world, including North Africa, these institutions have been less in evidence but the power of Western states as drivers of globalization is nevertheless evident in Amin's account. The neoliberal character of globalization is also strongly evident in the regional chapters on Central America and the Caribbean and South America. In the case of the former, Dierckxsens and Aguilar illustrate the role of Structural Adjustment Programmes and US foreign policy in leading to the reconfiguration of the region on neoliberal principles. Vizentini refers to the same factors – the Washington Consensus and US supremacy – as responsible for the shift to neoliberal globalization. The major dynamics – and meaning – of globalization as a neoliberal project imposed by the US and IFIs is taken as the starting point of the analysis. The question 'what is globalization?' is seen as a relatively straightforward one to answer. The same answer is given in the case of South Asia, where Khundker refers to 'enforced globalization' with the Structural Adjustment Programmes of the World Bank again seen as the main enforcers. The argument that neoliberal globalization is being forced on regions is common to many of the analyses of the regions which constitute the South. As such, it can be seen as a form of imperialism, an argument made with respect to East Africa where, in fact, the argument is made that the contemporary period is one of 'super-imperialism'. Kinyanjui and Kiruthu argue that the British Empire included a provision for the (paternalistic) care of its subjects whereas today's rapacious MNCs and IFIs share no such concerns.

In two other regions of Asia, South East and East Asia, the interpretation of globalization is again seen as neoliberalism but one in which the outcomes have been more mixed. For Bello, globalization in South East Asia has been a roller coaster ride with the upswing also responsible for globalization being seen as a benign force in East Asia in Tang's analysis. In both cases, the Asian financial crisis of 1997 has changed perceptions markedly. In all of these chapters, dominated by developing countries, the view of globalization as neoliberalism sponsored by the IFIs at the behest of Western powers is clearly evident. Indeed, this has been viewed as largely uncontroversial and the focus of many of the chapters has been on the impacts of globalization in these regions. Here, the impacts described have been overwhelmingly negative in economic and social terms. Economically, with the exception of South East and East Asia, globalization's impacts have been seen almost entirely negatively leading to increasing inequality and the curtailment or abandonment of national development objectives. In the place of the latter has come the increasing penetration of national and regional economies by transnational capital in both financial and direct investment forms. Social polarization has increased in many regions and whole regions – such as East Africa – remain mired in poverty with little immediate prospect of improvement despite long integration into international markets.

These analyses stand in contrast to those provided by Antoniades and Helleiner for Western Europe and North America respectively. In these cases, both authors raise the puzzling question why these two economic super-regions, without whose participation globalization could not occur, seem unsure what constitutes globalization. Absent in both cases, and in contrast to the regions discussed above, is any appeal to 'enforced' globalization at the behest of the IFIs. The regional perspectives offered here posit globalization rather as an external force but one that cannot plausibly be accepted as such given the importance of the regions themselves in the globalization process.

There is a puzzle too with respect to Central Europe. Here, as Kochanowicz points out, it was the process of globalization, in a technological sense, which eventually led to the collapse of the Soviet Union and freed the states of Central Europe from its grip. The demise of the Soviet Union ushered in a new period of global capitalism in which the former states of the Soviet bloc were integral to the new extended reach of capitalism. And yet, despite the place of the region within this new phase of the globalization process, the language of globalization is noticeable by its absence in the Central European case. Indeed, the role of internal factors and the language of transformation dominate even though the role of the IFIs and external agents such as MNCs and the Soros Foundation were very active in this transformation. Globalization, to use Kochanowicz's apt word, comes in disguised form in Central Europe. The meaning of globalization is different in this region and distinctive.

Regionalism and globalization

While the inter-regional themes exhibit some interesting differences, there are also issues which are common across the regions. One of the most important here is the relationship between regionalism and globalization. To some, these forces are complementary with regionalism being seen as the springboard for a more effective participation in the global economy. This view can be found in many of the regions. Antoniades finds this argument used widely within the Western European context where the EU is seen as a defensive mechanism needed to enable Europe to effectively compete on the world market. Helleiner documents the way in which NAFTA was seen by its architects as a mechanism for increasing competition within the region and thereby strengthening the region internationally. This same rationale can be found in the analyses of regional groups in West Africa, Southern Africa, South East Asia and South America for whom ECOWAS, SADC, AFTA and Mercosur respectively illustrate the regions' attempts to forge regional economic structures that will withstand global competition.

But while this strand of reasoning and motivation can be found in all of these regions, it is not the only one. Coexisting with this view of regionalism as a complementary – indeed necessary – process to that of globalization, is the argument that regionalism can be used as a bulwark against globalization, a mechanism for preserving regional autonomy, identity and values. This view is perhaps most clearly evident in Western Europe but can also be found elsewhere. Thus Vizentini describes Mercosur as a regional body intended to provide an alternative to economic integration with the US and global economies, and Walden Bello discusses how ASEAN *could* be transformed into a regional body offering an alternative to neoliberal globalization.

This points to a more general observation about regionalism, namely, its chameleon-like ability to be used for different purposes. Regionalism can be, and has been historically, used to either integrate with, or insulate from, the international economy. As such, it is not surprising to find that regionalism is being advocated in both of these uses in the current phase. It is not simply a question of whether regionalism is complementary to or competitive with globalization but which use is dominant in any particular region. The struggle for domination is being fought in regions across the world with the integrating forces currently in the ascendancy but with strong opposition in some regions arguing for regionalism's protective, insulating use. It is not surprising that this is not only being fought regionwide but has also resulted in intra-regional fissures.

Intra-regional dynamics

Underlying the role that regionalism plays are tensions between states within the regions about the role that regionalism should play. This is clear in South America where Brazil and Argentina have often been at loggerheads over the role and purpose of regional bodies. Chile too has also been a contributor to this with its greater support for initiatives with the US. In fact, there are several regional initiatives on offer in South America: Mercosur, FTAA and now the Venezuela/Bolivia/Cuba regional initiative (ALBA). In one single region, no less than three quite different regional visions are actively under consideration, each with very different conceptualizations of the relationship with globalization, and each vying for attention.

While South America provides the clearest example of this, the differences between what Antoniades identifies as the Anglo-Saxon and Continentalist views in Western Europe can also be seen as representing different visions of the relationship between regionalism and globalization. The use of globalization as a rhetorical weapon in North America also points to these intra-regional differences although here it is not between states but largely between state elites and sizeable proportions of their citizens.

The discussion to date has been in terms of regions with formal regional organizations. These are largely absent in East Asia. Some of the same intra-regional issues can be discerned however. Thus, Tang demonstrates that Japan and Hong Kong, for example, have responded to the Asian financial crisis with greater commitment to neoliberalism, whereas in China and South Korea a much more cautious approach has been taken which continues to stress the role of state developmentalism.

An implication here is that globalization has given a greater impetus for the collective actions of regions but has also led to intra-regional struggles on what the regional response should be.

Historical conjunctures

Evident from the regional perspectives presented here is the importance of historical conjunctures in explaining 'when globalization began' for the regions under discussion. Many contributors place the question of 'when globalization began' in a historical context which serves to highlight another central aspect of the globalization debate, namely, what is 'new' about the current phase.

Amin and Kinyanjui and Kiruthu take a historical approach in their analyses of the Arab World and of East Africa with the current phase seen as new forms of imperialism succeeding the old. Continuity is a feature here with changes representing the detail on an otherwise uniform historical surface. Other authors point more sharply to the neoliberal revolution of the 1980s as a starting point in contemporary globalization, a historical conjuncture which led to rather more radical changes in the regions under consideration. This would be relevant to the cases of Central America and the Caribbean, South America, South Asia and South East Asia. For Central Europe, the fall of the Soviet Union in 1991 is of central significance, while in North America the debates leading up to the implementation of NAFTA in 1994 are critical in understanding the region's relationship with globalization. In East Asia, Tang argues that for much of the post-war period, globalization was seen as a benign force, a view which remained largely unchanged until the Asian financial crisis of 1997. This analysis also finds strong resonance in Bello's account of South East Asia's experience.

In analysing globalization, regional histories are important as regionally specific historical events have framed what globalization means, what its impacts have been and how it has been resisted.

Regions and regionalisms

From the analyses presented in the chapters here it is evident that globalization can be understood from the perspectives of different regions. The framing of globalization's impacts has identifiable regional dimensions. Many of these have already been mentioned: neoliberalism in South America and South Asia and elsewhere, and transformation in Central Europe, for example. But the relationship between these regions and regionalisms shows considerable variation. In some cases, North America and Western Europe for example, the 'region' is defined by membership of the regional organizations, NAFTA and the EU respectively. In the case of West Africa and Southern Africa, the region is defined by relation to membership of ECOWAS and SADC. ASEAN plays the same role in region definition in South East Asia. Thus, for some regions, the link with regionalism is obvious and, indeed, definitional. In some cases, ECOWAS for example, the region pre-dated the regional organization and the latter evolved as a result of the perceived common interests of member states in the region. In other cases, however, the formation of the regional organization can be thought of as preceding or itself defining what constitutes the region. North America provides a good case in point where the concept of a North American 'region' arose only with the NAFTA. Mexico still sits ambiguously as a self-declared member of North America but still tied by history to the Central American region. ASEAN, formed as Bello points out in 1967 as an anti-communist regional organization, has evolved to represent and define a region.

In other regions, the link with regionalism is less apparent and in some cases entirely absent. In East Asia, for example, Tang points out that there are many countries which are potential members of the region and although this brings an inevitable arbitrariness to any definition of the region, it is still possible to speak meaningfully of an East Asian region. The absence of a regional organization contributes to the arbitrariness of definition. Central Europe has no regional organization and the definition of the region is based on shared history. In South America, as already noted, there is one region but multiple regionalisms.

The varying relationships between regions and regionalisms affect our understandings of globalization. In some of the chapters the impacts of globalization are filtered through regional organizations, in others not. In some cases, the response to globalization has been managed through regional organizations, in others not. The complex articulations of region and regionalism have highlighted different approaches to analysing the impacts and responses to globalization; 'regional perspectives' must be understood in these contexts.

Popular resistance

Neoliberal policies and the associated globalization process have generated diverse forms of resistance and opposition that have crystalized in the form of a worldwide anti-globalization movement. In many instances this movement is not particularly radical in that it is directed not against globalization per se, or against the system of global capitalism or imperialism behind it, but against globalization in its specific neoliberal form. The aim is to search for 'another world' associated with and brought about by a more ethical form of globalization. However, the readings in this and its companion volume also point towards more radical forms of regionwide opposition and resistance.

Some of these forces of resistance, as in North America and Western Europe, are located in the middle-class non-governmental sector of 'civil society', but the bulk of this anti-globalization movement is directed against corporate capitalism and its agenda of free trade and the free movement of capital in search of profit. This form of resistance – the 'anti-globalization movement' – is orientated towards the search for 'another world' in which the forces of 'economic freedom' are reined in and subject to considerations of, and a concern for, the public interest. However, this movement by and large is restricted to the 'North', the countries that make up the club of rich, industrialized countries in the OECD.

In the South of the global divide in wealth and incomes and economic power – that is on the periphery of the global economy (Africa, Latin America and the Caribbean, and parts of Asia) – the anti-globalization movement tends to take more virulent forms, in large part because the people in these areas are having to bear most of the social, economic and environmental, and political costs of globalization. There is no question that globalization is, as Galal Amin noted in regard to the Arab World, uneven in its workings. He established this pattern in a specific regional context but it is equally evident elsewhere, indeed everywhere. One conclusion that can be clearly drawn from each and all of the chapters in this volume is that globalization is a force of unequal development, making billionaires out of a small handful of individuals (see *Forbes's* super-rich) and spreading wealth among the upper and upper-middle strata of societies at the centre of the world system, while dispossessing and impoverishing a large part of humanity, subjecting it to conditions of environmental degradation, deterioration of living and working standards, social exclusion and exploitation.

Some of these conditions also exist at the centre of the system, in its North American and European heartland. But there is little question that people and countries on the South of the growing global divide bear the brunt of the globalization process. Thus, it is not surprising to read of the mounting and radical forms of popular resistance on the southern periphery – in South and Central America; in East, South and South East Asia. While regional anti-globalization movements, rooted in the popular sector of civil society, remain relatively weak in South and Southern Africa, this does not mean that the status quo cannot change over time. As Thompson shows in Chapter 9, South Africa is already showing signs of an increasing groundswell of social movement activity, even among those understood as more marginalized, and, the author argues, it is only a matter of time before this begins to manifest more broadly in the region. Ironically, she argues – and other authors in this volume confirm this – it appears that the more globalization processes and networks thicken, the more sustained the level and vehemence of civil society participation and resistance becomes. South America is an exemplar of this proposition. No region in the world, except for those societies 'in transition' from state socialism towards free market capitalism, has experienced as abrupt a transformation under the aegis of global capital and the 'new economic model' (witness Argentina, Bolivia, Brazil, Ecuador, Peru, and so on). And no region in the world has experienced as powerful forces of resistance against and opposition to the neoliberal agenda of structural adjustment and globalization. In this regional context the emergence of powerful anti-systematic movements, rooted in and led by indigenous communities, peasant farmers and landless rural workers, is bringing about another sea-change in national and regional politics. Neoliberalism in this context is imploding, defeated by forces of its own making.

The changing dynamics of globalization

The agents and forms of globalization presented in this volume represent analyses undertaken at a particular point in time. These may – or may not – change over time. As we have already noted, the authors of the regional chapters from the Arab World and East Africa stress continuity while other authors, especially from regions located in the South, view the IFIs straightforwardly as external agents imposing neoliberalism.

There are, however, other accounts of why the dynamics of globalization might be changing. One such account is that which suggests that the rise of the BRICs, as Goldman Sachs (1999) called Brazil, Russia, India and China, is changing the nature of globalization and intensifying competition. This has found expression in the analysis of Friedman (2005) who has proclaimed that as a result of technology and capital mobility, most production can take place in countries of either the North or the South and that, as a result, the world has become 'flat'.

The analyses presented in the chapters in this volume provide some insights into these claims. The first is that globalization has not produced a flat world but one still characterized by hierarchies; globalization is seen as the imposition of neoliberal policies in the regions of the South under the auspices of international institutions, while in Western Europe and North America these external actors are absent. In many regions this imposition is seen as a new form of imperialism. In short, the world is anything but flat.

The extrapolation of trends, upon which the Goldman Sachs report was based, is a dangerous business as Bello has shown for South East Asia, a region elevated to 'miracle' status where globalization was to have no downside. Even so, it is worth taking seriously the re-emergence of China. Several of the contributors to this volume – Bello for South East Asia and Khundker for South Asia, for example – raise the question of how regions should respond to economic competition from China. Will this be a force for unleashing greater neoliberalism on the regions as each one seeks to compete its way to the bottom of the international cost ladder? In which case, in terms of the dynamics analysed above, it is likely that regionalism will remain as a force for integrating into, and competing in, an increasingly competitive global market place. Or, as Bello suggests, will it lead to a counter action, a realization that regionalism and the development of regional economic structures are the best way to insulate regions from the vagaries of a new globalization process spurred by China? In the companion volume, Yu Keping documents that this has been a contentious debate within China itself – whether China will be swallowed up by a capitalist globalization or whether it will be able to forge a new path based on preserving its developmental objectives and national autonomy. This latter path, variously (and loosely) referred to as the 'Beijing Consensus' (Ramo, 2004) or perhaps 'globalization with Chinese characteristics', should it emerge will provide more challenges to regional efforts elsewhere in the world. The re-emergence of China gives a new context to the enduring question of the relationship between regionalism and globalization.

Conclusion: the utility of regional perspectives

A premise of this book is that despite its uniformity in practice (virtually the same policies and 'structural reforms', and the same agencies, are involved everywhere) globalization takes distinct national and regional forms. That is, in each country and in each region there are conditions and responses specific to that country and region that must be understood and taken into account in assessing the dynamics of the globalization process. These dynamics can be traced out on three levels: the implementation of 'structural reforms' in macroeconomic policies of the state under the Washington Consensus; the economic and social impacts of these reforms; and the strategic and political responses to these policy reforms by governments and all sorts of civil society organizations.

The analyses and perspectives of the authors in this volume provide clear evidence that globalization in its multiple forms and diverse phases has an important regional dimension. In the first instance, the national dimension of globalization needs to be established, as we have in the companion to this volume. This is because, notwithstanding the emergence of global institutions and forces that undermine the nation state and subjugate it to these institutions and forces, the nation state continues to be *the* most important repository of political power. This is evidenced not only by the activities of governments and state policies relative to globalization (mostly facilitating it, at times seeking to control it) and regionalism, but by the political dynamics of anti-systemic anti-globalization movements. These are directed, for the most part, against the state, or they involve a struggle over state power, the diminution of which has been greatly exaggerated by some scholars. However, the studies in this volume from a regional perspective show that there are distinct regional patterns in the structure of national experiences with, and responses to, globalization. There are important regional differences in the form that globalization takes in the 'history' of globalization, and in the responses of people and governments to it. Notwithstanding the apparent uniformity of the globalization process, reflected in a common ideology, the shared policy reforms and the same actors, these regional patterns are an important part of the fabric of our understanding of globalization. We trust that a close reading of the studies in this volume will contribute towards this understanding.

References

Friedman, T. (2005) *The World is Flat: A Brief History of the Twenty-First Century*, New York: Farrar, Straus & Giroux.
Goldman Sachs (1999) 'Dreaming with BRICs: The Path to 2050', *Global Economics Paper*, No. 99.
Ramo, J. (2004) *The Beijing Consensus*, London: The Foreign Policy Centre.

Index

CPSIA information can be obtained at www.ICGtesting.com
Printed in the USA
BVOW041857081111

275610BV00005B/4/P